PATIENTS AS VICTIMS

WILEY SERIES IN
**PSYCHOTHERAPY AND
COUNSELLING**

SERIES EDITORS
Franz Epting, *Dept of Psychology, University of Florida, USA*
Bonnie Strickland, *Dept of Psychology, University of Massachusetts, USA*
John Allen, *Dept of Community Studies, University of Brighton, UK*

**Patients as Victims: Sexual Abuse in Psychotherapy
and Counselling**
Derek Jehu

Eating Disorders: Personal Construct Therapy and Change
Eric Button

The Therapeutic Relationship in Behavioural Psychotherapy
Cas Schaap, Ian Bennun, Ludwig Schindler and Kees Hoogduin

Being and Belonging: Group, Intergroup and Gestalt
Gaie Houston

Life Stories: Personal Construct Therapy with the Elderly
Linda L. Viney

Psychoanalytic Counseling
Michael J. Patton and Naomi M. Meara

**Counselling and Therapy with Refugees:
Psychological Problems of Victims of War, Torture and Repression**
Guus van der Veer

**Feminist Perspectives in Therapy:
An Empowerment Model for Women**
Judith Worell and Pam Remer

**The Evolving Professional Self:
Stages and Themes in Therapist and Counselor Development**
Thomas M. Skovholt and Michael Helge Rønnestad

continued on back end-paper

PATIENTS AS VICTIMS

Sexual Abuse in Psychotherapy and Counselling

Derek Jehu

University of Leicester, UK

with specialist contributions by
**John Davis, Tanya Garrett,
Linda Mabus Jorgenson** *and*
Gary Richard Schoener

JOHN WILEY & SONS
Chichester · New York · Brisbane · Toronto · Singapore

Other Wiley Editorial Offices

John Wiley & Sons, Inc., 605 Third Avenue,
New York, NY 10158-0012, USA

Jacaranda Wiley Ltd, 33 Park Road, Milton,
Queensland 4064, Australia

John Wiley & Sons (Canada) Ltd, 22 Worcester Road,
Rexdale, Ontario M9W 1L1, Canada

John Wiley & Sons (SEA) Pte Ltd, 37 Jalan Pemimpin #05-04,
Block B, Union Industrial Building, Singapore 2057

Library of Congress Cataloging-in-Publication Data

Jehu, Derek.
    Patients as victims : sexual abuse in psychotherapy and
counselling / Derek Jehu, with specialist contributions from John
Davis . . . [et al].
        p.   cm. — (Wiley series in psychotherapy and counselling)
    Includes bibliographical references and index.
    ISBN 0-471-94044-5
    1. Sex between psychotherapist and patient—United States. 2. Sex
between psychotherapist and patient—Great Britain. 3. Sexually
abused patients. I. Title. II. Series: Wiley series on
psychotherapy and counselling.
RC489.S47J44   1994
616.89′023—dc20   93–42345
                                                            CIP

Typeset in 10/12pt Times from editor's disks by Text Processing Department,
John Wiley & Sons Ltd, Chichester
Printed and bound in Great Britain by Biddles Ltd, Guildford, Surrey

To Kit

Contents

Specialist contributors

John D. Davis, PhD, Department of Psychology, University of Warwick, Coventry CV4 7AL, U.K.

John Davis is senior lecturer in psychology at the University of Warwick and Consultant Clinical Psychologist for the Coventry District Health Authority, with special responsibility for the treatment of dissociative disorders. He directs the University of Warwick MSc course in psychotherapy, serves on the British Psychological Society's Standing Committee on Psychotherapy, and represents the Society on the Governing Board of the United Kingdom Council for Psychotherapy. He served on the Society's former working party on ethical guidelines for the practice of clinical psychology.

Tanya Garrett, Walsall Community Health Trust, Psychology Service, Ida Road Clinic, 78-80 Ida Road, Walsall WS2 9SS, U.K.

Tanya Garrett is a chartered clinical psychologist and Associate Fellow of the British Psychological Society. She is Principal Clinical Psychologist with Walsall Community Health Trust, where she manages the clinical psychology service to children, young people and families. She is currently undertaking MPhil/PhD research at the University of Warwick in the field of sexual contact between psychotherapists and their patients.

Linda Mabus Jorgenson, M.A., J.D. Spero & Jorgenson, 24 Thorndike Street, Cambridge, MA 02141, U.S.A.

Linda Jorgenson is a practising attorney and partner in the law firm of Spero & Jorgenson. In that role, Ms Jorgenson has seen over 200 victims of therapist/clergy/physician sexual misconduct. She successfully argued *Riley* v. *Presnell* 565 N.E.2d 780 (Mass. 1991), before the Massachusetts Supreme Judicial Court. *Riley* affirmed the application of the delayed discovery rule to victims of therapist sexual abuse, allowing the victim to file suit against the abuser when the victim realizes or "discovers" the harm inflicted by the therapist and its causes. Ms Jorgenson is a member of the Massachusetts House Committee on Sexual Misconduct by Physicians, Therapists and Other Health Care Professionals and is co-chairperson of the Civil/Criminal Statutes Subcommittee. She has written articles on sexual misconduct by psychotherapists and related topics such as post-termination sexual contact between therapists and patients, mandatory reporting requirements and criminalization of therapist sexual contact. She has made numerous presentations on this topic and has spoken at annual conferences of the American Psychiatric Association, the American Psychological Association and the American Academy of Psychiatry and the Law.

Gary Richard Schoener, Walk-In Counseling Center, 2421 Chicago Avenue South, Minneapolis, MN55404-3893, U.S.A.

Gary Schoener is a licensed psychologist and executive director of the Walk-In Counseling Center. He is the senior author of *Psychotherapists' Sexual Involvement with Clients: Intervention and Prevention*, and co-author of *Assisting Impaired Psychologists*. He has consulted in more than 3000 cases of sexual misconduct by professionals and is a member of the Task Force on Sexual Impropriety of the American Psychological Association and its Advisory Committee on the Impaired Psychologist. The Walk-In Counseling Center was the recipient of the 1977 Gold Achievement Award in Hospital and Community Psychiatry from the American Psychiatric Association.

Preface

My interest in the topic of this book began when treating adults who had been sexually abused in childhood, a substantial proportion of whom were similarly victimized by therapists in later life. I was precipitated into writing by my Investigatory Panel membership and my advisory role to Disciplinary Committees of the British Psychological Society. It seemed that there was a need for a reasonably concise and readily available presentation of the data, issues, opinions and regulatory provisions concerning the sexual abuse of patients by therapists in both the United States and the United Kingdom, and this book is an attempt to fill this gap.

To avoid tedious repetition, the term "therapist" is used generically to refer to psychotherapists and counsellors, regardless of the professions to which they belong, including psychiatry, psychology, counselling, nursing and social work. For the same reason, and because most abuse in therapy is perpetrated by male therapists on female patients, the male and female pronouns are used to refer to therapists and patients, respectively. As the focus of the book is on clinical rather than occupational, educational or other settings, the term "patient" is preferred to "client". The patients discussed are adults rather than children; the sexual abuse of the latter by therapists has much in common with that by others in positions of trust in the children's lives and there is already an appreciable literature on such abuse.

In part I, what constitutes sexual abuse in therapy is discussed, followed by the rationale for its proscription, and an exploration of the still controversial issue of the propriety of sexual relationships between therapists and their former patients.

Data on the epidemiology of sexual abuse by therapists in the U.S. and the U.K. is reviewed in part II. This includes publication of the results of the first survey of therapists on this topic undertaken in the U.K., those studied all being clinical psychologists.

Part III is devoted to various aspects of the topic of abusive therapists. Certain psychological characteristics that appear to enhance the risk of a therapist abusing his patients are identified, and a four-factor model of certain preconditions that must be present for abuse to occur is proposed. Finally, there is a discussion of the management of abusive behaviour by self-regulation, consultation, rehabilitation and treatment.

In part IV, the focus shifts to victimized patients. Some psychological characteristics that render patients vulnerable to sexual abuse by therapists are identified. The psychological consequences for patients of such abuse are discussed, followed by consideration of the psychological treatment of these consequences.

The legal and professional regulation of sexual abuse by therapists in the U.S. and U.K. is discussed in chapters 10 and 11, respectively, and its primary prevention is reviewed in chapter 12.

I am grateful to the two former patients who were willing to share their distressing experiences of victimization by therapists in appendices B and C.

It is my hope that this book will increase awareness of sexual abuse in therapy, as well as contribute to its reduction and to more effective help for patients who suffer in this way.

Derek Jehu
University of Leicester, 1993

Acknowledgements

John Davis and Tanya Garrett

The research reported in chapter 4 was carried out by Tanya Garrett under the supervision of John Davis in partial fulfilment of the requirements of the degree of MSc in psychotherapy at the University of Warwick. The authors are grateful to the British Psychological Society for assistance in the execution of the research and to all the clinical psychologists who contributed data.

Tanya Garrett's thanks go to Allan Norris and John Davis for their support; to Iain Liddell, Glyn Collis, Phil Spruce and Clive Eastman for the statistical advice; to Ann Newman, Joan Westwood, Pam Binns and Natasha Gray for their administrative help; and to Mathew Smith for the expert word processing consultancy.

Derek Jehu

My thanks go to the specialist contributors for their valuable chapters, to the necessarily anonymous writers of the autobiographical accounts in the appendices, to Jenny Fasal and Melanie Ward for publicizing my request for such accounts among the members of their self-help groups, and to Sheila Wesson for typing quickly, immaculately and cheerfully my innumerable drafts. I am grateful also to Michael Coombs and Wendy Hudlass of John Wiley for their encouragement and support; it has been a pleasure to work with them once again.

Linda Mabus Jorgenson and Gary Richard Schoener

We wish to thank Margaret M. Cleary, associate at Spero & Jackson.

Part I
ETHICS

1 Proscription of sexual activities

I will abstain from . . . abusing the bodies of man or woman
(Hippocrates, n.d., a, p. 301)

This ancient prohibition is reflected in the current ethical codes of most of the major mental health professions in both the United Kingdom and the United States of America, as the examples in Table 1.1 show.

The nature of the proscribed sexual activities is not specified in these codes, and traditionally it is the responsibility of the professions concerned to decide such matters. Thus, in England it has been held that serious professional misconduct is conduct "reasonably to be regarded as dishonourable by professional brethren of good repute and competency" (Halsbury, 1980, vol. 30, para. 125), and that "the Medical Acts have always entrusted the supervision of the medical advisors' conduct to a committee of the profession, for they know and appreciate better than anyone else the standards which responsible medical opinion demands" (*McCoan* v. *General Medical Council* [1964], All ER 143). Therefore, the opinions of therapists concerning the ethical acceptability of a range of sexual activities are reviewed next. It is recognized that these opinions do not in themselves constitute definitive ethical standards, but they do provide some guidelines as to what might be judged to be right or wrong according to more fundamental ethical criteria (see the section "Rationale for proscription", pp. 7–11).

Proscribed activities

Explicit acts

When performed by therapists with patients certain explicit sexual acts are widely regarded as improper, unacceptable and abusive. For instance, a survey

Table 1.1:   Examples of Proscription by Professional Organizations

Organization	Proscription
American	
American Association of Sex Educators, Counselors and Therapists	It is unethical for the therapist to engage in sexual activity with a client
American Psychiatric Association	Sexual activity with a patient is unethical
American Psychological Association	Psychologists do not engage in sexual intimacies with current patients or clients
National Association of Social Workers	The social worker should under no circumstances engage in sexual activities with clients
British	
British Association of Counselling	Engaging in sexual activity with . . . clients . . . is unethical
British Association for Sexual and Marital Therapy	Therapists must . . . not abuse their client–therapist relationship . . . sexually
British Psychological Society	A psychologist does not exploit the relationship . . . with the client for improper . . . sexual . . . gain
General Medical Council	The Council has always taken a serious view of the abuse of a doctor's professional position . . . to pursue a personal relationship of an emotional or sexual nature with a patient
	. . . where doctors attending a patient professionally have indecently assaulted or exposed themselves . . . such behaviour may . . . be treated as serious professional misconduct
United Kingdom Central Council for Nursing, Midwifery and Health Visiting	Avoid any abuse of your privileged relationship with patients . . . and of the privileged access allowed to their person

of psychologists in Missouri showed that they rated kissing, genital exposure, touching the breasts, fondling the genital area, oral sex and intercourse as always or almost always constituting misconduct (Stake & Oliver, 1991). Similarly, in a national survey of psychiatrists in the U.S.A. more than 95% of the respondents considered fondling, sitting on a lap, disrobing and genital contact to be inappropriate under any circumstances, and almost 90% thought that kissing could never be appropriate (Herman et al, 1987). The acts enquired about in these two surveys are only particular instances of a wide range of behaviour that is generally regarded as abusive, including some activities of a more bizarre nature (e.g. Pope, 1989a).

Suggestive acts

In the Missouri survey slightly lower ratings were given to sexual humour and suggestive looks and remarks, although they were still regarded as frequently constituting misconduct. In addition to the harassment they involve, such acts are often transitional steps taken by therapists in a sequence that may culminate in more complete sexual relationships with patients (Rutter, 1990).

Touching and hugging

The psychologists surveyed in Missouri rated touching and hugging as seldom constituting misconduct, 68% of the psychiatrists in the study by Herman et al (1987) considered that hugging could be appropriate in some circumstances, and 83% of clinical social workers in California had positive attitudes towards touching clients (Borenzweig, 1983). Such general acceptance of touching as appropriate in some circumstances accords with the numerous therapeutic purposes and benefits attributed to it in the literature, including the expression by therapists of congratulation, reassurance, support, comfort, consolation, solace, concern and caring, and the facilitation in patients of self-disclosure, self-exploration, and catharsis (e.g. Edwards, 1981; Goodman & Teicher, 1988; Levitan & Johnson, 1986; Pattison, 1973).

It is very important to recognize, however, that there are circumstances in which touching is not appropriate or beneficial. Correctly or incorrectly, patients may perceive it as sexual rather than nurturant, and a survey in the U.S.A. showed that 69% of psychiatrists believed that such misunderstanding occurs occasionally, frequently or always (Kardener, Fuller & Mensh, 1973). Being touched may evoke feelings of discomfort or shame in patients. They may be coerced to endure touching, and therapists may not desist when requested to do so. Therapists may use touch to evoke sexual arousal in themselves and/or their patients. In some cases this may be a further transitional step in a sequence towards more complete sexual relationships (Rutter, 1990).

Sexual attraction

Provided that it is not acted out, sexual attraction is not generally regarded as abusive. Thus, in a national survey of psychologists in the U.S.A., it was found that approximately 10% believed it to be unethical, and another 10% regarded it as unethical under rare circumstances (Pope, Tabachnick & Keith-Spiegel, 1987). Certainly, such attraction is statistically normal; for example, in another survey of U.S. psychologists 95% of men and 76% of women reported having been sexually attracted to patients on at least one occasion, while only 9% of men and 2% of women had acted out these feelings (Pope, Keith-Spiegel & Tabachnick, 1986).

The prevailing view in the literature is that the sexual attraction of therapists to some of their patients is a natural reaction which is to be expected. For instance, Pope and Bouhoutsos remark that "sexual attraction ... may be a completely natural part of the therapist's reaction to some patients. In some cases it may represent countertransference; in other cases it may represent an undistorted human reaction to another person" (1986, p. 36). Furthermore, in one of the surveys (Pope, Keith-Spiegel & Tabachnick, 1986), 63% of psychologists believed that their sexual attraction to patients had been beneficial to the therapy process in at least some instances, although the nature of the benefits is not specified. One might be the affirmation to patients of their attractiveness and desirability. In contrast, 49% of psychologists believed that their sexual attraction exerted a negative influence on therapy, although again the nature of the harm or impediment to the therapeutic process is not indicated directly. One possible adverse effect is the finding in the same survey that 63% of the psychologists reported that their sexual attraction to patients made them feel uncomfortable, guilty or anxious. In particular, they may fear that the attraction could get out of control and be acted out, which in turn might entail disadvantages such as reluctance to engage in perfectly proper discussion of patients' sexual problems, or even to premature termination of treatment or inappropriate referral to another therapist.

Sexual fantasies

Closely related to sexual attraction is the issue of therapists having sexual fantasies about their patients. This also is not generally regarded as abusive, always providing that the fantasies are not acted out with patients. Thus, Edelwich & Brodsky comment that "sexual fantasy is a normal and very common human experience. . . . Therapists and clients routinely fantasize about each other. Such fantasies become a problem only when they are acted upon" (1991, p. 14). There is some evidence to support the prevalence of fantasizing about patients in that among psychologists in the U.S.A., 46% reported engaging in such fantasizing on a rare basis, and 25% more frequently (Pope et al, 1987).

Conclusion

In summary, sexual humour, suggestive looks and remarks, kissing, nudity, fondling, oral sex and intercourse, among other sexual acts with patients, are widely recognized as constituting sexual abuse by therapists. Touching and hugging are not generally regarded as abusive, although there are circumstances in which they are inappropriate and potentially harmful. Finally, sexual attraction and fantasies are commonly viewed as natural reactions which are not in themselves abusive, provided that they are not acted out with patients. Some reasons why the sexual activities that have been identified here are judged to be unethical and abusive are discussed in the next section.

Rationale for proscription

There are several closely related and overlapping reasons for the ethical proscription of sexual relationships between therapists and patients, including those reviewed below.

Breach of trust

This is perhaps the most fundamental reason, from which many of the others are derived. As Marmor puts it, "The essential foundation on which the patient–therapist relationship rests is *basic trust*. On the implicit and explicit assumption that this trust will not be betrayed, the patient is encouraged to set aside her customary psychological defences and open herself completely to the presumably benign and therapeutic influence of the therapist's professional skill" (1972, p. 6). As a condition for this trust the therapist enters into a fiduciary relationship with the patient, in which he undertakes always to act in her best interests and to place these above his own. Clearly, a fiduciary relationship is breached if a therapist engages in sexual activity with a patient, because this is likely to be disadvantageous to her, as indicated below, and to be pursued for the benefit of the therapist rather than the patient. The need to avoid such breaches of trust and fiduciary relationships is recognized in the ethical codes of several professions, as shown in Table 1.2.

Violation of role

The role of therapist requires that occupants use their professional knowledge, judgement and skills for the benefit of patients. If therapists assume the dual

Table 1.2: Examples of Fiduciary Standards in Professional Organizations

Organization	Standard
American	
American Medical Association	Sexual misconduct . . . violates the trust the patient reposes in the physician and is unethical
American Psychiatric Association	The patient may place his/her trust in his/her psychiatrist knowing that the psychiatrist's ethics and professional responsibilities preclude him/her gratifying his/her own needs by exploiting the patient
British	
British Association for Sexual and Marital Therapy	It is the therapist's duty to act at all times according to the best interests of the client
British Association of Social Workers	Members . . . will give precedence to their professional responsibility over their own personal interest
British Psychological Society	Psychologists . . . shall . . . not exploit the special relationship of trust and confidence that can exist in professional practice to further the gratification of their own desires
General Medical Council	Good medical practice depends upon the maintenance of trust between doctors and patients and their families, and the understanding by both that proper professional relationships will be strictly observed
United Kingdom Central Council for Nursing, Midwifery and Health Visiting	. . . act always to promote and safeguard the interests and well being of patients . . . ensure that no action or omission on your part . . . is detrimental to the interests . . . of patients

role of lover with patients then the therapeutic role is likely to be violated. The therapist's objectivity and professional judgement may be impaired. His needs may be put before those of the patient, so that a conflict of interests arises between them. As indicated below, the process of therapy may be impeded or distorted, and the patient may be distressed and harmed (Kitchener, 1988).

Exploitation of vulnerability

The psychological vulnerability of many patients reduces their capacity to refuse or resist sexual advances by therapists who exploit any weaknesses. These are considered fully in Chapter 7, but they include the following characteristics. Due to low self-esteem, some patients have an excessive need for acceptance and approval from their therapists. The disclosure of sensitive and embarrassing personal information by patients can put them at the mercy of predatory therapists. The distress that brings patients into treatment makes them strongly dependent on their therapists for support, guidance and help. Finally, many patients are vulnerable to seduction because of the strong feelings of attraction, idealization and love they experience towards their therapists.

Misuse of power

The role of therapist confers considerable knowledge, expertise, credibility, authority and power on occupants in the eyes of patients. Their perception of these qualities coupled with the vulnerability discussed in the previous section results in a considerable power differential in favour of therapists, whose patients are likely to find it difficult to question or resist approaches from such powerful figures. For therapists to misuse this unequal power for their own sexual gratification is unfair and unethical.

It may also be sexist. The majority of abuse in therapy is perpetrated by male therapists against female patients (see part II), and to some extent this may reflect wider societal views of a traditional nature which endorse the appropriateness and acceptability of more powerful men pursuing and exploiting women for sexual purposes.

Absence of consent

The basic human right of self-determination requires that individuals make their own choices and control their own lives in so far as this is compatible with the rights of others. According to Beauchamp & Childress, "This means that the person ... should be ... able to exercise free power of choice, without the intervention of any element of force, fraud, deceit, duress, ... or other ulterior form of constraint or coercion, and should have sufficient knowledge and comprehension ... to enable him to make an understanding and enlightened decision" (1983, p. 66). It follows that the actions of therapists should be based on the voluntary and informed consent of patients, but for several reasons patients are unlikely to be able to give valid consent to sexual relationships with their therapists. The exploitation of vulnerability and misuse of power discussed above reduces or eliminates the necessary freedom of choice and action for patients. Furthermore, they may be unaware that sex between patients and therapists is inappropriate and unethical, and will almost certainly not fully comprehend the impairments to therapy and the iatrogenic effects that are likely to accompany such sex, as discussed below. More specifically, therapists sometimes deceive patients into believing that sex is a beneficial or necessary component of treatment. Thus, in these and other ways any apparent consent to sex by patients is invalidated by their limited freedom of choice and insufficient or inaccurate information.

Impairment of therapeutic process

Sexual abuse by therapists is likely to impair the process of therapy to the detriment of the patients involved. Thus, Kardener writes, "the physician, as a source of healing, support, and succour, becomes lost to his patient when he changes roles and becomes a lover. It is a frighteningly high price the patient must pay, since good lovers are much easier to find than good caretakers" (1974, p. 1135). Similarly, "when sexual intercourse begins, therapy ends" (Bouhoutsos et al, 1983, p. 194).

At the very least, sexual activity may divert time and effort that should be devoted to resolving the patient's problems. Abusive therapists may underestimate the severity of patients' problems so that they are perceived as normal individuals who are able and entitled to form validly consensual sexual and romantic relationships with whomever they please. Alternatively, patients' problems may be exaggerated or inflated in order to enhance and maintain their dependence on the therapist. The confusion, fear, resentment, loss of trust and other negative reactions that are commonly experienced by victimized patients are likely to affect adversely the therapeutic alliances between them and their therapists. More particularly, advice that would be beneficial to patients may not be given if it might contribute to the termination of sexual activity or remove the need for further treatment. For similar reasons, and to maintain the dependence and acquiescence of patients, certain problems such as unassertiveness may not be addressed adequately. Patients may not be referred to other professionals when this is necessary in case the sexual abuse is revealed to them. Likewise, abusive therapists may avoid supervision or consultation with other professionals. Either the patient or the therapist may terminate therapy prematurely and inappropriately in order to bring a sexual relationship to an end, or ostensibly to legitimize it because the victim is no longer a patient, as discussed below.

Iatrogenic effects

Sexual abuse by therapists can initiate, precipitate and exacerbate a wide range of psychological problems among victimized patients, thereby contravening the long-established ethical precept to "at least do no harm" (Hippocrates, n.d., b, p. 165). The now substantial body of evidence on these iatrogenic effects is presented in Chapter 8.

Disrepute of profession

Abusive therapists are liable to bring their professions into disrepute. Consequently, potential patients may be reluctant to seek the help they need from members of that profession, or even from other professions that are associated with it in the public mind.

Conclusion

Thus, the rationale for proscribing sexual relationships between therapists and patients includes breach of trust, violation of role, exploitation of vulnerability, misuse of power, absence of consent, impairment of therapy, iatrogenic effects and bringing professions into disrepute. It is for reasons such as these that certain acts, discussed in the section "Proscribed activities", are deemed to be abusive when they are performed with patients.

2 Former patients

The general consensus of opinion that it is unethical for therapists to engage in sexual activities with current patients does not extend to former patients. This is still an area of considerable controversy, which is reflected in several surveys of therapists' beliefs and in the ethical codes of their professions.

Beliefs

Herman et al (1987) conducted a national survey of psychiatrists in the U.S., of whom 1423 (26%) returned the questionnaire. Sexual contact with patients while treatment is in progress was considered to be always inappropriate by 98% of the respondents, while 30% believed it to be sometimes appropriate after termination.

Pope et al (1987) undertook a national survey of psychologists practising psychotherapy in the U.S., of whom 465 (46%) responded. Engaging in erotic activity with a current client was considered unquestionably unethical by 95% of the subjects, while 50% believed that becoming sexually involved with a former client fell into this category.

In another survey of a similar sample by Akamatsu (1988) responses were received from 395 subjects (39%), of whom 69% considered intimate relationships with former clients to be either very or somewhat unethical.

Thus, while sexual relationships with current patients are almost universally condemned as unethical, these three surveys indicate that opinion is much more equivocal about such relationships with former patients.

Ethics

This divergence and uncertainty among therapists is reflected in the ethical codes of their professional organizations. This is highlighted in Florida, where the Board of Psychological Examiners has ruled that for the purposes of determining the existence of sexual misconduct the psychologist–client relationship is deemed to continue *in perpetuity*, while in the same State the medical board permits sexual contact between psychiatrist and patient *immediately after termination*.

Several codes make no specific mention of sexual relationships with former patients, including those of the British Association of Social Workers, the British Psychological Society and the U.K. Central Council for Nursing, Midwifery and Health Visiting. The General Medical Council in the U.K. states that, "The question is sometimes raised whether the Council will be concerned with [sexual] relationships . . . between a doctor and a person whom the doctor has attended professionally in the distant past. In view of the great variety of circumstances which can arise in cases of this nature, the Council's judicial position has prevented it from offering specific advice on such matters" (General Medical Council, 1992, pp. 24–25).

The propriety of sexual relationships with former patients has been a controversial topic of debate in the American Psychological Association for several years. It was determined only in the December 1992 revision of the code, which includes the following provisions (American Psychological Association, 1992, p. 1605):

(a) Psychologists do not engage in sexual intimacies with a former therapy patient or client for at least two years after cessation or termination of professional services.
(b) Because sexual intimacies with a former therapy patient or client are so frequently harmful to the patient or client, and because such intimacies undermine public confidence in the psychology profession and thereby deter the public's use of needed services, psychologists do not engage in sexual intimacies with former therapy patients and clients even after a two-year interval except in the most unusual circumstances. The psychologist who engages in such activity after the two years following cessation or termination of treatment bears the burden of demonstrating that there has been no exploitation, in light of all relevant factors, including (1) the amount of time that has passed since therapy terminated, (2) the nature and duration of the therapy, (3) the circumstances of termination, (4) the patient's or client's personal history, (5) the patient's or client's current mental status, (6) the likelihood of adverse impact on the patient or client and others, and (7) any statements or actions made by the therapist during the course of

therapy suggesting or inviting the possibility of a posttermination sexual or romantic relationship with the patient or client.

In 1992 the British Association for Counselling (BAC) adopted as a temporary measure a statement for inclusion in its ethical code to the effect that "Engaging in sexual activity ... within 12 weeks of the end of the counselling relationship is unethical. If the counselling relationship has been over an extended period of time or been working in depth, a much longer 'cooling off' period is required and a lifetime prohibition on a future sexual relationship ... may be more appropriate" (British Association for Counselling, 1992, S.2.2.6). Subsequently, it was thought that a universal time limit is divisive and does not accommodate the diversity of the membership of the British Association of Counselling, that the dynamics of counselling may or may not go on forever, and that the issues that arise in sexual relationships with former clients also arise in other kinds of relationships. Therefore, a proposal is currently being considered to withdraw the 1992 statement and to replace it with "Counsellors remain accountable for relationships with former clients and must exercise caution over entering into ... sexual relationships. ... Any changes in the relationship must be discussed in counselling supervision. The decision about any change(s) ... should take into account whether the issues and power dynamics present during the counselling relationship have been resolved and properly ended" (British Association for Counselling, personal communication, 24 June 1993).

Post-termination sexual relationships are proscribed with varying degrees of specificity in the ethical codes of some other professional organizations; for example:

> Sexual involvement with one's former patient generally exploits emotions deriving from treatment and therefore almost always is unethical.
> (American Psychiatric Association, 1989)

> Sexual intimacy with former clients for two years following the termination of therapy is prohibited.
> (American Association for Marriage and Family Therapy, 1988)

> Therapists are responsible for making explicit to clients the appropriate boundaries to the therapeutic relationship, and for maintaining those boundaries both during and after therapy.
> (British Association for Sexual and Marital Therapy, 1991)

Rationales

The beliefs held by therapists and the views reflected in the ethical codes of their professions are determined by the extent to which it is considered that some of the reasons discussed in Chapter 1 for proscribing sex with current patients are also applicable with former patients.

Breach of trust

The case for proscription is that fiduciary relationships continue after treatment ends. For example, Gabbard & Pope argue that the obligation of confidentiality "is unaffected by termination or the passage of time after termination, [and] is but one form of recognition that the professional relationship does not dissolve or vanish upon ceasing of the therapy sessions" (1989, p. 120). Indeed, the Declaration of Geneva includes the statement that "I will respect the secrets that are confided in me, even after the patient has died" (Mason & McCall Smith, 1991, p. 440). Other post-termination obligations include the maintenance of records on patients, the liability to be subpoenaed to give evidence on their problems and treatment, and often availability for further consultation or therapy if necessary.

A somewhat contradictory view expressed by Appelbaum & Jorgenson is that "For most purposes, the fiduciary relationship ends when therapy is concluded. Therapists, for example, are not obligated to resume therapy at the request of former patients. ... Although some residual obligations remain—confidentiality is the best example—as a whole, the fiduciary duties are not of the same magnitude as during therapy" (1991, p. 1470).

Exploitation of vulnerability

While recognizing the considerable individual variation in residual psychological vulnerability between patients when treatment ends, it might be argued that most retain some vulnerability in that their presenting problems are not completely resolved. Alternatively, one might take the view that these problems are so substantially reduced after treatment ends that most former patients are not especially vulnerable to exploitation by therapists.

Another remaining source of potential vulnerability is the sensitive, personal information about patients that is still available to predatory therapists after treatment ends.

A major theoretical debate concerns the persistence after termination of transference reactions originating during therapy. According to Appelbaum & Jorgenson, "The existing data on this question ... are fragmentary, methodologically problematic, often based on single case reports, and in several instances susceptible to interpretations supporting both sides of the debate ...

we find it reasonable to assume both that some transference continues after the patient leaves the consulting room for the final time . . . and that for most patients the effect diminishes as time passes" (1991, p. 1470).

Gabbard & Pope offer a somewhat discrepant view. After reviewing the inadequate empirical data, they conclude that "The transference is never resolved. . . . These studies suggest that should either the therapist or the patient approach the other and enter into a sexually intimate relationship, the transference situation itself would be instantly reactivated and intensified" (1989, pp. 116–117).

Misuse of power

Those favouring the proscription of post-termination sex assert that the power differential between vulnerable, compliant patients and authoritative, dominant therapists remains considerable after therapy ends. For instance, Brown states that, "The therapist–client power differential remains after formal termination. . . . To the extent that vestiges of this power differential remain, a sexual relationship is unethical . . . the burden of proof that all vestiges of power differential is removed should be on the therapist" (1988, p. 249). Similarly, according to Gabbard & Pope, "The distorted transferential reactions, the realistic intrapsychic representations, and the aspects of the formal professional relationship, all of which endure past the termination . . . indicate that—however much therapists may wish to conceal, discount, or deny it—there is a profound power differential between therapists and their patients regardless of termination" (1989, p. 121).

Another view is that the power remaining with therapists after termination is so reduced that the risk of its misuse for sexual purposes is minimized. Thus, Appelbaum & Jorgenson consider that, "As far as the therapist's potential for coercing the patient into sexual contact is concerned, that should decrease substantially after therapy is over. The implicit threat that treatment will be withheld if the patient refuses sex is now defused. . . . On the other hand, personal information revealed in the course of therapy might still be used to manipulate the former patient into agreeing to sexual contact. . . . The therapist's potential for coercive influence on the patient has diminished but has not disappeared altogether" (1991, p. 1470).

Absence of consent

Those who believe that patients remain vulnerable and therapists powerful after treatment ends will tend towards the view that former patients cannot give valid consent to post-termination sex with their therapists. This view is likely to be strengthened to the extent that such sexual relationships are believed to impair the therapeutic process and to have iatrogenic effects, as discussed below. This is especially the case if patients are unaware of these potential disadvantages, or if they are deceived by therapists into thinking that there are no such risks or that sex after termination is unquestionably appropriate and ethical.

Impairment of therapeutic process

The legitimation of sexual relationships between former patients and therapists could distort the process of therapy prior to termination (Gabbard & Pope, 1989). The possibility of such a relationship in future might lead patients to present themselves in the most favourable light, by acting to please their therapist and by refraining from disclosing embarrassing or shameful information that might deter him as a potential lover. Problems that could prolong therapy might not be mentioned so that sexual gratification is not delayed. The prospect of a relationship with the therapist might divert the attention and efforts of patients from improving relationships with other significant people in their lives. Finally, patients might fear that disclosure of events such as having been sexually abused in childhood or raped as an adult, or of problems such as promiscuity, might signal their future sexual availability to predatory therapists. Therapists might also conduct therapy with the possibility in mind of patients becoming lovers, thus entailing many of the adverse effects on the therapeutic process with current patients that were discussed in Chapter 1.

One aspect of an appropriate termination of therapy is the internalization of the therapist in symbolic form within the patient, who can then continue to benefit from his therapeutic influence. For instance, Geller, Cooley & Hartley (1981–82, p. 123) cite self-statements by former patients such as:

> When I am faced with a difficult situation I sometimes ask myself, "What would my therapist do?"

> In a sense, I feel as though my therapist has become part of me.

> I try to solve my problems in the way my therapist and I worked on them in psychotherapy.

> I am aware of a particular emotional atmosphere which gives me the sense that my therapist is "with me".

The former therapist who is or has been the patient's lover may no longer be such a beneficial internal resource, perhaps because his image has been damaged by subsequent breach of trust, exploitation or misuse of power.

It is by no means uncommon for former patients to seek further consultation or treatment with their earlier therapists, sometimes many years after the original therapy ended. As discussed in Chapter 1, if the therapist has become the patient's lover he is no longer available to her as a therapist.

Iatrogenic effects

Although specific evidence is lacking, it is certainly conceivable that post-termination sex with therapists could contribute to the psychological problems of victimized patients that are discussed in Chapter 8.

Furthermore, a therapist's sexual involvement with a particular former patient may entail adverse effects for other current or former patients who learn of the relationship. They may be jealous and suffer lowered self-esteem in the belief that they were not attractive or special enough to be chosen as his lover. There may be feelings of insecurity arising from having trusted someone who has proved to be untrustworthy, and who might even share confidential information about them with his lover.

Disrepute of profession

If it is thought that therapists commonly have sexual relationships with their former patients and that this is regarded as acceptable and ethical, then some potential patients may be deterred from seeking the help they need from any of the therapeutic professions.

Solutions

A range of possible solutions to the dilemma of the ethical status of sexual relationships between therapists and their former patients can be categorized into those proposing (i) no proscription, (ii) absolute proscription and (iii) the conditional proscription of such relationships.

One extreme and apparently rare solution is to condone all sexual relationships between therapists and former patients. One instance of this cited above is the decision of the medical board in Florida to permit sexual contact between psychiatrist and patient immediately after termination. The rationale usually provided for solutions in this category is that consenting adults have the right to enter into relationships with whomever they wish, and reference is sometimes made to the freedom of association provisions in the U.S. constitution. As we have seen, one argument against this viewpoint is that former patients may not be able to give valid consent to sexual relationships with their therapists.

At the other extreme is another apparently rare solution, that such sexual relationships should never be permitted under any circumstances. An example of this view is the decision of the Florida Board of Psychological Examiners cited above, which deems the psychologist–client relationship to continue in perpetuity. Against such views, Appelbaum & Jorgenson argue that "Although an absolute ban, if observed, would afford complete protection from the negative consequences of sexual relationships between therapists and former patients, it would do so at the cost of precluding relationships that may involve no more problems than many relationships routinely sanctioned in our society" (1991, p. 1472), and "given the general presumption that persons' choices should be respected, there are insufficient grounds to warrant an outright ban on sexual contact after termination of therapy. Rather, more selective interventions are justified to minimize the likelihood that impaired decisions will be made or adverse effects occur" (1991, p. 1471).

This approach requires identification of those conditions that would justify proscribing sexual relationships between therapists and former patients. The following subsections describe the conditions that might be considered in this context, together with the American Psychological Association's provisions concerning sexual relationships with former patients quoted above.

Vulnerability

If former patients remain psychologically vulnerable after therapy ends then this could justify the proscription of sex with their therapists. For instance, in Minnesota this is a criminal offence when the former patient is "emotionally dependent" on the therapist, such dependence being defined as meaning "that the nature of the ... former patient's emotional condition and the nature of the treatment provided by the psychotherapist are such that the ... former patient is unable to withhold consent to sexual contact or sexual penetration by the psychotherapist" (Minnesota Criminal Sexual Conduct Code, 1985, S.609.341). More broadly, several classes of patient are mentioned in the literature as being especially vulnerable to post-termination sexual exploitation. They include those who are severely disturbed or chronically disordered, those whose problems include promiscuity, those with a history of sexual or physical abuse in childhood, and those who are socially isolated and lonely (see Chapter 7).

The deliberate exploitation of patients' vulnerabilities by therapists for their own sexual gratification will almost certainly be considered unethical. An example of this is a civil suit in which it was found that the behaviour of a psychiatric resident constituted malpractice and intentional infliction of emotional distress. The patient had sought treatment for substance abuse and "seductive behaviour". After therapy ended the resident who had treated her smoked marijuana and drank alcohol with her and commenced a sexual relationship, through which she became pregnant. The court noted that his actions were intended to exploit the former patient's specific vulnerabilities (*Noto* v. *St. Vincent's Hospital and Medical Center of New York* (1988) 142 Misc. 292 537 N.Y.S. 2d 446, Supreme Court).

Power

A closely related condition meriting the proscription of post-termination sex is misuse by therapists for their own gratification of any residual power differential between them and their former patients.

Consent

If former patients do not give valid consent to sexual relationships with their therapists then these relationships are unethical. Consent may be lacking because of the "emotional dependence" discussed above, or because therapists have deceived patients, perhaps by misinforming them that post-termination sex is quite appropriate and ethical or that it is perfectly consistent with the patient's treatment and recovery. For example, in Minnesota it is a criminal offence if sex "occurred by means of therapeutic deception", meaning "a representation by a psychotherapist that sexual contact or sexual penetration by the psychotherapist is consistent with or part of the patient's treatment" (Minnesota Criminal Sexual Conduct Code, 1985, S.609.341). Similar provisions in the U.K. are discussed in Chapter 11.

Harm

If former patients are in any way harmed or distressed by sexual relationships with their therapists then this justifies the ethical proscription of these relationships. An example of this is the legal recognition in Wisconsin that "Any person who suffers ... a physical, mental or emotional injury caused by ... sexual contact with a therapist who ... has rendered to that person psychotherapy counseling or other assessment or treatment ... has a civil cause of action against the psychotherapist" (Wisconsin Act 275, 1985, S.895.70). Civil suits on similar grounds can also be pursued in the U.K. (see Chapter 11).

Therapy

Some sources suggest that the nature of the treatment undergone by former patients can influence whether post-termination relationships with their therapists are unethical. Thus, Gonsiorek & Brown propose that such sexual contact is always and forever prohibited with patients who have received "psychotherapy in which the transferential relationship plays a primary or central role ... in which there exists a ... power differential between client and therapist; in which therapy is long term (eg more than one year); and in which ... the client comes to consciously or subconsciously perceive the therapist in a parental or powerful authority role" (1989, p. 299).

Termination

Prior to the 1992 revision of their code, the Ethics Committee of the American Psychological Association stated that "If ... it seems that the treatment ended in order to give the appearance of compliance with the ethical proscription against psychologist–client sexual intimacies, the committee will find that behavior a clear violation. ... Such terminations are seen as subterfuge" (American Psychological Association Monitor, 1987, June, p. 45).

The subterfuge may be overt or covert, in that therapists may themselves terminate treatment inappropriately and prematurely in order to pursue sexual relationships with former patients while preserving the appearance of compliance with ethical requirements. Alternatively, therapists may convey to patients the message that if they take the step of terminating treatment then sex will be possible without any ethical contravention (Gonsiorek & Brown, 1989).

Timing

One of the most frequent proposed solutions to the ethical dilemma of post-termination sex is that it should be permitted only after a specified period of time (most usually two years) has elapsed since the end of therapy. Appelbaum & Jorgenson review these solutions and propose that:

> concerns about allowing patients to enter into sexual relationships with former therapists can be addressed by precluding the initiation of therapist–patient sexual contact until a substantial period of time has elapsed after the end of treatment. We suggest one year as a period that appropriately balances the interests involved, although we recognize that any line drawing is largely arbitrary. ... During this one year period, no social contact or communication at all ... would be permitted.
> (1991, p. 1471)

The benefits claimed for such a waiting period include reductions in the vulnerability of patients, the misuse of power by therapists, the lack of valid consents and impairment of the therapeutic process, although we saw above that all of these claims are subject to dispute. Appelbaum & Jorgenson recognize that there may be difficulties in determining when treatment ends and in monitoring the waiting period, and that post-termination sex might need to be absolutely proscribed for certain classes of especially vulnerable patients, such as those mentioned above.

Conclusion

Rather than either condoning or banning all sexual relationships between former patients and their therapists, it seems preferable to proscribe them selectively when certain conditions exist. These include the continuing psychological vulnerability of patients, the misuse of power by therapists, the absence of valid consent, the infliction of harm or distress on patients, any impairment of the therapeutic process, termination for the purpose of starting a sexual relationship, and the commencement of such a relationship too soon after treatment is ended. Such conditions could be standardized in legal provisions and ethical codes, or they could be individualized on a case-by-case basis. It is not expected or intended that this solution would open the door to widespread post-termination sex, because one or more of the conditions justifying its proscription is likely to be present in the vast majority of cases, leaving only a very small number as ethically acceptable exceptions.

Part II
EPIDEMIOLOGY

3 Epidemiology in the U.S.A.

Tanya Garrett

Until relatively recently the issue of the sexual abuse of patients in psychotherapy had received little attention in the theoretical and research literature. It is now an established area of attention in the U.S.A. It is clear from American research that sexual contact between psychotherapists and their patients is a significant problem, but that, like rape and child sexual abuse, it is underreported. In the U.S.A., half the money for malpractice cases is spent on complaints regarding sexual intimacy (Pope, 1991). About 13% of allegations of professional misconduct handled by the American Psychological Association (APA) insurance trust in 1981, and 18% of the complaints to the APA ethics committee in 1982 involved sexual offences. Yet suits and complaints are filed in only about 4% of cases, and only half of these are completed (Bouhoutsos, 1985).

The process of data collection in this field has been problematic. Butler & Zelen (1977) were threatened with expulsion from a professional organization when they suggested research into the field of therapist–patient sexual intimacy, and when early research was allowed, the results were suppressed (Forer, 1968, cited in Bouhoutsos, 1985). Not until the 1970s, at least in the U.S.A., was concerted attention given to the problem (Bouhoutsos, 1985), with a proliferation of research and theoretical papers.

Possible reasons for such interest include the increasing number of women in psychology and related professions, the growth of the women's movement and the development of consumerism. This last development has been slower in the U.K., which, together with a cultural difference between the two countries in their attitudes and openness towards sexual issues, as well as the fact that most U.S. therapists are in private practice whereas most psychotherapy in the U.K. takes place within public settings, may partially explain the silence in the

U.K. concerning sex between therapists and their patients. Further, the accumulating professional and public interest in therapist–patient sexual contact may in part be due to the fact that a few therapists began to assert publicly that it could be a legitimate practice (e.g. McCartney, 1966; Shepard, 1971). In addition, patients in the U.S.A. began to press legal actions against therapists who violated the prohibition on sexual contact with patients (Pope & Bouhoutsos, 1986).

Prevalence of abuse

Generally speaking, the research has yielded no differences in any respect between the main American psychotherapy professions of clinical psychology, psychiatry and social work. No empirical evidence is available to date to indicate the extent of sexual contact between other professionals and lay psychotherapists and counsellors, and their patients. As shown in Table 3.1, most surveys have found that, overall, something under 10% of professional psychotherapists have had sexual contact with their patients.

Table 3.1:　Proportions of Therapists Reporting Sexual Contact with Patients

Profession and source	%
Psychiatrists	
Kardener, Fuller & Mensh (1973)	5
Pope, Levenson & Schover (1979)	7
Derosis et al (1987)	7
Gartrell et al (1987)	7
Psychologists	
Pope, Keith-Spiegel & Tabachnick (1986)	6
Pope, Tabachnick & Keith-Spiegel (1987)	2
Social workers	
Gechtman (1989)	4

Pope, Tabachnick & Keith-Spiegel (1987) found significantly lower rates of sexual contact with patients than previous studies: only 2% of therapists reported having had sex with a patient. Similarly, Gechtman (1989) found that 4% of social workers had engaged in sexual relations with their patients. On the basis of such more recent surveys, Pope (1990) suggests that the rate of therapist–patient sexual involvement is declining in the U.S.A. However, drawing inferences about actual changes in therapists' sexual behaviour is problematic because surveys do not specify when the sexual behaviour occurred (Williams, 1992). In addition, reporting practices, particularly by male psychotherapists, may have changed in recent years (Stake & Oliver, 1991) because of the increased publicity accorded to the sanctions that have been applied to sexually abusive professionals.

Abusive acts

Most researchers have included a definition of sexual contact in their surveys, which may limit the range of sexual acts that respondents describe. However, from the available information, the sexual acts that take place between therapists and their patients include suggestive behaviour, erotic kissing, fondling, massage, genital exposure, masturbation, oral–genital contact, anal intercourse and vaginal intercourse (Bouhoutsos et al, 1983; D'Addario, 1977; Gartrell et al, 1986; Kuchan, 1989; Valiquette, 1989; Vinson, 1984).

Sexual intercourse occurs in anything between 41% (Holroyd & Brodsky, 1980) and 83% of cases where sexual contact has taken place (D'Addario, 1977), with other studies suggesting figures somewhere in between; for example, 58% (Bouhoutsos et al, 1983) and 75% (Vinson, 1984).

Serial abuse

In the limited evidence available, there is some discrepancy between the proportions of abusive therapists reported to have had sexual relations with more than one patient. It is important to note, however, the broad research finding that therapists who have sexual contact with one patient are at a high risk of re-offending.

In the study of psychiatrists conducted by Gartrell et al (1986), 33% of the respondents who admitted having a sexual relationship with patients had abused from 2 to 12 patients. Holroyd & Brodsky (1977) found that 80% of the clinical psychologists who had sexual contact with patients in their study had done so with more than one patient, and one therapist had victimized 10 patients.

Course of abuse

Initiation

Information on which participant in therapy initiated sexual contact is provided in a national survey of psychiatrists in the U.S.A. (Gartrell et al, 1986), in an inquiry to Californian psychologists about their patients who had been sexually abused by previous therapists (Bouhoutsos et al, 1983), and in a study in Montreal of volunteers who had been abused by therapists (Valiquette, 1989). The results of these surveys are shown in Table 3.2.

Table 3.2:   Initiator of Sexual Contact

Source	Initiator			
	Therapist	Patient	Therapist and patient	Disputed/ mutual/ undetermined
Gartrell et al (1986)	11	32	57	—
Bouhoutsos et al (1983)	42	6	—	52
Valiquette (1989)	67	14	20	—

These investigations also provide data on when sexual contact commenced, again with varied results, as shown in Table 3.3. In addition, Derosis et al (1987) state that the overall rate of sexual contact with patients by their psychiatrist respondents was 6.6%, whereas if the post-termination cases were dropped, the rate fell to 6.1%.

Table 3.3:   Commencement of Sexual Contact

Source	Time (%)		
	During therapy	After termination	During last session or immediately afterwards
Gartrell et al (1986)	27	63	—
Bouhoutsos et al (1983)	96	4	—
Valiquette (1989)	78	—	22

In the study of attitudes conducted by Gartrell et al (1987), 30% of psychiatrists said that post-termination sexual contact with patients could sometimes be acceptable. Interestingly, 74% of the respondents who had had sexual contact with patients believed that such contact could be acceptable, and indeed used this as a means of rationalizing their behaviour.

Duration

Gartrell et al (1986) report the length of therapist–patient sexual relationship as between one sexual encounter (19%) and over 5 years (17%), with other categories as follows: less than 3 months, 26%; 3–11 months, 17%; and 1–5 years, 21%.

Termination

For those patients whose sexual contact with their therapist began while therapy was in progress, the most detailed information available is derived from the patients described by Bouhoutsos et al (1983). Therapy ended immediately after the first sexual contact in 34% of cases, while for the remainder it continued beyond this point. Both therapy and sexual contact ended simultaneously for 55% of these patients, therapy ended while sex continued for 27%, and therapy continued while sex ended for 18%. Therapy was terminated by the patient in 67% of cases, by the therapist in 15% and by someone else in 1%.

The 20 abusive therapists described by Butler & Zelen (1977) stated that therapy was terminated immediately after the first sexual contact in 25% of cases, while in 30% it continued with sexual contact and in 45% without such contact.

In Valiquette's study of abused volunteers, therapy ended after the first sexual contact in 36% of cases. It was terminated by the patient in 61% of cases, by the therapist in 27% and by both parties in 12%.

Gender variables

The most striking research finding to emerge concerning the therapists and patients who become sexually involved concerns status. The vast majority of the therapists are older men (Bouhoutsos et al, 1983) and most of the patients are younger women (e.g. Kardener, Fuller & Mensh, 1973; Pope, Keith-Spiegel & Tabachnick, 1986; Pope & Vetter, 1991).

The earliest information about the characteristics of therapists who become involved with their patients was provided by Dahlberg (1970), based on cases of patients whom he had treated and who had had sexual relationships with their therapists. These therapists were always male. It has been found that a greater number of the complaints made against women psychiatrists tend to be for homosexual involvement (Mogul, 1992).

Generally speaking, when the overall figures are broken down by gender of therapist, the percentage of male therapists who engage in sexual intercourse with patients rises to around 10%, and it becomes clear that women offenders form only a tiny minority of the total number. For example, Gartrell et al (1986) surveyed U.S. psychiatrists, and found that 7% of male and 3% of female psychiatrists had had sex with patients. Other surveys indicate figures of 3% and 12% for women and men, respectively (Pope, Levenson & Schover, 1979), 2% and 8% (Derosis et al, 1987), 2% and 9% (Pope, Tabachnick & Keith-Spiegel, 1987) and 0.6% and 5% while therapy was ongoing (Holroyd & Brodsky, 1977).

This last study found that 8% of men and 1% of women had ever had sex with patients. Gechtman's (1989) study of social workers revealed no erotic contact between female social workers and their clients.

Bouhoutsos et al (1983) asked Californian clinical psychologists about their patients who had been sexually abused by previous therapists. The general breakdown supports the preponderance of male therapist–female patient dyads: this was so for 92% of cases. In 2% of cases, a female therapist had been sexually involved with a male patient.

A small percentage of therapist–patient sexual relationships involve same-sex pairs. Gartrell et al (1986) found that in 3% of the cases of sexual contact between psychiatrists and their patients the liaison involved a male therapist and a male patient, and in 2% a female therapist and a female patient. Somewhat different findings on same-sex relationships between psychiatrists and their patients are reported by Mogul (1992), who reviewed complaints to the American Psychiatric Association Ethics Committee. Only two (2%) of 86 complaints against male psychiatrists involved male patients, while six (75%) out of eight complaints against female psychiatrists involved female patients. The variations across the findings of these two studies may well be due to sampling differences between psychiatrists responding to a national survey and those against whom ethical complaints had been made.

Some surveys have not, however, shown significant gender differences in sexual contact with patients. These surveys have for the most part, although not exclusively, been conducted more recently (Stake & Oliver, 1991; Akamatsu, 1988; Pope, Tabachnick & Keith-Spiegel, 1987). It has been suggested (Pope, Tabachnick & Keith-Spiegel, 1987) that this apparent decrease in the rate of sexual contact with patients by male practitioners may be accounted for by an actual decrease in abuse as a consequence of the increased attention that sexual misconduct has received in recent times. Of more concern is the possibility that offenders are less willing to disclose their sexual contact with patients because of the increasing likelihood that sanctions will be applied (Stake & Oliver, 1991).

Gonsoriek (1989a) suggests that the abuse of male patients may be underreported, particularly if it was perpetrated by a male therapist. Possible reasons for this include the socialization of men to exclude the perception of themselves as powerless victims; thus, self-blame may occur when men are sexually abused by their therapists. Although sexual activity with a same-sex partner does not necessarily mean that either person is homosexually oriented, if a male victim fears that he is homosexual because of such a sexual contact with his therapist homophobia in society may mean that he is less likely to report the abuse for fear of disapprobation. In addition, those patients whose sexual orientation is homosexual may fail to complain about a sexually abusive psychotherapist because this might be viewed as disloyal to the gay community or could entail public revelation of the patient's sexual orientation.

Holroyd & Brodsky (1977) surveyed clinical psychologists' attitudes towards erotic and nonerotic physical contact with patients and found that male therapists are more likely to see benefits in nonerotic contact for opposite sex patients. Male therapists are also more likely to consider having sex with a patient than are female therapists (Pope, Keith-Spiegel & Tabachnick, 1986).

Thus, sexual contact between therapists and their patients must be viewed within the broader context of gender and therefore power issues in psychotherapy.

Age variables

The available research suggests that there is a significant discrepancy between the ages of the therapists who become sexually involved with patients, and the patients. The sexually abusive therapists reported by Dahlberg's (1970) patients were over 40 years of age, 10 to 25 years older than the patients. Gartrell et al (1986) found that the average age of such therapists was 43, while the average age of the patients was 33. Similarly, Bouhoutsos et al (1983) describe average ages of 42 and 33 for therapists and patients, respectively.

Professional variables

In terms of professional characteristics that distinguish offenders from non-offenders, it is clear that while offenders are more likely to advocate and use nonerotic touching of patients, they do not differ on most variables from therapists who do not have sex with their patients (Holroyd & Brodsky, 1980).

The evidence concerning a possible link between personal therapy and sexual contact with patients is somewhat equivocal. Gartrell et al (1986) surveyed U.S. psychiatrists, and found that offenders were more likely to have had personal therapy. However, in Gechtman's (1989) sample of social workers, no significant association emerged between personal therapy and erotic involvement with patients.

Pope, Keith-Spiegel & Tabachnick (1986) argue that educator–student sex models later therapist–patient sex. For female respondents, engaging in sexual contact as a student with educators was related to later sexual contact as professionals (although the extent to which this was with patients is not specified): a figure of 23% as compared with 6% who had not had sexual contact with educators. For male respondents, the number who had been sexually involved with educators was too small to test the relationship. In summary, many female therapists who have sexual relationships in their professional roles were themselves sexually involved with their own teachers, supervisors or therapists (Folman, 1991; Pope, 1989a).

A survey by Kardener, Fuller & Mensh (1976) showed that the freer physicians are with nonerotic physical contact, the more statistically likely it is for them also to engage in erotic practices with patients. Holroyd & Brodsky (1980) found that clinical psychologists who had sex with patients advocated and used nonerotic contact with opposite sex patients more often than did other therapists. Those who had non-intercourse sexual contact, however, did not differ from other therapists in their use of nonerotic touching. So, "the differential application of nonerotic hugging, kissing and touching to opposite sex patients but not to same sex patients is viewed as a sex-biased therapy practice at high risk for leading to sexual intercourse with patients" (p. 807).

Holroyd & Brodsky (1977), in a survey of the attitudes of clinical psychologists towards erotic and nonerotic physical contact with patients, found male therapists to be more likely to see benefits in nonerotic contact for opposite sex patients.

Conclusion

A wide range of sexual acts are perpetrated with patients by abusive therapists belonging to all the main psychotherapy professions in the U.S.A., including intercourse in more than half the cases. Typically, the therapist is male and the patient female. Almost half of such relationships appear to last for less than three months, although some last for more than five years. The limited and inconsistent evidence concerning serial abuse, the initiator of the sexual contact and the time of its initiation precludes any generalization on these topics at present. From the findings on termination, in so far as they are comparable across studies, it appears that in between a quarter and a third of cases, therapy is terminated immediately after the initial sexual contact, while in the remainder therapy continues with or without further sexual contact. Whenever it occurs, termination of therapy is instigated by the patient in at least two-thirds of cases.

While the data available from the studies discussed here provide important information, in terms of broad upper or lower limits, about the problem of the sexual abuse of patients by psychotherapists, there are a number of methodological limitations in the research which must be considered when interpreting it. The most obvious issue is that of sampling bias, in terms of the motivation of research volunteers, in particular their motives to participate or not to participate, a question for which no clear answers are available. In addition, the demographic characteristics of the population of sexually abusive therapists, particularly in terms of behaviour around the returning of questionnaires, are unknown. Thus, it is difficult to draw inferences about the larger population of sexually abusive therapists on the basis of such studies (Williams, 1992).

Clearly, much work in this field remains to be undertaken, particularly in terms of attempting to establish more precisely the extent and nature of, as well as contributory factors to, the sexual abuse of patients by psychotherapists. Williams (1992) suggests that future research to complement existing data might target the naturalistic behaviour of populations; for example, complaints filed against therapists in professional, regulatory and legal settings could be integrated with information about numbers of therapists practising and numbers of patients being treated. In this way, estimates of minimum incidence and changing patterns of sexual contact between patients and their therapists could be obtained.

4 Epidemiology in the U.K.

Tanya Garrett and John Davis

Over the last two decades, North America has seen a wealth of empirical research (Chapter 3) aimed at both estimating the extent to which psychotherapists become sexually involved with their patients, and understanding the phenomenon. It has taken some time for the issue to gain prominence in the U.K., and still longer for research efforts to begin. In recent times, there has been considerable media coverage of therapist–patient sexual contact but no surveys concerning the question have been published to date.

In an effort to begin to address the absence of U.K. research in this field, and to encourage debate around the issue of sex in psychotherapy, we undertook the first national U.K. survey of clinical psychologists in 1992.

Clinical psychologists were targeted in this instance because we anticipated ready access to and a good response from members of our own profession, most of whom are engaged in therapeutic work. Other researchers, it is hoped, will follow suit with other professional and non-professional groups to establish a broad data set for the U.K. Research in America, however, has found few differences of relevance between the main therapy professions: psychology, psychiatry and social work (Borys & Pope, 1989).

This chapter presents some of the findings of the survey with particular reference to those clinical psychologists who disclosed sexual contact with their patients. Other findings from the study will be reported elsewhere.

Methodology

In January 1992 an anonymous questionnaire (Appendix A), covering letter and return-addressed envelope were sent to a random sample of 1000 members of the Division of Clinical Psychology of the British Psychological Society (total membership 2421). It was intended that members would be directly mailed by the British Psychological Society, excluding corresponding, affiliate and overseas members. The exclusion was designed to ensure a sample of qualified psychologists practising in Britain, but due to an administrative error, some trainee clinical psychologists were included. Exclusions totalled 183 Division members, so the sample was taken from a population of 2238.

The questionnaire was developed to gather information about respondents' personal and professional circumstances, to ascertain their attitudes towards and experience of physical and sexual contact with patients, and to assess their experience of sexual contact in student–educator and personal therapy relationships. Finally, questions were included about their experience of treating patients who had had sexual contact with previous therapists and their knowledge of clinical psychologists who had become sexually involved with patients. Space was provided for further comments.

The development of the questionnaire was informed by previous research in the U.S.A. Questions were included in areas that have been shown to be associated with sexual contact between therapists and patients in the U.S.A. That is, respondents were asked to give their age and gender (Dahlberg, 1970), to state whether they had undertaken personal therapy (Gartrell et al, 1986), to report their experience of physical contact with patients of both sexes, and to give their views of possible benefits, to students/trainees, of sexual contact with educators. They were asked to specify whether they had experienced sexual contact themselves with an educator during their training or with their therapist if they had been in personal therapy (Pope, Keith-Spiegel & Tabachnick, 1986).

We also wished to examine the salience in Britain of variables that had not emerged from the North American research as being significantly associated with sexual contact with patients. Respondents were therefore asked to report their marital status and sexual orientation, the length of time since they had qualified, their therapeutic orientation and specialty, and whether they had treated patients who had been sexually involved with previous therapists.

It was hypothesized that the risk of sexual involvement with patients might increase with the amount of clinical work undertaken and with the number of patients treated in long-term therapy. Heavier caseloads expose therapists to a wider range of patients and subject them to greater stress. Long-term therapy increases attachment and dependency, and generally intensifies transference and countertransference reactions. Such practices could predispose therapists to become sexually involved with their patients. Thus, questions in these areas were formulated. It was also felt important to ask about therapists' experience of sexual attraction to patients, on the basis that this is an essentially normal process in therapy and that denial of attraction may dispose therapists to act out sexually (Pope & Bouhoutsos, 1986). Respondents were asked to specify why they had not felt such an attraction, as well as to specify why they had not engaged in sexual relations with a patient, in order to elicit more meaningful information in these areas.

To assess the parameters of abuse, specific questions were formulated for those respondents who had engaged in sexual relations with a patient. For example, they were asked about the total number of occasions of sexual contact over their lifetime, distinguishing between sexual contacts with current and discharged patients. Additionally, in order to establish the extent to which attempts were made to separate the sexual contact from therapy, respondents were asked to identify the location of the sexual contacts with current patients.

More detailed information was gathered about the nature of the sexual contacts that had occurred between respondents and their patients by enquiring about a specific contact. To avoid any systematic bias in the selection of contacts, respondents were asked to select the most recent sexual contact they had had with a patient, if there had been more than one. Here, the authors were particularly interested in the severity of the contact and any coercion involved, and therefore asked questions about the forms of sexual contact that had occurred, whether the therapist aimed to inflict pain on the patient, and any steps that may have been taken to prevent the patient from disclosing to others.

Questions about the way in which the sexual involvement came about, who initiated the contact and the perceived degree of consent on the part of the patient were designed to establish respondents' attributions regarding responsibility and consent. We hypothesized that those therapists who become sexually involved with patients may be likely to rationalize such contact by viewing it as consensual, disregarding the differences in power that are present in the therapy relationship. For similar reasons, we included a question about the effects respondents thought the sexual contact had exerted on the patient.

We recognized that inviting respondents to disclose their own experiences of sexual contact with patients would inevitably result in a conservative estimate of the prevalence of such contacts. We therefore included questions that would provide an alternative perspective on prevalence, at the same time providing some comparative information across professions. To this end, respondents were asked to specify whether they had treated patients who had been sexually involved with a previous therapist of any profession, and to indicate whether they knew through other sources of clinical psychologists who had had sexual contact with patients.

Finally, an attempt was made to ascertain the extent of reporting of therapists, both clinical psychologists and members of other professions, known by respondents to be exploiting patients sexually. Respondents were also asked whether they had taken any action to prevent the continuation of such contacts, and if not, why not. These questions were prompted by North American evidence that therapists rarely take action against colleagues who breach the sexual boundaries of therapy (Gartrell et al, 1987).

Return rate and demographic information

In subsequent presentations of data, distributions that do not sum to 100% signify that not all respondents completed the item in question.

The usable return rate was 58%. A total of 588 questionnaires were returned, of which 581 were completed. Of the seven remaining, six were returned blank, because the recipient had either never practised or was a trainee and did not feel that it was appropriate to complete the questionnaire. The seventh was not returned, but the recipient wrote to indicate that s/he did not wish to complete the questions. In addition, one individual wrote back expressing doubts about the validity of the study and about the appropriateness of requesting intimate information of this nature.

Of the respondents, 60.7% were female and 37.6% male. Their mean age was 39 years (range 24–78; S.D. 9.14) and the mean length of post-qualification practice as a clinical psychologist was 11 years (range 0–40; S.D. 8). Most respondents were married (60.5%) or in a stable relationship (20.8%). Many (12.5%) were single and 4.3% were separated or divorced. Only 0.9% were widowed. The majority of respondents described themselves as heterosexual (96.4%), with 1.5% stating that they were bisexual and 1.7% homosexual.

Respondents' professional practice

In terms of therapeutic orientation, respondents were asked to indicate the three orientations that most influenced their practice. The results for this question are given in Table 4.1. This suggests that the sample is predominantly cognitive-behavioural in orientation, with a modest psychodynamic element, and a rather weaker flavouring of systemic and humanistic influences.

Subjects were also asked to specify their main area of clinical work (Table 4.2) and their main work setting (Table 4.3). Thus, the majority of respondents worked predominantly with an adult population. Substantial minorities worked mainly with children and with people with learning difficulties, and a few respondents worked mainly with the elderly, with those with physical health problems or in the field of neuropsychology. Of the small percentage identifying "other" as their main specialty, responses included work in social services and

Table 4.1: Respondents' Therapeutic Orientations: Percentages Acknowledging Influence of Given Orientation (Section 1, Question 6)

Orientation	First influence	Second influence	Third influence
Behavioural	29.4	27.3	13.2
Cognitive	32.6	30.8	11.7
Psychodynamic	20.3	10.9	19.3
Systemic	11.9	10.9	17.8
Humanistic	9.3	10.9	16.0
Other	5.3	1.4	3.1

Table 4.2: Respondents' Main Areas of Clinical Work (Section 1, Question 7)

Specialty	Percentage of respondents
Adults	54.0
Children/young people	13.9
Learning difficulties	12.9
Elderly	5.2
Physical health	3.6
Neuropsychology	3.8
Other	4.5

Table 4.3: Respondents' Main Work Setting (Section 1, Question 11)

Setting	Percentage of respondents
National Health Service	88.3
Private practice	4.0
Social services	0.9
Voluntary agency	0.7
Other	4.3

universities. Clearly, the vast majority of respondents were employed mainly in the National Health Service. A small minority were mainly engaged in private practice or "other" settings. Only a very small number worked mainly for social services or a voluntary agency.

Respondents spent a mean 14 hours per week in face-to-face patient contact (Section 1, Question 8) (range 0–60; S.D. 7.57) and had a mean 12.9% of their patients in long-term therapy (Section 1, Question 9) (range 0–100; S.D. 21.1). Most respondents worked predominantly on a short-term basis with patients (Section 1, Question 10): a mean 67% of their patients were in short-term therapy (range 0–100; S.D. 30.25). A substantial minority of respondents had undertaken personal therapy (44%).

Attitudes towards and prevalence of sexual contact with patients

Although 2.8% of the sample did not respond when asked whether they believed that patients could ever benefit from sexual contact with a psychotherapist (Section 3, Question 1), 3.6% responded positively to this question, with 93.6% responding negatively.

Twenty respondents, constituting 3.4% of the sample, admitted to having engaged in what they regarded as sexual contact with current or discharged patients. However, a further three respondents (0.5% of the sample) did not respond to this question (Section 3, Question 2). Of these twenty, only five had replied positively to the earlier question asking whether they believed that patients could ever benefit from sexual contact with a therapist.

Twelve of the twenty disclosing psychologists were male, and seven were female. One respondent did not specify his/her sex. The contacts of most of these psychologists (fifteen of the twenty) were heterosexual in nature. Two of the twenty, one male and one female, reported homosexual contacts. The remaining three respondents omitted this item.

In terms of marital status, eight of the twenty described themselves as married, six as in a stable relationship, five as single and one as separated/divorced. The majority of the group (fifteen of the twenty) were heterosexual, four were homosexual and one was bisexual. Most (sixteen of the twenty) reported sexual contact with only one patient, one with two patients, two with three patients and one with six patients (Section 3, Question 4a). Almost all the psychologists (eighteen of the twenty) described their main employment as in the National Health Service, one was mainly in private practice and one did not respond to this question. Most had not undertaken personal therapy at any time (eleven of the twenty), eight had done so and one respondent did not complete this question.

The modal total number of occasions on which respondents had had sexual contact with patients was just one (six respondents). Three individuals reported two occasions, one reported four, one reported five, one reported six and one reported ten occasions. Two psychologists described multiple sexual contacts with patients: one estimated over 800 occasions of sexual contact, and one 1000. Five respondents who had had sexual contact with patients did not respond to this question (Section 3, Question 4b).

The sexual contacts reported by the majority of the respondents (thirteen of the twenty) were with discharged patients only. For all but one of these individuals, the contacts had been with one discharged patient only: the other reported sexual contact with three discharged patients (Section 3, Question 4c). Six respondents had had sexual relations with current patients only; four of the six reported sexual contact with one current patient, one with two current patients and one with three current patients (Section 3, Question 4d). One individual reported sexual contact with both current and discharged patients (five current and one discharged).

When the seven psychologists who had engaged in sexual relations with current patients were asked the circumstances in which this occurred, four stated that it had happened only during therapy sessions, one only outside therapy, and two both within and outside therapy sessions (Section 3, Question 4e).

Respondents were asked to specify whether they had previously disclosed their sexual contacts with patients, and if so, to whom. One of the twenty did not respond to this question. Of the remainder, it is noteworthy that only two had not previously disclosed to anybody. Of the seventeen who had disclosed, twelve described recipients of more than one role category; the mean number of role categories checked by the seventeen disclosers was 2.3 (range 1–5). Colleagues proved the most popular choice of confidante, targeted by thirteen of the seventeen, closely followed by friend/partner (twelve); less commonly chosen were manager (five), personal therapist (four), supervisor (three) and unspecified other (two). It would appear, therefore, that at least among practitioners willing to disclose sexual contact in an anonymous survey, the contact had not in general been a secret shared only between therapist and patient (Section 3, Question 4f).

When respondents were asked to consider a specific patient with whom they had had sexual contact, the most recent if there had been more than one (Section 3, Question 4g), eleven reported that the patient had been female, six that the patient had been male and three did not respond. The patient's age was given by all but four respondents; the mean age was 30 years (range 18–41; S.D. 7.9). None of the sample disclosed sexual contact with a child. The types of sexual contact that occurred between psychologists and their most recent patient are given in Table 4.4 (three of the twenty disclosers did not answer this question).

All respondents who answered the relevant question (sixteen of the twenty) stated that their sexual contact with the patient had been consenting and did not involve the infliction of pain on the patient. Initiation of sexual contact was considered by eleven of the twenty respondents to have been mutual, while six attributed initiation to the patient, one to himself and two did not respond.

For five respondents, the sexual contact disclosed had been a once-only episode. The sexual involvement had lasted less than 3 months for four respondents, between 3 and 11 months for two respondents, and more than 5 years for four respondents. Two respondents did not answer the question on the length of sexual involvement.

Table 4.4:   Types of Behaviour in Most Recent Sexual Contact

Type of behaviour	Number of respondents engaging in behaviour
Kissing	12
Non-genital touching/holding/fondling	12
Hand–genital contact	11
Vaginal intercourse	8
Oral–genital contact	7
Anal penetration	1
Other	2

Ten respondents reported that they had no current contact whatsoever with the patient, three had continuing social but no sexual or therapeutic contact, two had continuing therapeutic but no sexual contact and one had continuing therapeutic and sexual contact; three were married to or in a committed relationship with the patient. One psychologist did not respond to this question. Of the twenty respondents, eight expressed current concern about their sexual contact with the patient in question, ten were unconcerned and two did not state whether or not they were currently concerned.

Nature of sexual contacts with patients

Most of these reports of sexual contact with patients are restricted either to current or to discharged patients. Only one respondent stated that he had engaged in sexual contacts with both current and discharged patients. Some respondents reported a single sexual contact with either a current or a discharged patient, while others reported multiple sexual contacts with a single patient. There were others who had engaged in sexual contact on a single occasion with more than one current or discharged patient, and some respondents who had had sexual contact with more than one current or discharged patient on a number of occasions. In the following case profiles, the respondents are grouped according to these categories. Where information was not provided about the number of sexual contacts that occurred between a respondent and his/her patient, it has been classified in the category which best seems to fit the information given.

Sexual contacts with current patients only

Multiple sexual contacts with one current patient   Psychologist A admits to having had sexual contact with one then current patient, not detailing the number of occasions on which this occurred. He had previously disclosed this contact to a colleague and to a friend/partner. The patient was a woman in her 40s with whom he engaged in kissing, non-genital touching/holding/fondling, hand–genital contact, vaginal intercourse and oral–genital contact. He states that the patient gave full consent to the contact and that no pain was inflicted upon her. He was sexually involved with the patient for between 3 and 11 months and currently has no contact whatsoever with her. He states that sexual contact was mutually initiated and occurred after a close relationship developed within treatment sessions. This was followed by contact outside sessions, eventually developing into a sexual relationship. He states that he believes that the contact directly had "no great adverse effects" upon the patient but the sexual involvement led to a "sidelining" of the therapeutic relationship and loss of trust. He now feels concerned about the contact. He explains that he took no direct steps to dissuade the patient from disclosing the contact as she volunteered an assurance of confidentiality.

Single sexual contact with one current patient   Psychologist B had sexual contact with one then current patient on one occasion. B had previously disclosed this contact to a colleague, to her supervisor and to a friend/partner. The patient was a man in his 40s, with whom she engaged in non-genital touching/holding/fondling. She states that the patient gave full consent to the contact and that pain was not inflicted upon him. She no longer has contact with the patient. She states that she became involved with him as a first-year trainee when visiting him at home. She naively made erotic contact with him as a response to his distress concerning his homosexual orientation. When asked to specify the effects she believed this contact had on the patient, she states that she does not know. She now feels concerned about the contact, which she says was initiated by the patient. She explains that she took no steps to dissuade the patient from disclosing the contact, but discussed it with her supervisor and explained to the patient that it was a mistake.

Psychologist C disclosed sexual contact with one current patient on one occasion. He had previously disclosed this contact to a colleague and to a friend/partner. The patient was a young, teenage woman with whom he engaged in non-genital touching/holding/fondling. He states that the patient gave full consent to the contact and that pain was not inflicted upon her. He currently has no contact with the patient. He states that he became sexually involved with her when "she was very flirtatious and came and sat upon my lap". He states that he has no idea of the effect of the contact on the patient but estimates that this would be very little since she was "a very flirtatious and seductive person with several members of staff". He now feels unconcerned about the contact, and states that the contact was initiated by the patient. He indicates that he took no direct steps to dissuade her from disclosing the contact. He discussed his feelings about it with a colleague.

Psychologist D reported sexual contact with one current patient on one occasion. D had previously disclosed this contact to a colleague, to her manager and to a friend/partner. The patient was a man in his 30s who, on a home visit, made verbal sexual suggestions to her while encouraging his dog to keep her in her chair. No further detail is given by the respondent, who states that the patient gave full consent to the contact and that pain was not inflicted on him. She no longer maintains contact with him. She states that the incident occurred on an initial assessment visit. When asked to specify the effects she believes this contact had on the patient, she states that it is "hard to assess" but that it was agreed that it would be appropriate for her to avoid further contact and to pass his case on to a colleague. She now feels concerned about the contact, which she says was initiated by the patient. She states that she took no steps to dissuade him from disclosing the contact.

Sexual contacts with more than one current patient   Psychologist E states that he had sexual contact with three current patients, not detailing the number of occasions on which this occurred. He had previously disclosed this to a colleague and to his personal therapist. The most recent patient with whom he had sexual contact was a woman in her 40s with whom he engaged in kissing and non-genital touching/holding/fondling. He states that the patient gave full consent to the contact and that no pain was inflicted upon her. He has been erotically involved with her for more than 5 years and still has both therapeutic and sexual contact with her. He does not mention how he became sexually involved with the patient, nor the effects which he believes the involvement has had on her. He feels concerned about the involvement, which he states was mutually initiated. He denies having taken steps to prevent the patient from disclosing the contact.

Psychologist F admits to having had sexual contact with two current patients. Since the total number of sexual contacts F reported was two, she clearly had just one sexual contact with each patient. She had previously disclosed these contacts to a colleague, to her manager and to a friend/partner. The last patient with whom she had sexual contact was a man in his 20s, who exposed himself to her and invited her to masturbate him. She did not comply with his request. She states that the sexual contact was initiated by the patient. It is not clear what part, if any, this respondent believes herself to have played in bringing about or colluding with the sexual episode, though her current "concern" about it and her experience of an unspecified sexual incident with another patient suggest that she does not view herself simply as a victim of abuse by her patients. She confirms that this was the only sexual incident between them, and she currently has continuing therapeutic contact with him free of any sexual contact. Following the incident, she established as conditions for continued therapeutic involvement that the patient must be properly dressed and must not touch her. She believes that the incident had a positive effect on the patient in that she has continued to see him and he now uses therapy appropriately. She is now concerned about the sexual episode. She did not take steps to dissuade the patient from disclosing the incident, and in fact persuaded him to discuss it jointly with herself and his key worker. She adds, "I suspect that I have not filled this in correctly. It would be easier if you defined 'sexual contact'".

Sexual contacts with discharged patients only

Single sexual contact with one discharged patient   Psychologist G admits to sexual contact with one discharged patient on one occasion. G had previously disclosed this contact to her personal therapist. The patient was a woman in her early 30s with whom she engaged in kissing and hand–genital contact. She states that the patient gave full consent to the contact and that no pain was inflicted upon her. She reports no continuing contact with the patient. She states that sexual contact occurred through her giving in to the patient's demands. When asked to specify the effects she believes this contact had on the patient, she states that it "woke her up to reality". She now feels concerned about the contact, which she says was initiated by the patient. She explains that to dissuade the patient from disclosing the contact, she "explained the effect on her future career" (i.e. on the psychologist's career).

Psychologist H admits to sexual contact with one discharged patient on one occasion. He had previously disclosed this contact to a friend/partner. The patient was a woman, whose age he does not give, with whom he engaged in kissing, non-genital touching/holding/fondling, hand–genital contact and vaginal intercourse. He states that the patient gave full consent to the contact and that pain was not inflicted upon her. He currently has no contact with the patient. He states that sexual contact occurred with the patient as a result of mutual attraction. He is unable to say what impact the contact might have had on her. He now feels unconcerned about the contact, which he described as mutually initiated. He claims that he took no direct steps to dissuade the patient from disclosing the contact.

Multiple sexual contacts with one discharged patient   Psychologist I states that sexual contact took place on four occasions with one patient whom the respondent states was current, but whom her account suggests was in fact discharged when sexual contact occurred. The psychologist had previously disclosed this contact to a colleague, to her manager, to her supervisor and to a friend/partner, as well as in a supervision group some time later. The patient was a man in his 30s, with whom she engaged in kissing, non-genital touching/holding/fondling and vaginal intercourse. She states that the patient gave full consent to the contact and that pain was not inflicted on him. The contact lasted between 3 and 11 months, and the psychologist currently has no contact whatsoever with the patient. However, for 2 years afterwards she continued to have social contact with him, but no sexual or therapeutic contact. She states that the contact occurred after she felt attracted to him, but contained her feelings during therapy, which was unsupervised. After he ceased to be a patient, she became socially and subsequently sexually involved with him. When asked to specify the effects she believed this contact had on the patient, she states that it was probably unhelpful and repeated a pattern he had followed of becoming very involved with helpers from other agencies. This was not known to her until later. She now feels concerned about the contact, which she says was mutually initiated. She explains that she took no steps to dissuade the patient from disclosing the contact, but discussed the ethical issues with him at the time. She also informed him that she had sought professional guidance and advice about the morality of the situation, even though he had been discharged. The patient disclosed the contact to friends, to colleagues and to the person who sought help for him.

Psychologist J states that he had sexual contact with one discharged patient on "too many occasions to count". He had previously disclosed this contact to a colleague and to a friend/partner. The patient was a woman in her late 30s with whom he engaged in kissing, non-genital touching/holding/fondling, hand–genital contact, vaginal intercourse and oral–genital contact. He states that the patient gave full consent to the contact and that pain was not inflicted on her. He has been sexually involved with her for more than 5 years and is currently married to or in a stable relationship with her. He states that sexual involvement began 4 years after therapy had ended when they had both moved to another town. He believes that the effects of the contact on her have been positive. He now feels unconcerned about the contact, which he says was mutually initiated. He states that he has taken no steps to dissuade her from disclosing the contact.

Psychologist K admits to having been sexually involved with one discharged patient. He had not previously disclosed this contact, and gave no further details. He states "I need to emphasize that it was an ex-patient who I had seen only twice. Eight months later we met in a gay bar in of all places, X [a city abroad]! I guess we took it from there but didn't have sex/physical contact till a few months later, once we agreed to meet up in Y [a city in the U.K.], and emphasized we were friends. But now so many years down the line (we have been together 11 years) we are lovers—still trying to have children". It is unclear whether this implies a heterosexual relationship or refers to adoption by a homosexual couple.

Psychologist L admits to having had sexual contact with one discharged patient on ten occasions. He had not previously disclosed this contact. The patient was a woman in her late 20s, with whom he engaged in kissing, non-genital touching/holding/fondling, hand–genital contact, vaginal intercourse, oral–genital contact and anal penetration. He states that the patient gave full consent to the contact and that pain was not inflicted on her. He was sexually involved with her for less than 3 months and reports no continuing contact with her. He states that sexual contact with her occurred because of mutual weakness and vulnerability, but states that "the responsibility was and is mine alone". He believes that the effect of the sexual involvement is "continuing emotional damage" to the patient. He now feels concerned about the contact, which he sees as having been mutually initiated. He says that he took no direct steps to dissuade the patient from disclosing the contact.

Psychologist M admits sexual contact with one discharged patient on three occasions. He had previously disclosed this contact to a colleague, to his manager and to a friend/partner. The patient was a woman in her early 30s with whom he engaged in kissing, non-genital touching/holding/fondling, hand–genital contact, vaginal intercourse and oral–genital contact. He states that the patient gave full consent to the contact and that no pain was inflicted on her. The sexual contact lasted for less than 3 months and he maintains no current contact with the patient. He states that sexual contact occurred following correspondence after her discharge. The psychologist moved from the city in which he had resided and arranged to meet the patient there 2 years later. It is unclear whether he made the arrangement to meet the patient at the time of discharge or whether he recontacted her 2 years later. He states that they "both felt it had been a glorious weekend but very much an unrepeatable interlude that had 'rounded off' our relationship". He now feels unconcerned about the contact, which he describes as having been mutually initiated. He reports having taken no direct steps to dissuade the patient from disclosing the contact. He continues, "I have felt sexual attraction to clients both before and since the one with whom I had a brief sexual relationship. In no other case, however, have I contemplated acting on it. The lady in question and I were aware of mutual non-transference attraction (had we met in any other circumstances that attraction plus the desire to act upon it would have been there). We became friends after discharge—admittedly because of that attraction—and the sexual contact took place within that context. We continued to be friends after the contact until we both became involved with others whom we married. I cannot now contemplate acting on sexual attraction to a patient— either during or after therapy. Many of my patients are now survivors of child sexual abuse and to do so—even if I could rationalize it to myself—would be a repeat of using a position of vulnerability to obtain sexual gratification. My patients are very much now confined to 'work time' professional relationships. I find other women outside of work attractive too but have no desire to act upon it because of my love and commitment towards my wife and children. The friendship with this lady (patient) grew from our meeting through work and the sexual relationship grew out of that. She was, and is, very much the exception in my professional life—I still remember her with great affection".

Psychologist N admits having been sexually involved with one discharged patient, but does not detail on how many occasions sexual contact occurred. She had not previously disclosed this experience. She does not say whether the patient was male or female and gives few details about the involvement, but does mention that their liaison has lasted for more than 5 years and that she is currently married to or in a committed relationship with the individual. Their sexual involvement does not currently cause her any concern.

Psychologist O, who does not state his/her own gender, admits to having had sexual contact with one discharged patient on six occasions. He/she had previously disclosed this contact to a colleague. The patient was a woman in her mid-20s, with whom he/she engaged in kissing, non-genital touching/holding/fondling and hand–genital contact. The psychologist states that the patient gave full consent to the contact and that no pain was inflicted upon her. The sexual contact lasted for less than 3 months and the psychologist currently has continued social contact with the patient, but no sexual or therapeutic contact. This individual states that sexual involvement with the patient occurred following re-establishment of contact by the patient after discharge, and that they met socially rather than professionally. He/she states that the sexual contact raised issues about the patient's commitment to her existing boyfriend and was distressing for her for much of the period that it continued. Now, the psychologist believes, the sexual contact has little or no effect on the patient. The psychologist now feels unconcerned about the contact, which is described as having been mutually initiated. He/she asserts that no direct steps were taken to dissuade the patient from disclosing the contact.

Psychologist P states that sexual contact occurred between himself and one discharged patient on two occasions. The sexual contact occurred about 6 months after the patient had been discharged and moved abroad. He had previously disclosed this contact to a supervisor and friend/partner. The patient was a woman in her early 20s and the psychologist was at that time in his mid-20s. He reports engaging in kissing, non-genital touching/holding/fondling, hand–genital contact, vaginal intercourse and oral–genital contact with the patient. He states that the patient gave full consent to the contact and that pain was not inflicted on her. He describes the sexual contact as a single sexual encounter (though this would appear to contradict his earlier statement that sexual contact occurred on two occasions) and no longer has any contact with the patient. He states that he became sexually involved with her when he was lonely and inexperienced as a trainee therapist, and attributes the involvement to the mutual liking between them. Regarding the impact the contact might have had upon her, he states that he wrote to her a number of years later expressing guilt and she reassured him that she had not been harmed. He now feels unconcerned about the contact, but states that he would not repeat it even if he were single. He describes the contact as having been mutually initiated, and reports that the patient travelled from a country in northern Europe specifically to see him. He explains that he took no direct steps to dissuade her from disclosing the contact. He continues, "I believe *no* therapist should engage in a sexual relationship with a client in treatment. There may be a case for 'allowing' it after a reasonable period of discharge provided the patient obtains support/counselling from another source. Subsequent to my experience, I asked female therapists to take over two patients who became over-involved with me and I found it difficult to continue my role as an effective therapist. Both had been subjected to sexual abuse in childhood or adolescence. Without my experience gained it would have been easy for an inappropriate sexual relationship to develop. This would definitely have been *damaging* to the patients involved if it had occurred".

Psychologist Q discloses sexual contact with one discharged patient, but does not specify the number of occasions on which sexual contact occurred. He had not previously disclosed this contact. He does not give the age or sex of the patient, but it is clear from his subsequent comments that the patient is a woman. He does not specify the nature of the sexual contact that took place, whether she gave full consent to the contact or whether he inflicted pain upon her. He is currently married to or in a committed relationship with the patient. He states that he became sexually involved with her 9 months to a year after discharge when they met again through mutual friends. After his divorce, he started going out with the patient. In terms of the impact the contact might have had upon her, he states that she changed her lifestyle and commenced a degree. She now lives with the psychologist and is head of a department in a higher education establishment. The psychologist does not state whether he feels concerned or unconcerned about the involvement, which he says was mutually initiated. He says that he made no attempt to dissuade the patient from disclosing the contact, as she was no longer in therapy with him. He continues, "The therapeutic relationship is a very special one in which the therapist has an advantage since he/she can be seen by the patient as an understanding, benign, knowledgeable person who has the patient's interests at heart (almost altruistic) and will be able to improve their life and help solve their difficulties and problems. The therapist may be the first person to listen and understand the patient's problems. If the therapist changes this relationship the trust and the advantages to the patient can be detrimental as the relationship will change. Also it is *never* worth your whole professional life, standing, etc., which will always be in jeopardy and trusting it to a person who usually cannot manage their own lives and can now hold power over the therapist. In the course of one's life patients sometimes make covert or blatant passes or let it be known to the therapist that they would like the relationship to become sexual but in these cases it may be an aspect of their pathology or need for 'love' which they are not getting from their partners or through socially acceptable ways, e.g. a person lacking in social skill, etc. I have utilized such instances firstly by explaining the therapeutic relationship, describing the limits and then directing the patient's needs more appropriately".

Psychologist R admits to sexual contact with one discharged patient on two occasions. He had previously disclosed this contact to a colleague. The patient was a woman in her early 20s. They engaged in kissing, hand–genital contact and oral–genital contact. He states that the patient gave full consent to the contact and that pain was not inflicted on her. He describes his involvement with the patient as lasting for one sexual encounter (though this would appear to contradict his earlier statement that sexual contact occurred on two occasions) and currently has continuing social contact with the patient, but no sexual or therapeutic contact. He states that he became sexually involved with the patient almost 25 years ago, when they were both very immature and unsettled in their personal lives. There was a physical attraction and a shared sense of humour/philosophy of life. In terms of the impact the contact might have had upon the patient, he states that there was certainly no long-term harm, and he does not believe that either of them got caught up in the relationship at the time. He now feels unconcerned about the contact, which he says he initiated himself. He explains that he took no direct steps to dissuade her from disclosing the contact. He continues, "I saw Anne [the pseudonym used for the patient by the respondent] perhaps 15–20 times over a year-long period in [specifies dates] after she had been discharged from hospital. On two occasions our contacts became sexual. I moved away from the area within a year or two but have kept written contact 2–3 times a year with Anne and have seen her twice. Her life remained very unsettled until [specifies period a few years later] and during this time she wrote to me and occasionally phoned and in the broadest sense of the word I believe our contact was therapeutic—the more recent letters are on a friendship level. Anne has married, developed a good career and achieved national success in a leisure pursuit. We both knew what we were doing was wrong. I fully appreciated the thorough unprofessionalism of my actions, though did not believe it would harm my friend—but in retrospect I don't think that was a mature decision– it could have gone seriously wrong but I believed Anne to be more stable than her admission to hospital suggested. As I say, this was almost 25 years ago and the action of a very immature young man. I can still treat myself to the odd fantasy when seeing a female to whom I'm attracted but I leave it at that. Good luck with your dissertation."

"PS I've just re-read what I have written and if it isn't obvious there is almost a confessional aspect to this. My Catholic/Freudian friends tell me that confession is good for you so I expect I can relax now and wait for the good feelings to roll in, if it wasn't for my anxieties (just about manageable) about disclosure".

Multiple sexual contact with more than one discharged patient Psychologist S admits to sexual contact with three discharged patients. She states that it is impossible to quantify the number of occasions on which sexual contact has occurred as she had long-term relationships with two of the patients, but estimates over 1000. She had previously disclosed her involvement to a colleague, to her manager and to her personal therapist. The most recent patient with whom she had sexual contact was a man in his 30s with whom she engaged in kissing, non-genital touching/holding/fondling, hand–genital contact, vaginal intercourse and oral–genital contact. She states that the patient gave full consent to the contact and that pain was not inflicted on him. The sexual involvement lasted for more than 5 years and she currently has continuing social, but no sexual or therapeutic contact with him. She states that the contact occurred following an immediate mutual attraction. At the second session, the patient declared that he had only kept his appointment because of this attraction, and did not feel the need for therapy. She continues, "I knew I had to do something before a therapist–patient pattern developed and revealed my attraction to him. I immediately discontinued therapy". There appears to be some ambiguity in this statement and it is unclear whether the respondent means that she herself revealed her attraction to the patient or that she was concerned that the "pattern" would reveal her attraction to him. It appears likely that the former is the intended meaning here. When asked to specify the effects she believed this contact had on the patient, she states that this was positive since they had a "very good, committed relationship and are now good friends". She now feels unconcerned about the contact, which she says was mutually initiated. She says that she took no steps to dissuade the patient from disclosing the contact.

Sexual contacts with both current and discharged patients

Psychologist T admits to sexual contact with six patients, one after discharge and five while the patients were in therapy. His sexual contacts with current patients number five in all, i.e. one with each patient, but the total rises to over 800 when his relationship with the discharged patient is included. The sexual contacts with current patients occurred only within therapy sessions. He had previously disclosed the contacts to a colleague, to his personal therapist and to a friend/partner. The most recent patient with whom he had sexual contact was a teenage man with whom he engaged in hand–genital contact. He states that the patient gave full consent to the contact and that pain was not inflicted on him. The patient was then, and continues to be, in therapy with him, but there has been no further sexual contact following this solitary occasion. He states that the sexual contact occurred because the patient was concerned about penile size and, having poor literary skills, was not sure about how to use condoms. In terms of the impact the contact might have had upon the patient, he states that the patient felt mildly embarrassed, but was reassured by feedback about the size of his penis and clearer about the use of condoms. The psychologist now feels unconcerned about the contact, which he claims was initiated by the patient. He states that he took no direct steps to dissuade the patient from disclosing the contact. He continues, "The sexual contacts referred to within therapy are not mutual and arose from concerns about penile size, tight foreskins, uncertainty about correct use of condoms, fibrous scar on penile shaft causing crooked erection and explaining surgical strategies in sex reassignment. None were orgasmic or directly construed as a sexual contact by the clients as far as I know. The other contact was a 4-year relationship which was embarked upon after the client had been discharged for 6 months. Over a three or four session contact it became explicitly discussed that he and I found each other sexually and physically attractive prior to therapy as we had met on one previous social occasion. As we were falling in love, I terminated the contract, transferred the case to a colleague and maintained a prohibition on contacting him for 6 months. As soon as the 6-month embargo was ended he contacted me proposing a meeting. We became lovers for 4 years. When I was counselling teenage gay men, I was frequently propositioned within sessions, either verbally or by the lad rubbing an erection through his trousers. I was tempted on many occasions but refused the invitations. I regard the five contacts within sessions as mildly to moderately abusive in that I should have suggested that they consult a medical practitioner; there was secondary sexual gratification for me; but the contact itself was no more than what a medical practitioner would do or might do. Where erection was achieved the client masturbated to arousal [sic]. A female supervisor frequently unzipped my trousers and attempted to arouse me to erection manually or orally. I was embarrassed, confused, but felt foolish if I objected or complained".

Discussion and recommendations

The prevalence of sexual contact between clinical psychologists and their patients as disclosed in this study broadly accords with the recent figures obtained in North American research (Gechtman, 1989). An examination of the details of the cases where sexual contact occurred between therapist and patient suggests that the phenomenon is complex, perhaps more complex than has to date been recognized: for example, a substantial minority (36.8%) of these psychologists were women (seven out of nineteen who specified their gender). However, it should be noted that this subsample is nonetheless unrepresentative of the full sample of respondents, where 61.7% of those who gave their gender were women. North American surveys do not provide a clear picture in terms of the percentages of male and female therapists who engage in sexual behaviour with patients. While some surveys would suggest that substantially more men have sexual contact with their patients (e.g. Gartrell et al, 1986; Pope, Levenson & Schover, 1979; Bouhoutsos et al, 1983), others have found no significant difference between the sexes (e.g. Stake & Oliver, 1991; Akamatsu, 1988).

There is at present a debate in the field of psychotherapy (Miller, 1993) concerning the legitimacy of sexual contact with current patients versus that with discharged patients. Clinical psychologists are currently being asked to comment on whether ethical codes should permit sexual contact with discharged patients at all, or, for example, after a specified period following discharge. One of the issues to be considered in this context is the potential harm that such contacts could cause to patients (see Chapter 2).

An extension of this debate might lead us to question whether a distinction should be made between a single sexual contact with a single patient, and more sustained sexual contact with one or more patients. This introduces the issue of the therapist's fitness to practise, since the therapist who has a series of sexual contacts with patients could be considered to be unfit to practise because of potential harm to patients. By contrast, the therapist who engages in a single sexual contact with one patient may have been coerced in some way by the patient or advances may have been made towards the therapist by the patient (as occurred for some respondents in this survey), or the therapist may subsequently have realized the potential damaging effect of his or her actions and perhaps sought help to prevent recurrence of sexual contact with patients. It has certainly been argued that such therapists are more amenable to rehabilitation (Schoener & Gonsoriek, 1988).

An additional factor to be considered may be the duration of the contact between therapist and patient. Some of the respondents in this survey have argued that lasting post-termination sexual relationships can have a positive effect upon patients, and, indeed, should not be viewed differently from any other sexual relationship.

Six out of the twenty clinical psychologists who disclosed sexual contacts had such contact with current patients only. A seventh had sexual contact with both current and discharged patients. For three of these seven psychologists, their avowed breach of sexual boundaries was confined to a solitary occasion with a single patient. In addition, according to respondents' accounts, most of the reported sexual contacts with current patients involved some coercion towards the therapist (Psychologist D), advances by the patient (Psychologists C and F), or naiveté on the part of the therapist (Psychologist B).

Over half (14) of the disclosures concerned sexual contact with one or more discharged patients. Some of these involve long-term relationships with a former patient or sexual contact some years later. There was one respondent who disclosed multiple sexual contacts with a number of discharged patients.

It would be misleading to assume that the therapists who disclosed sexual contact with patients had not considered the effect of the sexual contact upon the patient, or simply did not consider this issue. The majority of respondents voiced their current concern about the effects upon the patient(s) of the sexual contact. Many stated that sex with a patient had occurred at a difficult or vulnerable time in their lives or when the therapist was immature or naive. These factors appear to be largely independent of the status of the patient (i.e. whether current or discharged). However, one therapist openly admits an element of abuse in his sexual contacts with patients, and in many other cases there appear to be no "mitigating" factors mentioned by respondents. It is pertinent, then, to recall here the finding (Pope & Vetter, 1991) that harm occurred to patients in 80% of the cases in which therapists engaged in sex with a patient even after termination of therapy.

In the light of the current debate about the legitimacy of sexual contact with discharged patients, it is clearly essential for future research to examine in greater detail the issue of post-termination sexual relationships, in particular their effect upon the patient. Such research would inform this debate in terms of providing systematic data. However, it must be borne in mind that some therapists may terminate therapy in order to embark upon a sexual relationship with the patient. This would suggest that the therapist may not always have the best interests of the patient in mind, if the patient's psychological distress (the reason for seeking therapy) was subordinated to the sexual desire of the therapist by the premature termination of therapy.

We also need to question some of the gender-based theoretical understandings of the phenomenon of therapist–patient sexual contact that have been developed if such a substantial proportion of therapists who engage in sexual contact with their patients are female. That is, it has been argued on the basis of findings that it is largely male therapists who sexually abuse female patients, that male ascendancy over women in our society is translated into the therapy situation, and thus legitimizes and enables men's exploitation of women. Although the gender argument may have relevance in terms of explaining some cases of sex in therapy, additional factors should be considered, while bearing in mind that it may be that male therapists are less likely to report sexual contact with female patients (and possibly male patients) because of recent publicity accorded to such cases and the adverse consequences for male therapists of such reporting, for example in terms of malpractice actions (see Chapter 2).

It is important that further surveys are conducted with other groups of therapists and counsellors to extend our knowledge of the phenomenon of therapist–patient sex, and to establish the validity of the findings of this survey, in particular the issue of prevalence. However, it is equally important that the therapy and counselling professions pay heed to the findings of this research and attend to their stance on the matter, as well as to questions of prevention and means of addressing the problem of sexual contact between therapists and their patients once it has occurred.

Part III
ABUSIVE THERAPISTS

5 Risk characteristics and preconditions for abuse

In this chapter some psychological characteristics that appear to enhance the risk of therapists abusing their patients are identified, and several preconditions for the occurrence of abuse are conceptualized.

Risk characteristics

Certain psychological characteristics appear to enhance the risk of a therapist sexually abusing his patients. These characteristics have been identified largely by clinical observation rather than by systematic research; consequently, little quantitative data is currently available on their prevalence among abusive therapists. In particular, it is important to appreciate that the information available is derived from male perpetrators and nothing is known about any possible gender differences in the distribution of these or other characteristics. It should be noted that they are not regarded as being mutually exclusive or as constituting a typology of abusers.

Distressed

A large proportion of abusive therapists appear to suffer some form of personal distress. For example, in a group of twenty psychiatrists and psychologists, 90% reported having been "vulnerable", "needy" and/or "lonely" when the sexual contact occurred, and these problems were related to unsatisfying or broken marriages. In the same group, 55% said they were frightened of intimacy (Butler & Zelen, 1977). Other reported sources of distress include low self-esteem, depression, concerns about sexual adequacy or orientation, mid-life crises and professional burnout.

Isolated

In addition to lacking close personal relationships, as mentioned above, abusive therapists are often professionally isolated individuals who do not communicate or consult with their peers and are unwilling to seek help from another therapist.

Grandiose

Some abusive therapists exhibit features of a narcissistic personality disorder such as having a grandiose sense of self-importance and "specialness", together with a grossly excessive valuation of their own capacities and achievements (American Psychiatric Association, 1987). There is a tendency to believe that they are superior to other therapists, are able to treat patients whom others cannot help, and that they are unique in being able to provide what a patient needs— sometimes including her sexual satisfaction. Such therapists feel competent and entitled to use unorthodox therapeutic approaches—perhaps including sexual contact—which are beyond the more limited powers of lesser therapists. Being overconfident in themselves, they do not deign to seek help or advice from others. Very often patients perceive them as charismatic gurus.

Dominating

Commonly, abusive therapists appear to have strong propensities to control and subjugate their patients, sometimes humiliating them in a sadistic manner (Smith, 1984). In the group of twenty abusive psychiatrists and psychologists studied by Butler & Zelen (1977), 70% stated that they had a more dominant and/or fatherly role, and 15% described themselves as domineering and controlling in their interactions with patients.

Antisocial

Abusive therapists exhibiting these characteristics are sometimes labelled psychopathic or sociopathic, or given the diagnosis of antisocial personality disorder (American Psychiatric Association, 1987). According to Gabbard, "The absence of a mature moral sense in these therapists makes it difficult for them to experience other people as separate individuals with feelings of their own.

Hence, patients who come to them for help are seen merely as objects to be used for their own sexual gratification. The therapist has no empathy for the victim nor concern for the harm that might come to the patient" (1991, p. 652).

Schoener & Gonsiorek (1989) identify the impulsive and sociopathic character disorders in abusive therapists. The former "have long-standing problems with impulse control: some may even have had legal difficulties. . . . If there is a long history of inappropriate behavior it may include . . . sexual harassment of staff members or trainees, or poorly controlled sexual behavior in their personal lives. . . . While severe consequences are pending they show guilt, remorse, and depression. . . . However, they rarely have any true appreciation of the effect of their behavior on their victims, and they tend to deny that they have caused any harm" (1989, p. 403). Sociopathic abusers share many of these features but "they tend to be far more deliberate and cunning in their sexual exploitation of clients. Typically, they are cool, calculating, and detached, and they are expert at seducing a range of clients and at covering their tracks" (Schoener & Gonsiorek, 1989, p. 404).

Conclusion

Clearly, not all therapists who exhibit one or more of the characteristics of distress, isolation, grandiosity, domination or antisocial behaviour will abuse their patients. These characteristics appear to enhance the risk of abuse but for this to occur certain preconditions must exist, which are considered next.

Preconditions for abuse

For a therapist to sexually abuse a patient he must:

1. Be motivated to abuse.
2. Overcome any internal inhibitions he may have against doing so.
3. Overcome any external constraints.
4. Overcome any resistance from the patient.

This so-called four-factor model was first proposed by Finkelhor (1984) in respect of sexual offenders against children but it appears to be equally applicable to abusive therapists.

Motivation

As discussed further in the conclusion to this section, knowledge of the motives for abuse may help to *explain* why it occurs but it does not constitute an *excuse* for the perpetrators, who must be held responsible for their actions. The following subsections discuss the more common motives that are experienced or expressed by therapists.

Sex   Perhaps the most obvious, but not necessarily the most frequent, motive for abuse is the sexual gratification of the therapist, who may be particularly liable to exploit patients for this purpose if other sexual relationships are lacking or unsatisfying in his life. As discussed above, some therapists with antisocial characteristics are also motivated to use patients for their gratification, regardless of the victims' feelings or suffering.

Love   This appears to be a frequently cited motive for the sexual abuse of patients. Among 84 abusive psychiatrists, 65% said that they had been in love with the patients they victimized, and 92% believed that these patients had been in love with them (Gartrell et al, 1986). In another study of 20 offenders, 55% reported having loved the patients concerned (Butler & Zelen, 1977). Clearly, there are likely to be response biases in proclamations of love for their victims by abusive therapists. With varying degrees of awareness, they may rationalize their transgressions as arising from "true love", or they might advance this in a conscious and deliberate attempt to legitimize and excuse their abusive acts— especially if the perpetrator has antisocial characteristics.

The professed love of therapists for their patients is often regarded as a countertransference reaction rather than genuine, romantic love, although this is a difficult discrimination, both theoretically and empirically (Maroda, 1991). Controversy exists over the precise definition of countertransference (e.g. Greenson, 1974; Grossman, 1965), but there is general agreement that it involves the transfer of attitudes acquired in the past to the present, so that the therapist's perception of the patient is distorted and his feelings towards her are inappropriate and unrealistic. "Genuine" loving relationships are influenced by past experience also, but it is suggested that they have relatively greater freedom from the distortion and unreality of countertransference reactions. Thus, the professed love of a therapist for his patient might fall at any point on a continuum, at one end of which is relatively undistorted and realistic genuine love, while at the other end is the distorted and unrealistic love of a countertransference nature. Incidently, it is not essential to confine countertransference concepts to psychoanalytic theory; equivalent processes are described and accounted for in other approaches, such as schema theory (e.g. Beck & Freeman, 1990; Jehu, 1992; McCann & Pearlman, 1990; Young, 1990).

Distress   Therapists who are experiencing personal distress may turn to their patients for the reassurance, support, comfort and intimacy that are lacking in their everyday lives. Typically, a role reversal occurs whereby the therapist's needs are given priority over those of the patient, and she assumes responsibility for looking after him, often including fulfilling his sexual desires. Thus, Schoener & Gonsiorek describe therapists who "have long-standing and significant emotional problems. ... Their work tends to be at the center of their lives and most of their personal needs are met in the work setting" (1989, p. 403); and Pope & Bouhoutsos describe the process of what they call "role trading", in which "The patient's role is to care for, please, and gratify the wants and needs of the therapist. ... The therapist becomes the talker, the patient the listener. The life and needs of the therapist become the focus. The legitimate needs of the patient become secondary or denied altogether. ... Sexually gratifying the therapist is but one of many ways in which the patient fulfils this function" (1986, p. 6).

Narcissism   Among 84 abusive psychiatrists, 19% said that they intended sexual contact to enhance the patient's self-esteem and/or to provide a restitutive emotional experience, and 18% said it was intended as a therapeutic intervention (Gartrell et al, 1986). Varying proportions of the same sample reported that they believed sexual contact to be appropriate for treating sexual dysfunction (18%), enhancing the patient's self-esteem (11%), providing a corrective emotional experience for the patient (8%), changing a patient's sexual orientation (7%) or shortening a grief reaction after a significant loss (6%) (Herman et al, 1987).

These therapeutic intentions and beliefs in some cases may reflect the narcissistic or grandiose characteristics of the therapists concerned. They may regard themselves as having special powers and superior capacities which render them uniquely able to provide what the patient needs, together with an entitlement to use unorthodox methods that most therapists would eschew. These methods may include sexual contact, which has been described as resulting from the therapist succumbing "to the illusion that a magically curative copulation will resolve the patient's illness which has resisted all the more sophisticated psychotherapy techniques" (Searles, 1979, p. 431).

Power   Sexual abuse may be motivated by the power and control that some therapists desire over their patients. According to Smith "the patient becomes the object first of psychological subjugation that may, as the therapist becomes bolder, become a form of physical subjugation. Such therapists enjoy a sense of triumph as they take custody of the patient's body as well as her mind" (1989, p. 61).

Coercion Some patients, particularly those with a borderline personality disorder, may coerce their therapists to engage in sex with them by threatening to become violently angry or to harm themselves if the therapist does not comply with their wishes. Such threats and consequences can be extremely frightening and the therapist may feel that he dare not resist the demand for sex. Thus, Gutheil states that "Borderline rage is an affect that appears to threaten or intimidate even experienced clinicians to the point that they feel or act as though they were literally coerced—moved through fear—by the patient's demands; they dare not deny the patient's wishes. Such pressure may deter therapists from setting limits and holding firm to boundaries for fear of the patient's volcanic response to being thwarted or confronted" (1989, p. 598). Furthermore, "Many of the women with a borderline level of ego organization ... are also self-destructive and suicidal. Such depression and suicidal despair may lead the psychotherapist to justify any sexual transgression with the assertion that only acceding to the patient's sexual demands will keep her from killing herself" (Eyman & Gabbard, 1991, p. 669).

Internal inhibitions

When a national sample of psychotherapists in the U.S. were asked why they refrained from sexual involvement with clients to whom they were attracted the most frequent reasons given were that it would have been unethical, countertherapeutic or exploitative, an unprofessional practice, against the therapist's personal values, or that he/she was already in a committed relationship. Less frequent reasons included fear of censure or loss of reputation, fear of being damaged, fear of retaliation by the client and the illegality of sexual involvement (Pope, Keith-Spiegel & Tabachnick, 1986). These and any other internal inhibitions must be overcome as a necessary second precondition for abuse to occur.

This can be accomplished by certain forms of behaviour such as the misuse of *alcohol or drugs* which have disinhibiting effects, or by *poor impulse control* so that inhibitions are bypassed rapidly and often with limited awareness.

Another way of overcoming internal inhibitions is the deployment of certain cognitive-affective mechanisms or defences which influence the potential perpetrator's perceptions of, and feelings about, the abuse. One such mechanism is variously termed psychogenic amnesia, motivated forgetting or *repression* and it is exemplified by the finding that over 80% of 20 abusive therapists "could not recall or were unwilling to recall the events which led directly to the sexual contact. ('I feel like I was particularly unconscious during that time, and I don't remember much of that aspect of the relationship'). One may recognize in this 'forgetting' the conflict-blocking involved" (Butler & Zelen, 1977, p. 142). This finding may also reflect some element of *dissociation*, whereby the perpetrator cognitively disengages himself from the abusive situation so that it is as if it is not happening, or he depersonalizes and feels different from his usual self so that in effect it is not really he who is abusing the patient. The defence of *denial* may be manifested in statements such as "It wasn't abusive because we didn't have intercourse", "It wasn't distressing or harmful to the patient" or "No one will ever know what happened". *Minimization* may be deployed so that the abuse is played down in statements such as "It was only a bit of fun", "We only petted" or "It only happened once". A range of *rationalizations* may be advanced to excuse the abuse, including:

- Our relationship is "special" and different from those of other therapists with their patients.
- I am in love with her.
- She/is seductive/started it/wanted it/consented to it/enjoyed it/needed it.
- Our sexual relationship is part of her therapy and will help to resolve her problems.
- I had to agree to sex to stop her becoming enraged or harming herself.
- Sex only happens outside therapeutic sessions.
- Therapy has terminated so there is nothing wrong in having sex.
- She is already promiscuous/sexually experienced so one more lover won't matter.
- It is normal for a man to have sex with any available woman.

External constraints

A therapist may be motivated and have overcome his internal inhibitions but certain external constraints may still restrain him from abusing a patient. Thus, overcoming such restraints constitutes a third necessary precondition for abuse to occur. The customary privacy of therapeutic sessions, particularly in independent practice, affords some opportunity for abuse, and this may be enhanced by arranging appointments when other members of staff are absent, perhaps late in the evening or at weekends. Therapists may also contrive opportunities for sexual relationships by visiting patients in their homes or arranging to meet them socially outside therapeutic sessions. In order to maintain secrecy and the continuance of the abuse, therapists may also keep their patients relatively isolated by not referring them to other professionals when this is indicated, and may avoid supervision of their work with victimized patients or fail to disclose the sexual nature of their relationships with them to the supervisor.

Patients' resistance

Because of certain inadequacies and vulnerabilities discussed in Chapter 7 some patients will offer little or no resistance to sexual approaches from their therapists, but to the extent that such resistance is manifested then it must be overcome as a fourth and final precondition for the occurrence of abuse. This task might be addressed by means of boundary violations, persuasive communications, exploitation of relationships with patients and encouraging them to use drugs or alcohol.

Boundary violations Sexual relationships between therapists and patients very often begin with the gradual erosion of customary boundaries between professional and personal relationships, and perpetrators sometimes report that they found themselves behaving atypically with patients whom they subsequently sexually abused. Such boundary violations commonly include unorthodox therapeutic arrangements, suggestive talk, physical contact, extratherapeutic relationships and excessive self-disclosure by the therapist (Epstein & Simon, 1990; Simon, 1989, 1991).

A variety of *unorthodox therapeutic arrangements* may occur. Sessions may be increased in frequency or lengthened, held outside normal working hours when other members of staff are not present, or held at locations other than the customary professional setting, such as when unnecessary or inappropriate house calls are made. Unusually large proportions of sessional time may be spent in personal conversation rather than on therapeutic tasks. Treatment may be terminated prematurely to permit the commencement of a sexual relationship, which the therapist therefore claims to be ethical, or to enable such a relationship to continue treatment might be prolonged unnecessarily. Fees may be reduced or waived in circumstances when this would not be normal practice.

In addition to sexual jokes, *suggestive talk* might include intrusive questioning of patients about their sex lives to satisfy the therapist's curiosity and perhaps feed his fantasies rather than because such inquiry is clinically necessary and appropriate. Sexual innuendoes are another example; for instance, a therapist may tell a patient that he finds her very attractive and would like to get to know her much better if she were not his patient.

In their survey of U.S. psychologists Holroyd & Brodsky found that "The therapist at risk for intercourse with patients is likely to be one who typically touches opposite-sex patients but not same-sex patients. Thus, . . . the stage may be set for unethical sexual involvement with patients" (1980, p. 810). *Physical contact* such as touching, hugging and kissing may constitute exploitation of the patient's wish to be physically comforted in non-sexual ways. In other cases, it is represented as appropriate treatment to desensitize the patient's sexual inhibitions and anxiety, and these problems are sometimes overdiagnosed by therapists who abuse their patients in this way.

Proper boundaries may be transgressed by entering into *extratherapeutic relationships* with patients, which are also referred to as dual or multiple relationships. Thus, potentially abusive therapists may relate to patients in a variety of roles such as social acquaintances, personal friends, voluntary helpers, business associates and financial advisors. In most circumstances this would be deemed unethical; for instance, the American Psychological Association states that "A psychologist refrains from entering into or promising another personal ... financial, or other relationship ... if it appears likely that such a relationship reasonably might impair the psychologist's objectivity or otherwise interfere with ... his or her functions, or might harm or exploit the other party" (1992, p. 1591).

A final example of boundary violation is excessive *self-disclosure* by potentially abusive therapists. Consequently, their patients are often unusually and inappropriately well-informed about many aspects of the therapist's personal life such as his own problems and love relationships.

Persuasive communications Therapists may attempt to persuade patients to enter into a sexual relationship by indoctrinating them with certain messages and arguments. These often reflect the therapist's own rationalizations and might include statements such as:

- Sex is a necessary and appropriate part of your treatment.
- Sex will make you feel better.
- Sex will not harm you in any way.
- I am uniquely able to provide the sexual experiences you need.
- It is all right to have sex as long as it happens outside therapy sessions.
- It is all right to have sex after treatment is ended.
- I am in love with you.
- Sex could lead to a long-term relationship.
- Our relationship is special and not subject to the usual rules.
- Adults have the right to have sex with anyone they wish.
- No one will ever know what happens.
- Because you are disturbed no one will believe you if you complain.
- It is your fault because you turned me on and then continued to come and see me.

Exploitation of relationship Therapists may exploit various aspects of their relationships with patients in order to overcome their resistance to sexual advances. Thus, the power differential between them may be exploited so that the therapist's authority, power and control is exerted to coerce the patient into complying with his sexual wishes and demands. Psychological pressure may be applied or therapists may physically intimidate or assault their victims. The psychological vulnerability of patients, including their strong dependence on therapists, places them at risk for sexual exploitation. Similarly, this may be facilitated by the transferential or genuine feelings of love for their therapists experienced by some patients. Finally, the role reversal whereby patients assume responsibility for looking after their therapists may include gratifying his sexual desires.

Drugs and alcohol   The use of these substances is sometimes promoted and encouraged by therapists in order to disinhibit patients and thus overcome any resistance they might otherwise have to engaging in sex.

Conclusion

Thus, it is suggested that the four factors—therapist motivation, overcoming internal inhibitions, overcoming external constraints and overcoming patient resistance—are all necessary preconditions for the sexual abuse of patients by therapists. Unless all of these conditions are met abuse will not occur. This constitutes a more comprehensive and balanced explanatory model than a monolithic focus on any single cause.

As indicated above, this model in no way excuses the abusive behaviour or reduces the therapist's total responsibility for its occurrence. As Gutheil puts it, "the clinician always bears the burden of clinical, ethical, and moral codes and constraints flowing from the professional role; the patient does not. Consequently, in an instance of sexual misconduct, it is the clinician and only the clinician who can be counted culpable, blameworthy, or—in certain circumstances—liable or criminal" (1991, pp. 661–662).

6 Management of abusive behaviour

The primary prevention of sexual abuse in therapy, and its legal and disciplinary regulation are considered in part V. In this chapter, several strategies for managing potential or existing abuse are discussed, including self-regulation, consultation, rehabilitation and treatment.

Self-regulation

If therapists monitor carefully their own feelings and behaviour they can become aware at an early stage of any tendencies or developments that might result in the sexual abuse of patients. These include the risk factors and preconditions for abuse discussed in Chapter 5, such as:

1. Personal distress or professional isolation.
2. Narcissistic, dominating or antisocial tendencies.
3. Experiencing sexual desire or feelings of love for patients.
4. Using drugs or alcohol, or rationalizations and other defences to overcome internal inhibitions.
5. Attempting to overcome any resistance from patients by means of boundary violations, persuasive communications or exploitation of the therapeutic relationship.

Therapists who identify the operation of such contributory factors may then be able to curb them so that the potential for abuse does not escalate. Thus, in a survey of psychologists by Stake & Oliver (1991), 69% of the respondents said that they worked through feelings of sexual attraction to clients by themselves.

Some examples of how this might be accomplished include pursuing emotional and sexual satisfaction in their own lives rather than through their therapeutic relationships, acknowledging the countertransferential nature of their feelings of love, discontinuing any boundary violations, and attending to ethical, legal and clinical reasons for not abusing patients, such as those cited in the section "Internal inhibitions" in Chapter 5.

Another way in which therapists can self-regulate potential or existing abuse is to terminate treatment, with or without referral to another professional. According to the evidence cited in Chapter 3, in the study by Bouhoutsos et al (1983), after sexual contact, treatment was terminated by the therapist in 15% of cases and mutually with the patient in 17%, while in Valiquette's (1989) study the equivalent proportions were 27% and 12%. Butler & Zelen (1977) reported that 25% of the therapists in their sample terminated treatment immediately after the onset of sexual behaviour, and although 5% of the sample felt that in such circumstances the patients should be referred to another therapist, no such referrals were made. Among Stake & Oliver's (1991) respondents, 22% dealt with sexual attraction to patients by referring them to another therapist. Thus, in summary, it appears that between one-quarter and one-third of therapists terminate treatment with patients whom they have abused, and the proportion of such patients who are referred to another therapist is variously reported as nil and 22%.

While terminating treatment in order to commence a sexual relationship is generally accepted as unethical (see Chapter 2), some controversy remains over the clinical desirability of termination as a means of avoiding or ending sexual abuse. For example, Rutter argues that if the therapist "continues to be so overcome by his non-professional feelings toward her that he cannot maintain the highest standard of professional behavior, he must end their relationship with extreme care. In doing so he must clearly communicate to her that she is not to blame for this ending" (1990, p. 196). Edelwich & Brodsky admit that there are rare instances when a referral is called for, but they are generally opposed to this on the grounds that "There may not be a more suitable clinician available to take the case. The client may suffer iatrogenic damage from delay, discontinuity, and feelings of rejection. Both the client and clinician are denied the experience of working out uncomfortable issues" (1991, p. 237). Ideally, potential or existing abusive therapists will bear these opposing views in mind when deciding whether to terminate treatment.

Consultation

Another approach to managing sexual involvement with patients is for therapists to seek assistance from a friend, relative, colleague or supervisor. Discussing the issues explicitly with another person who views them more objectively can help to clarify the therapist's confusion over his feelings and actions. In a survey of U.S. psychiatrists 41% of abusers consulted colleagues about sexual involvement with patients (Gartrell et al, 1986). Very similarly, in another study, 40% of abusive psychiatrists and psychologists sought help from a friend or colleague (Butler & Zelen, 1977). Finally, among U.S. psychologists, feelings of sexual attraction to patients were discussed with the therapist's own therapist in 19% of cases, and with a supervisor in 49% (Stake & Oliver, 1991). As reported in Chapter 4, among 20 psychologists who had abused patients in the U.K., 13 had disclosed this to colleagues, 12 to friends or partners, 5 to managers, 4 to personal therapists, 3 to supervisors, and 2 to unspecified others, a total of 17 (85%) having disclosed to at least one other person. Thus, it seems that consultation is sought by approximately 40% to 85% of sexually involved therapists. Sometimes this occurs within the context of ongoing supervision, as discussed in Chapter 12.

Rehabilitation

The aim of rehabilitation programmes is to help suitable abusive therapists to return to practice without further risk to patients. These programmes may include personal therapy for the offender but they are more comprehensive, often covering such matters as his professional practices, work settings, clientele and supervision. Some offenders may themselves seek rehabilitation, but more commonly they are referred by supervisors, employers or regulatory boards, or as a consequence of legal proceedings. I have been able to find only one programme described in the literature. This is conducted at the Walk-In Counseling Center in Minneapolis, and it includes components for the assessment of candidates, the planning of rehabilitation programmes and the evaluation of the offender's progress, as outlined below (Schoener & Gonsiorek, 1988, 1989).

Assessment

The aims of this component are to ascertain the factors contributing to the sexually abusive behaviour and to determine the candidate's suitability for rehabilitation. It is not designed to investigate whether abuse occurred, and cannot be conducted if the candidate denies that it happened.

The first step in assessment is the gathering of information on several topics. A detailed description of the abuse is obtained, often from letters of complaint, transcripts of legal or disciplinary proceedings, and interviews with victims, offenders and other informants. The personal adjustment of the offender is assessed with particular attention to the risk factors and preconditions for abuse discussed in Chapter 5. His practice style is also investigated with regard to these issues; for example, whether he is prone to violate boundaries. Likewise, inquiry is made about the setting in which he practises, including matters such as privacy, office furnishings, home visits and other extramural meetings, and the provision of supervision. The nature of the patients he treats is examined; for example, whether they tend to be female or victims of previous abuse. Finally, any situational factors that might have contributed to the abuse are ascertained, perhaps including career changes, marital problems, a chance social encounter with the victim, or life experiences or interests that she has in common with him.

On the basis of all this information a hypothesis to explain the abuse is formulated, in the light of which a decision can be reached on the candidate's suitability for rehabilitation (see the section on "Efficacy", p. 75), and a programme can be planned if this is appropriate.

Programmes

These commonly include several components, discussed below. Personal therapy may be prescribed; certain temporary or permanent limitations may be placed on the offender's professional practice, such as that he will not treat female patients. He may be required to have close and effective supervision (Schoener, 1989a,b,c). Individually appropriate further education and training may be desirable. Modifications in his therapeutic style may be mandated, such as complete abstinence from physical contact with patients. Occupational changes may be recommended, perhaps involving withdrawal from work of a therapeutic nature, or transfer from private to public practice where collegial influences and controls are stronger and supervision can be exercised.

One of the possible programme components mentioned above has been criticized recently. A medical board had permanently prohibited an offending psychiatrist from treating females. Subsequently Bursztain & Gutheil commented, "cases where such contact has occurred are also characterized by other serious breaches of the standard of care, such as the failure to focus on the development of a therapeutic alliance. ... Until the offending clinician demonstrates that such failures have been remedied, we are concerned that the clinician who cannot be considered competent to treat women should be considered competent to treat men. Moreover, ... such ... measures perpetuate the traditional stereotypes of women as 'the weaker sex' ". (1992, p. 1276).

Evaluation

Evidence is required on the offender's progress in the rehabilitation programme and the extent to which he has achieved the changes necessary for him to resume therapeutic practice without further risk to patients.

Efficacy

At present no systematic data are available on the outcome of rehabilitation programmes with abusive therapists, and there are methodological difficulties in gathering such evidence (Furby, Weinrott & Blackshaw, 1989; Pope, 1990). The prospects of successful rehabilitation are thought not to be high; for instance, the California licensing boards for psychologists, social workers, and marriage and family counsellors reviewed rehabilitation attempts and concluded that for abusive therapists the "prospects for rehabilitation are minimal and it is doubtful that they should be given the opportunity to ever practice psychotherapy again" (Callanan & O'Connor, 1988, p. 11). It is also thought that poor candidates for rehabilitation include serial offenders, particularly those who abuse again while undergoing rehabilitation, and those who show no remorse or believe that sex with patients is not harmful (Brodsky, 1989).

Fundamental doubts are expressed that offenders should ever be allowed to practise therapy again (Pope, 1990; Sonne & Pope, 1991). It is argued that judges who take bribes or teachers who victimize children are never allowed to resume these roles and that the sexual abuse of patients by therapists is an equally basic breach of trust and should attract similar consequences. Moreover, the reinstatement of "rehabilitated" therapists may be damaging to the reputations of the professions concerned, and it also raises the question of whether future patients of these therapists are to be told of their previous abuse as a necessary condition of an informed consent.

Treatment

Personal therapy is probably most appropriately conducted as part of a more comprehensive rehabilitation programme. Like rehabilitation, treatment cannot be implemented if the offender denies the abuse, and his informed consent and motivation to change are essential preconditions (Howard League, 1985, pp. 114–118; Perkins, 1991, pp. 167–173). In this section the person rendering the treatment is referred to as the therapist and the recipient of treatment as the offender. Apart from a fictional case study (Pope, 1987a), there appears to be only one description of a treatment approach with these offenders in the literature. Individual psychotherapy was provided over 10 to 30 months for 20 "neurotic" offenders. It is emphasized that this approach may not be suitable for other types of offender and it should be "viewed as a set of working hypotheses, not final recommendations" (Gonsiorek, 1989b). In the light of this current lack of information it seems reasonable to extrapolate from approaches developed with sex offenders in general and to investigate their applicability and efficacy with abusive therapists specifically.

Most of these approaches utilize both indirect and direct treatment strategies, although this is a somewhat arbitrary distinction. Components from both strategies are drawn upon to constitute individualized treatment programmes for particular offenders, and these programmes are reviewed with the offenders concerned as the bases for their informed consents and therapeutic contracts.

The indirect strategy assumes that components of treatment aimed primarily at alleviating certain problems that are assessed as contributing to the offender's abusive behaviour will, if successful, have the secondary effect of eliminating this behaviour. These problems might include several discussed above, such as:

1. Personal distress, including life crises, anxiety disorders and depression.
2. Sexual dysfunction or dissatisfaction.
3. Marital conflict or disruption.
4. Other interpersonal dysfunctions, including difficulties in communication, perspective taking, anger management and problem solving.
5. Misuse of drugs or alcohol.

The treatment of these wide ranging problems is beyond the scope of this book and reviews are available elsewhere (e.g. Barlow, 1985; Bellack & Hersen, 1990; Bellack, Hersen & Kazdin, 1992; Hawton et al, 1989).

The direct treatment strategy encompasses components aimed primarily at controlling the abusive behaviour. Some of these are discussed next, including withdrawal, covert sensitization, guided self-dialogue, imagery rehearsal, behavioural rehearsal, bibliotherapy, victim empathy training, cognitive restructuring, schema-focused cognitive therapy and relapse prevention. Space precludes extensive consideration of these procedures, but references are cited in which more detailed descriptions are available.

Withdrawal

This is perhaps the most basic means of controlling potentially abusive behaviour. Offenders may be advised that if they experience impulses towards re-offending which they find difficult to control then it may be appropriate for them to withdraw from the risky situation. Even a brief break may enable them to interrupt the chain leading to the abuse and to implement other methods of self-control such as those discussed below.

Covert sensitization

(Brownell, Hayes & Barlow, 1977; Cautela, 1967; Hayes, Brownell & Barlow, 1978; Lichstein & Hung, 1980)

The aim of this procedure is for the offender to associate events early in the chain leading up to sexual activity with aversive fantasies so that the chain is interrupted and the activity becomes less attractive and erotic. As a preliminary, he is given training in relaxation techniques.

Some scenes of events early in the chain are developed, the reason for selecting early events being that it is easier for offenders to interrupt the chain at this stage than later when impulses become increasingly irresistible. One example of such a scene is: "You are feeling lonely and depressed when a patient you like comes for treatment. You think how attractive she looks and how marvellous it would be if she became your lover. She seems understanding and sympathetic so you tell her how you feel and start to hug and kiss her".

Similarly, some aversive scenes are developed in which the events depicted in the abusive scenes are followed by unpleasant, disturbing consequences; for instance: "As you make these advances the patient is shocked, she jumps up, shouts at you to stop, runs out of the room, you hear her crying and telling the receptionists and patients in the waiting room what you had done, and you see that a senior colleague is there also. You feel sick and are terrified about what this will mean for your job and career".

In contrast, some relief scenes are developed in which the offender controls his abusive behaviour and experiences feelings of well-being for having done so; for example: "Although you feel attracted to your patient you think of the dangers and adverse consequences of acting out these feelings and stop yourself from making sexual advances to her. You feel an enormous sense of relief that you have not put yourself at risk or distressed your patient. You feel quite proud that you can be attracted to a patient without exploiting her".

During treatment sessions the offender closes his eyes and relaxes, and then is asked to imagine an abusive scene followed sometimes by an aversive scene and sometimes by a relief scene. These pairings are repeated several times in a session and they are tape-recorded so that the offender can increase his exposure to them between sessions. He is advised also to imagine an aversive scene whenever there is a possibility that he might re-offend in a real-life situation, so that covert sensitization is used as a means of self-control.

Guided self-dialogue (Meichenbaum, 1985; Meichenbaum & Genest, 1980)

This procedure is based on the principle that thoughts can influence feelings and actions. Therefore, it is useful for offenders to prepare with their therapist suitable statements that the offenders can say to themselves when there is a risk that they might re-offend. These self-statements or self-instructions can deter the offender from further abusive behaviour. Examples of such statements are: "It's OK to be attracted to the patient as long as I don't make any move", "If I do nothing the urge will go away and I will feel good", "It is wrong to have sex with a patient", "Freud said that the patient's falling in love is induced by the analytic situation and is not to be ascribed to the charms of the analyst's person", and "If I make sexual advances I could lose my job/ruin my career/be sued/break up my marriage/distress or harm my patient". Such statements can be written on index cards to which the offender can refer as reminders when necessary.

Imagery rehearsal (Hall, 1989)

This procedure enables offenders to rehearse and practise dealing with potentially abusive situations in imagination as a bridge to doing this in real life. They are relaxed and asked to imagine a situation in which they are at risk of re-offending, including their feelings of sexual attraction and arousal. Instead of acting out these feelings offenders are asked to imagine themselves dealing with them appropriately using the control techniques they have learned, such as withdrawal, covert sensitization and guided self-dialogue. Finally, they should imagine the positive feelings of well-being associated with successful control. A hierarchy of situations may be worked through in this way from the least to the most risky. A variant of this procedure is covert modelling, in which offenders imagine therapeutic models acting appropriately in such situations.

Behavioural rehearsal (Meichenbaum, 1985)

Another way for offenders to rehearse and practise control techniques in preparation for real life is in role plays with their therapists. These can include role reversals so that therapists can demonstrate and model appropriate behaviour for offenders.

Bibliotherapy

It may be useful to capitalize on the academic and professional backgrounds of offenders by encouraging them to increase their knowledge of sexual abuse in therapy by reading the relevant autobiographical, clinical and research literature, and discussing this critically with their therapists. While such knowledge is unlikely in itself to control abusive behaviour, it may facilitate and enhance the implementation of other techniques.

Victim empathy

In their discussion of this procedure, Hildebran & Pithers describe its purpose as follows: "Offenders gained an intellectual understanding of the precursors that led to victimizing others, and they developed an awareness of what they needed to do to refrain from abusing again, but they lacked the emotional recognition of the victims' trauma that could energize a dedication to implementing what they had learned. . . . Offenders must develop emotional motivation, as well as cognitive understanding, in order to feel committed to utilizing . . . tools they have been offered" (1989, p. 236). This section discusses some of the ways in which this aim can be pursued.

Offenders can be given reading assignments, including material on the reactions of victims, discussed in Chapter 8, as well as autobiographical accounts (e.g. Appendices B and C; Bates & Brodsky, 1989; Freeman & Roy, 1976; Plaisil, 1985; Walker & Young, 1986). They may be asked to write reports for discussion with their therapists on their conclusions from these readings and how they apply to their own victims.

Prescribed reading may be supplemented by exposure to video material in which victims describe their experiences and reactions, often with quite dramatic effect on offenders. After discussion of this material they may be asked to write an account of their own abusive behaviour from the perspective of the victim, and on the basis of this may role play the victim with the therapist. The original account is often revised and deepened after it is discussed and role played. It may then be used as a basis for a letter to the victim in which the offender accepts responsibility for the abuse, expresses his regrets and shows understanding of the distress and harm it has caused. Depending on the circumstances, this letter may or may not be sent. In either case it is a useful therapeutic experience for the offender.

At this stage meetings are sometimes arranged with the offender's own victim(s) and/or with patients abused by other therapists. The victims' accounts of their experiences and reactions together with questions from the offender may further enhance his empathy with their emotional pain and other problems.

Cognitive restructuring (Beck, 1976; Beck & Emery, 1985; Beck et al, 1979; Burns, 1980; Hawton et al, 1989; Murphy, 1990)

Most offenders develop distorted cognitions or beliefs that contribute to or support their abusive behaviour. Some examples of these cognitions are shown in Table 6.1, which is based on a categorization derived from Bandura (1977) and Murphy (1990). It follows that the therapeutic correction of such cognitions is likely to reduce the risk of re-offending. Cognitive restructuring is one corrective approach, which comprises helping offenders to identify any beliefs that may be contributing to their abusive behaviour, assisting them to recognize the distorted nature of these beliefs and exploring with them more accurate and appropriate alternatives to the distorted beliefs.

These aims are pursued by means of a variety of procedures but common to many of them is a Socratic style of questioning. The therapist does not in a didactic manner tell the offender what his beliefs really are or what he should be thinking. Instead, the therapist asks appropriate and well-timed questions to induce the offender to discover this information for himself. For example, the therapist might ask questions along the lines of: "what is the evidence . . .?" for a certain statement the offender has made, or "what other possible explanations could there be . . .?" for a certain event. In short, the style of the therapist is to ask questions rather than to give answers.

The sources cited at the beginning of this section contain details of several procedures for the identification of cognitions, including interviews, instant replay, remote recall, role play, induced imagery and offender recording (see also Chapter 9).

These sources also present a range of common errors in thinking which may help offenders to recognize the distorted nature of their beliefs, such as dichotomous thinking, over-generalization, mislabelling, selective abstraction, disqualifying the positive, arbitrary inference, magnification and minimization, emotional reasoning, should statements and misattribution.

Several procedures for exploring more accurate and appropriate alternatives to distorted cognitions are discussed in the same sources. One such procedure is *cost–benefit analysis*, which can motivate offenders to change their belief systems (Jenkins-Hall, 1989). With therapeutic assistance, they can list the potential costs and benefits of offending, as illustrated in Table 6.2.

The *provision of information* such as that indicated in the sections on "Bibliotherapy" and "Victim empathy" can also contribute to the exploration of alternative beliefs; for instance, by increasing the offender's awareness of the harm he may inflict on his victims.

An offender's beliefs may be subjected to *logical analysis* to determine whether the evidence necessarily entails the conclusion he has drawn and what alternative conclusions there might be. Thus, because the patient accepted his invitation to dinner he might have concluded that she wanted a sexual relationship with him. Clearly, other possible conclusions include that:

Table 6.1: Cognitive Distortions of Abusive Therapists

Categories	Cognitions
Justifying sexual contact	
Moral justifications	I loved her
	I was the only one who could satisfy her
	Sex was therapeutic
	Treatment had been terminated
	Sex only occurred outside sessions
	I didn't charge her for sessions when we had sex
Psychological justifications	I can't remember how we came to have sex
	I had been drinking
	I was powerless to control my urges
	My wife is not interested in sex
	My wife doesn't understand me
	I had split up with my wife
	I was lonely
	I was under stress
Palliative comparisons	We didn't have intercourse, we only petted
	Sex only happened once
	I only had sex with one patient
Euphemistic labelling	It was only a bit of fun
Misperceiving consequences	
Minimizing consequences	The patient wasn't harmed
	She'll soon get over it
	It's no big deal
Ignoring consequences	There is no reason for me to worry about the patient I had sex with
Misattributing consequences	She is distressed because her current therapist is incompetent
Devaluation and misattribution	
Devaluation	She was promiscuous anyway
	She was incestuous
	She was a "borderline"
Misattribution	She came on to me
	She said she loved me
	She agreed to sex
	She enjoyed it
	She didn't resist
	She threatened suicide if we didn't have sex
	She would have become violently angry if I hadn't agreed to sex

1. She was lonely and welcomed his company without being aware of or desiring any possible sexual consequences.
2. She lacked the power to turn down his invitation.
3. To turn down his invitation would indicate an unacceptable lack of trust in him.
4. She might fear that he would not continue to treat her if she turned down his invitation.

An offender may magnify events so that he predicts the direst consequences for himself. In such circumstances the therapist may be able to *decatastrophize* the situation by widening the offender's perspective so that he takes all the relevant information into account when he makes his predictions. For example, he may believe that a certain patient offers the only opportunity for an understanding and loving relationship he will ever have in his life. He might be helped to see that appropriate treatment could enable him to enter a social network outside his practice and to establish a relationship with a partner who is not his patient.

The procedure termed *distancing* refers to the process of an offender shifting from a subjective to an objective perception of his own beliefs, so that they are no longer regarded as self-evident truths but rather as hypotheses that may or may not be valid. For example, an offender may be absolutely convinced that his victim provoked his advances and was responsible for what happened. If he is exposed vicariously to sexual contacts between other therapists and their victims then he may acknowledge that these victims were not to blame and consequently begin to shift towards accepting responsibility for his own abusive behaviour. Such exposure might be arranged through reading personal accounts by victims or viewing equivalent video material.

Table 6.2:   Cost–Benefit Analysis of Offending

Costs		Benefits	
1.	Distress/harm to patient	1.	Sexual gratification/reassurance/comfort/love for offender
2.	Offender's guilt/depression/low self-esteem	2.	Control over patient
3.	Retaliation by patient	3.	Avoidance of patient's suicide/rage
4.	Professional alienation/censure		
5.	Legal/disciplinary proceedings		
6.	Break up of marriage		
7.	Rejection by friends		

Table 6.3:   Example of Reattribution

Distorted beliefs	Alternative beliefs
The patient was responsible because she:	The patient was not responsible because she:
1. Did not object to my sexy jokes and innuendoes	1. Trusted her therapist to respect and care for her
2. Agreed to have a drink with me in the evening	2. Needed him to continue treating her
3. Did not resist physically when I kissed her afterwards	3. Regarded him as a powerful and authoritative figure whom it would have been difficult to oppose
	4. Had been indoctrinated with the belief that she did not have the right to say "No" when she was sexually abused in childhood

Offenders may blame their victims for the sexual acts that occurred between them. The procedure of *reattribution* is aimed at a more appropriate assignment of responsibility by showing that the facts do not support the attribution of blame to the victim, as illustrated in Table 6.3.

Finally, an offender's beliefs can be challenged and alternatives explored by *role reversals*, in which the therapist plays the role of an abuser who declaims his distorted beliefs while the offender role plays someone who disputes these beliefs, such as an employer, senior colleague, disciplinary board member or plaintiff's lawyer.

Schema-focused cognitive therapy (Beck & Freeman, 1990; McCann & Pearlman, 1990; Young, 1990)

Schemas are cognitive structures that organize experience and behaviour. They contain certain very fundamental and core beliefs about oneself, other people and the world in which one lives. More particularly, they interpret and attach meaning to events. It is postulated that distorted schemas contribute to personality disorders (see Chapter 8), and the aim of schema-focused cognitive therapy is to weaken such schemas and to strengthen more adaptive alternatives so that the associated disorders are ameliorated. This form of intervention is discussed more extensively in Chapter 9, the present chapter being restricted to its application to the narcissistic and antisocial disorders, which are those most commonly reported among therapists who sexually abuse their patients (Beck & Freeman, 1990).

The grandiosity and narcissism of these therapists are described in the sections on risk factors and motivation in Chapter 5; some key features of the *narcissistic personality disorder* are summarized in Table 6.4. (American Psychiatric Association, 1987; Beck & Freeman, 1990), and core schemas associated with this disorder are shown in Table 6.5 (Beck & Freeman, 1990, pp. 49, 361).

Grandiosity can be restructured by exploring alternative schemas which emphasize what the offender has in common with other people rather than his perceived differences from them. Examples of these alternatives include: "One can be human, like everyone else, and still be unique", "Everyone is special in some way", "I can enjoy being like others, rather than always having to be better" and "I don't really need constant attention and admiration from everyone to exist and be happy" (Beck & Freeman, 1990, p. 249).

Table 6.4:   Features of Narcissistic Personality Disorder

Grandiosity
1.   Grandiose sense of own importance, achievements, "specialness", uniqueness, and superiority

2.   Entitlement to special favours and treatment

3.   Exemption from rules that apply to others

4.   Expectation of constant attention, admiration, deference, and compliance from others

Hypersensitivity to evaluation
1.   Reacts to criticism with feelings of rage, shame or humiliation

Lack of empathy
1.   Lack of empathy for feelings of others

2.   Regards others as inferior

3.   Focuses exclusively on personal gratification

4.   Exploits others to achieve own ends

Table 6.5:   Schemas Associated with Narcissistic Personality Disorder

1.   I'm a very special person
2.   I deserve special dispensations, privileges and prerogatives
3.   I'm superior to others and they should acknowledge this
4.   I'm above the rules
5.   Other people should satisfy my needs
6.   People have no right to criticize me

Similarly, hypersensitivity to evaluation can be restructured by exploring alternative schemas such as: "Everyone has flaws" and "Feedback can be valid and helpful. It's only devastating if I take it that way" (Beck & Freeman, 1990, p. 249). This feature of narcissism can also be addressed by imaginal and *in vivo* desensitization, in which the offender is gradually exposed to a hierarchy of critical evaluations. Finally, he can acquire and implement the range of skills for coping with stress that are discussed in Chapter 9.

Lack of empathy can be restructured by exploring alternative schemas such as: "Other people have needs and opinions that matter too" (Beck & Freeman, 1990, p. 249). All the procedures described in the section on victim empathy are applicable to this task as well as to enhancing the offender's appreciation of the feelings of his victims. More considerate ways of behaving towards other people are also promoted. Thus, the cognitive, affective and behavioural aspects of empathy are addressed.

In addition to these specific interventions for various aspects of the narcissistic personality disorder an important component of schema-focused cognitive therapy is a corrective relationship with the therapist. In particular, limits need to be set on narcissistic attitudes and behaviour in treatment so that appropriate and acceptable behaviour by the offender is maintained and the rights of the therapist are respected. Any attempted transgressions constitute opportunities for the identification and restructuring of distorted schemas. Furthermore, therapists can provide accurate feedback on their reactions to the offender's behaviour, thus enhancing his awareness of its effects on others.

The *antisocial personality disorder* is discussed as a risk factor in Chapter 5 and its key features include lack of remorse or guilt, callousness or shallow affect, impulsiveness or poor behavioural control, promiscuous sexual behaviour, manipulation of others, pathological lying and failure to accept responsibility for one's own actions. Among the associated schemas are: "I need to look out for myself", "If people don't take care of themselves that's their problem", "Others are exploitative and therefore I am entitled to exploit them back", "I am entitled to break the rules because they are designed to protect the 'haves' not the 'have nots'" and "I can get away with things so I don't need to worry about bad consequences" (Beck & Freeman, 1990, pp. 26, 48, 49, 361).

The process of schema-focused therapy for antisocial personality disorder can be conceptualized as guiding the offender through a hierarchy of moral functioning. Prior to treatment he thinks only in terms of self-interest, basing choices on obtaining rewards or avoiding immediate punishment. Thus, he exploits a victim without regard to her interests or the consequences to himself. At the second level, the offender shows some concern for specific people under certain conditions where he stands to gain or lose. Thus, he might take into account a victim's needs and wishes in the service of his own longer term self-interest, perhaps pretending some romantic feelings or having some social involvement so that she continues to comply with his sexual demands. At a third level, the offender shows greater abstract ability to consider the wider society, so that rules such as those enshrined in ethical codes are respected. He also acknowledges the needs of others so that he is concerned about their welfare and values relationships with them. Consequently, he is more likely to desist from exploiting patients and to seek a stable and satisfying relationship outside his practice.

Offenders with antisocial personality disorder are most likely to be motivated to engage in treatment if they can see advantages to themselves in doing so. Cost–benefit analyses as described above are useful tools for this purpose, in addition to clarifying the positive and negative consequences of operating at different levels of moral functioning and of certain actions by the offender. Additionally, the identification of distorted schemas and the exploration of alternatives are addressed by the restructuring procedures discussed above and in Chapter 9.

Relapse prevention (Laws, 1989; Pithers et al, 1988)

The aim of this component in treatment programmes is to provide offenders with the means of maintaining beneficial changes after formal therapy has ended. It is assumed that they are never "cured" and will always be tempted to re-offend, consequently they need to be able to deal appropriately and effectively with such temptations. These assumptions are discussed with offenders as a rationale for the intervention.

Sexual abuse does not just happen "out of the blue". It is the culmination of a chain of events, and the first step in relapse prevention is the recognition by the offender of the sequence of precursors leading to his abusive behaviour (Nelson & Jackson, 1989). Typically, this sequence comprises:

1. A negative mood state, such as sadness, loneliness or anger.
2. Fantasies of performing the abusive acts.
3. Distorted cognitions about this behaviour (see Table 6.1).
4. Passive planning of how it might be acted out without risk to the offender (often rehearsed during masturbation).
5. Implementation of the plan.

This final step often involves "apparently irrelevant decisions" (AIDs), which place the offender, often without conscious intent, in "high risk situations" (HRSs) that threaten his self-control. For example, when in the vicinity of a patient's home he might decide to visit to check on her progress (an AID), and thus find himself alone with her, in privacy, consuming alcohol and in quasi-social circumstances (an HRS).

It is likely to be difficult for offenders to control their abusive behaviour when they are in high risk situations. Consequently, they are encouraged to disrupt the sequence of precursors at the earliest possible point, when interdiction is relatively easy. As discussed above, during treatment they will have acquired a range of skills that can be deployed for this purpose, including withdrawal, covert sensitization, guided self-dialogue and cognitive restructuring. It is useful for offenders to develop individualized "maintenance manuals" containing, among other things, details of their sequence of precursors and of the coping strategies available for its disruption, to which they can refer for information and prompting. Finally, although relapse prevention was developed as a method of self-regulation it can facilitate external supervision. The sequence of precursors can be shared with a supervisor, who can monitor their occurrence and the offender's responses, perhaps in collaboration with his colleagues or employers.

Efficacy

As in the case of rehabilitation programmes, at present there is no systematic evidence available on the efficacy of treatment for abusive therapists. Moreover, opinions on the efficacy of treatment for sexual offenders are generally equivocal and varied. For instance, on the basis of their comprehensive review, Furby, Weinrott & Blackshaw conclude that "There is as yet no evidence that clinical treatment reduces rates of sex offences in general and no appropriate data for assessing whether it may be differentially effective for different types of offenders" (1989, p. 27). A somewhat less negative view is taken by Marshall et al, who conclude, "In our review ... we have attempted to answer the question: 'Can sex offenders be effectively treated so as to reduce subsequent recidivism?' We believe that the evidence provides an unequivocally positive answer ... although ... not all programs are successful and not all sex offenders profit from treatment. Comprehensive cognitive/behavioral programs and those programs that utilize antiandrogens in conjunction with psychological treatments seem to offer the greatest hope for effectiveness and future development" (1991, pp. 480–481). Thus, at present no firm conclusions can be reached on the effectiveness of treatment with abusive therapists, and the arguments discussed in the section of the efficacy of rehabilitation are applicable also to treatment programmes.

Conclusion

Potential or existing abuse may be managed by the strategies of self-regulation, consultation, rehabilitation or treatment. This last strategy might include procedures to improve control over abusive behaviour, such as withdrawal, covert sensitization, guided self-dialogue, imagery rehearsal, behavioural rehearsal, bibliotherapy, victim empathy training, cognitive restructuring, schema-focused cognitive therapy and relapse prevention. The efficacy of these strategies and procedures with abusive therapists is not known at present.

Part IV
VICTIMIZED PATIENTS

7 Psychological vulnerability to abuse

Some psychological characteristics rendering patients vulnerable to sexual abuse by therapists are reviewed in this chapter, while the associated demographic characteristics are considered in part II. The whole chapter is based largely on information concerning female victims of male therapists, and while much of the discussion may be applicable to other gender dyads this remains to be demonstrated empirically.

There are no known psychological characteristics among patients that inevitably predict and determine that they will be abused by predatory therapists. Many victims, however, do exhibit one or more characteristics that appear to enhance their vulnerability to such abuse. Some of these are reviewed below, and it is emphasized that they overlap and are not mutually exclusive; neither do they constitute a typology of vulnerable patients. Moreover, in no way does the identification of these characteristics imply that the patient is to blame for the abuse; as discussed in part I, ethically, the therapist is always fully responsible.

Love for therapist

A patient's genuine or transferential love for the therapist may render her vulnerable to sexual exploitation. Sexual advances by him may be construed and accepted as a natural component of what she perceives as a romantic, loving relationship. Conversely, she may express her feelings towards him in seductive behaviour, which he fails to manage appropriately (Klopfer, 1974; Rappaport, 1956; Saul, 1962).

Care of therapist

The phenomenon of role reversal or role trading between patient and therapist is described in Chapter 5. The therapist's needs and wishes are given priority over those of the patient, who assumes responsibility for his care and gratification. Thus, she may feel that she has an obligation and duty to fulfil his sexual desires, thereby rendering herself vulnerable to exploitation. As discussed below, a propensity to take care of others may stem from having been socialized into this role during an abusive childhood.

Approval by therapist

A patient may have an exceptionally strong need for approval by her therapist. Consequently, she may welcome any signs that he regards her as "special" and comply with his sexual demands in order to obtain and retain his approval. The exaggerated need for this is likely to be associated with low self-esteem, perhaps resulting from a history of lack of appreciation and rejection by significant others, often from childhood onwards.

Dependence on therapist

Vulnerability to sexual abuse may arise from a patient's overdependence on her therapist. She may be convinced of her own helplessness and need for someone stronger to rely on. Consequently, she may feel impotent to resist or evade sexual demands from her more powerful therapist, and fear that any attempt to do so will result in him abandoning her. It is understandable that many patients feel weak and incapable when they are unable to cope with their own problems and are forced to seek and rely on what they perceive as competent and trustworthy professional help. In the longer term, some patients will have experienced overcontrolling, dominating, unloving or abusive parenting, which undermined their self-confidence, a point returned to below.

Knowledge limitations

Some patients are vulnerable because they lack sufficient and accurate knowledge of the impropriety of sexual relationships with their therapists. They may never have been exposed to this information, or it may have been denied or repressed so that they are not aware of it, or it may be distorted by cognitions such as those in Table 6.1. As discussed in Chapter 6, predatory therapists commonly indoctrinate victims with these distorted beliefs to persuade them to comply with their sexual demands, and patients are generally reluctant to challenge assurances given to them by their therapists.

Power over therapist

One way in which a patient can achieve some power and control over her therapist is by entering into a sexual relationship with him. For instance, this may make him dependent on her for his sexual gratification, and his reputation and career are in her hands. Risks to the therapist such as these are especially relevant when one considers that the wish for power may well be associated with feelings of anger and hostility towards him. Thus, paradoxical as it may seem, a patient's wish for power may render her vulnerable to exploitation by a predatory therapist.

Dissociative reactions

Patients may be vulnerable to sexual abuse by therapists because they respond to their advances with various dissociative reactions. These are discussed in Chapter 8, on the consequences of such abuse, but they include disengagement, depersonalization and multiple personality disorder. Patients may disengage cognitively from the abuse situation so that it is as if it is not happening. They may depersonalize so that they feel different from their usual selves and it seems that the abuse is not happening to them. Finally, some patients experience the abuse as happening to one of their alter multiple personalities rather than to their host personality. The following is an example of a patient's description of her dissociative reactions to a sexual encounter with her therapist:

> I did what I have always done in the past. I shrank inside my mind and nearly disappeared. I had the "internal me" (the real me) that hid when I was afraid, and I would leave the "external me", the "pretend me" (which was my body without my mind), to deal with the real scary stuff. The "pretend me" could stand anything and feel nothing. The "real me" sang songs until it was over.
>
> (Armsworth, 1989, p. 560)

As suggested in this quotation, a tendency to dissociate often originates in childhood; this is discussed below.

Borderline personality disorder

Among the diagnostic criteria for this disorder are (American Psychiatric Association, 1987):

1. Unstable and intense interpersonal relations, alternating between extremes of overidealization and devaluation.
2. Impulsiveness in areas such as sex.
3. Inappropriate, intense, uncontrolled anger.
4. Recurrent suicidal behaviour.
5. Chronic feelings of emptiness or boredom.
6. Frantic efforts to avoid abandonment.

It is readily understandable how such characteristics can render borderline patients vulnerable to sexual abuse by therapists, and Gutheil (1989) has proposed several circumstances in which this may occur. The threats of "borderline rage" or of suicide (Eyman & Gabbard, 1991) if the patient is thwarted may intimidate the therapist into acceding to her sexual wishes. The dependency of a borderline patient may lead her to expect the therapist to meet all her needs, including sexual gratification, and he may react with rescue fantasies and over-involvement towards her. She may experience confusion over appropriate boundaries and limits between herself and the therapist, which may be conducive to violations by both participants. Finally, manipulativeness and a sense of entitlement among borderline patients can induce therapists to behave towards them in ways that are at variance from their usual professional practice. The association between borderline personality disorder and abuse in childhood is discussed below.

Child abuse history

Victims of sexual, physical or emotional abuse in childhood tend to be revictimized in later life in a variety of ways, including *spouse abuse* (Armsworth, 1989; Briere & Runtz, 1987; Russell, 1986; Walker 1985), *separation or divorce* (Russell, 1986), *rape* (Armsworth 1989; Atkeson, Calhoun & Morris, 1989; Fromuth, 1986; Kluft, 1990; Runtz & Briere, 1988; Russell, 1986), *prostitution* (James & Meyerding, 1977; Silbert, 1984; Silbert & Pines, 1981, 1983; Vitaliano, James & Boyer, 1981), *unwanted pregnancy* (Wyatt, Guthrie & Notgrass, 1992), *accidents* (Sedney & Brooks, 1984) and *sexual abuse by therapists* (Armsworth, 1989, 1990; De Young, 1981; Kluft, 1990; Pope & Vetter, 1991). Systematic evidence on this last category of revictimization is sparse, but Armsworth (1989) reported that 7 (23%) of 30 incest survivors became sexually involved with a helping professional. This prevalence rate for professional abuse of incest victims is almost certainly higher than the equivalent rate for non-victims, although specific evidence on this point appears to be lacking. Several related ways in which the alleged association between child abuse and later revictimization might arise are considered next.

Learned helplessness

Children feel powerless when they are abused, in that their own wishes and sense of mastery over what happens to them are persistently overridden by the offender, and any attempts to obtain support from others are often found to be ineffective. This leaves them with a profound sense of helplessness, to which one response is to abandon any attempt to control events and become passive and submissive, which carries the risk of revictimization in later life. Such reactions have been referred to as learned helplessness (Abramson, Seligman & Teasdale, 1978; Peterson & Seligman, 1983; Seligman, 1975) and impaired perceived self-efficacy (Bandura, 1977, 1982). They are illustrated in the following description by a patient of her immediate response to therapist abuse:

> I did nothing when he approached me, I was there but I was not there. It was as if I was a voiceless, mindless, selfless creature frozen in cement. I could not think, I could not feel, I could not move, I just stayed and let it happen.
>
> (Armsworth, 1990. p. 551)

Unassertiveness

Victims of child abuse may have failed to acquire social skills such as assertiveness which would have strengthened their ability to resist revictimization. These deficiencies may be due at least in part to the victim's modelling of her mother's passivity and misuse with a dominant father-figure, a situation that is typical of the families of origin of many child victims (Jehu, 1988). An oppressed and demoralized mother is in a poor position to transmit appropriate interpersonal expectations and skills to her daughter.

Low self-esteem

Many victims of child abuse have low self-esteem, including self-blame and self-denigration (Jehu, 1988, 1989, 1991a,b, 1992). Often they believe themselves to have been responsible for the abuse, which gives rise *inter alia* to feelings of guilt and self-hatred. Consequently, these victims may accept that they deserve to suffer and be punished by various forms of revictimization throughout their lives. Being abused in childhood may also signify to victims that compared to others they are worthless, inadequate and inferior. Such self-denigration, together with self-blame, may lead victims to believe that they have no right to deny or resist later exploitation by others.

Need for approval

As indicated above, emotional abuse in childhood, including lack of appreciation or rejection by significant others, is likely to result in low self-esteem. This lack of an internal sense of self-worth renders victims excessively dependent on some external criterion of worth such as the approval of others. This has to be sought constantly and it leaves victims vulnerable to manipulation, exploitation and revictimization by those whose approval is needed.

Excessive dependency

Factors such as learned helplessness and feelings of inadequacy and inferiority may lead victims of child abuse to become excessively dependent on others—including therapists—who are perceived as strong and powerful. Such sources of support and strength may be relied upon also in an attempt to redress the lack of protection and nurturance experienced during an abusive childhood. This life event may also destroy a victim's trust in her own perceptions, judgements and decisions so that she becomes dependent on others in these respects. Consequently, she may exhibit some characteristics of a dependent personality disorder such as (American Psychiatric Association, 1987):

1. Inability to make everyday decisions without an excessive amount of advice, reassurance or help from others.
2. Agreeing with people even when she believes they are wrong, through fear of being rejected.
3. Undertaking unwelcome tasks in order to be liked by others.

As indicated above, other possible consequences of excessive dependence are the idealization and overvaluation of the therapist by the patient, subordinating herself to him, her compliance with his wishes and demands, and fear of being abandoned by him in the event of non-compliance. In any of these ways overdependent patients may be at the mercy of exploitative therapists who appear to offer the prospect of nurturance and security.

Parentification

This is the term used by Gelinas (1983) to describe the role confusion or role reversal that is common in the families of origin of abused children (Jehu, 1988). Their mothers, who are often oppressed and incapacitated, tend to turn to a daughter for assistance. Thus, the daughter takes on what are normally parental responsibilities for domestic tasks, child care, family finances and meeting the emotional needs and demands of family members. The child is taught and expected to subordinate her own needs to those of others, which assume priority for her, and this expectation and role tend to persist into later life so that she accepts and meets the responsibility of caring for her therapist, including satisfying his sexual desires.

Oversexualization

This term implies that a relationship must include a sexual component, however inappropriate it may be, or that the relationship is perceived to have such a component when none exists. In one group of previously sexually abused women patients 51% reported that they had oversexualized their relationships with men, and on a Belief Inventory the following items were endorsed as partly, mostly or absolutely true by various proportions of these patients (Jehu, 1988):

1. "No man could care for me without a sexual relationship" (68%).
2. "I've already been used so it doesn't matter if other men use me" (54%).
3. "I don't have the right to deny my body to any man who demands it" (48%).

There are several possible reasons for the oversexualization of relationships among previously sexually abused women. They may not be able to distinguish sex and affection because of the confusion of parental love and sexuality in childhood. They may have a compulsive need for sex as proof of being loved and of being an adequate woman. Their sexual attractiveness and favours may be a means of exercising power over men. They may feel that they do not have any right to deny sex to a man. Finally, sexuality can serve a self-punitive function for victims in that it may be accompanied by sexually transmitted disease, unwanted pregnancy, abortion, rape or abuse by a therapist.

Dissociation

The nature of dissociative reactions and their implications for the vulnerability of patients to exploitative therapists is discussed above. Because children often cannot escape physically from abusive situations they commonly detach themselves mentally through various dissociative reactions, which then tend to persist as responses to abusive situations in adulthood. There is now a substantial body of evidence for such an association between abuse in childhood and dissociation in later life (e.g. Briere & Runtz, 1987, 1988; Chu & Dill, 1990; Putnam, 1989, 1991; Ross, 1989; Sanders & Giolas, 1991; Strick & Wilcoxon, 1991).

Borderline personality disorder

Similarly, the features of this disorder and its implications for vulnerability to therapist abuse are discussed above, and there is substantial evidence for its association with abuse in childhood (e.g. Harney, 1992; Herman, Perry & van der Kolk, 1989; Landecker, 1992; Ogata et al, 1990; Paris & Zweig, 1992; Zanarini et al, 1989).

Conclusion

Among the psychological characteristics that appear to enhance a patient's vulnerability to sexual abuse by her therapist are her genuine or transferential love for him, assumption of responsibility for his care, need for his approval, dependence on him, limitations in her knowledge relevant to the abuse, wish for power and control over the therapist, dissociative reactions, borderline personality disorder and a history of abuse in childhood.

This association between childhood abuse and revictimization by therapists might be mediated by factors which include the patient's learned helplessness, unassertiveness, low self-esteem, need for approval, excessive dependency, parentification, oversexualization of relationships, dissociation and borderline personality disorder.

This psychological approach to explaining vulnerability in no way implies that patients are to blame for being abused by therapists, who retain complete ethical responsibility for their actions.

8 Psychological consequences of abuse

Predominantly adverse psychological consequences for patients following sexual involvement with their therapists are reported in several studies, some of which are reviewed here. Bouhoutsos et al (1983) obtained information from 318 Californian psychologists in respect of 559 of their patients who had been sexually intimate with a previous therapist. These patients were reported as experiencing negative, positive, or no effects from this abuse, although these outcome categories were not mutually exclusive and mixed outcomes occurred in some cases. Negative effects on personality were reported to have occurred in 34% of the patients, including depression, loss of motivation, impaired social adjustment, significant emotional disturbance, suicidal feelings or behaviour and increased drug or alcohol use. Hospitalization was necessary in 11% of cases and 1% committed suicide. Sexual, marital or intimate relationships worsened for 26% of the patients. Negative feelings about having been sexually involved with their therapist were experienced by 29%. In contrast to these adverse effects, 16% of the patients were reported to have become healthier or to have improved emotionally and/or in sexual relationships, and in 9% of cases no effect was deemed to have occurred.

Further analysis of the data showed that respondents who were themselves sexually intimate with patients reported positive effects from previous sexual involvements with therapists in 32% of their cases, compared to 11% of cases reported as experiencing positive effects by respondents who were not themselves abusers (Holroyd & Bouhoutsos, 1985). Positive effects were also more likely to be reported when the patient alone or the patient and therapist mutually initiated the sexual intimacies rather than the therapist alone, although in many of these cases negative effects occurred later (Bouhoutsos et al, 1983; Pope & Bouhoutsos, 1986). An additional possible reason for the reported positive outcomes is that some negative effects such as post-traumatic stress reactions might be delayed in their onset and therefore not apparent to the respondents at the time of the inquiry.

This is the major study currently available on the iatrogenic effects on patients of sexual involvement with their therapists but it does have some important limitations. The response rate was low (16%). It was restricted to psychologists practising in California. Patients who became intimate with their therapists more than three months after termination were excluded. Lastly, there were unknown selection biases in that victimized patients who did not re-enter therapy with any of the psychologists surveyed were not covered in the study.

A national survey of psychologists in the U.S. was conducted by Pope & Vetter (1991) with a response rate of 50%. These respondents reported on 958 patients who had been sexually intimate with their therapists. Hospitalization considered to be at least partially a result of the intimacies was required in 11% of cases, and 14% attempted suicide, while 1% committed suicide.

Psychiatrists in the U.S. were surveyed by Gartrell et al (1986) with a response rate of 26%. The respondents reported on 3031 patients who acknowledged sexual involvement with previous therapists. This was assessed as always harmful to the patients by 87% of the respondents, as sometimes helpful or inconsequential by 6%, as helpful in all cases by 1%, while 6% did not indicate their assessment. Those respondents who were themselves repeated offenders against patients reported the previous sexual involvement as always harmful in 39% of cases, compared to equivalent estimates of 70% by one-time offenders and 88% by non-offenders.

Feldman-Summers & Jones (1984) recruited volunteers for a comparison of a group of women who had been sexually involved with their therapists with a second group who had been so involved with other health care practitioners, and with a third group who had no such involvement. In comparison with this third no-involvement group, those previously involved with their therapists reported that they were more mistrustful and angry towards men and therapists as a result of the abuse they had suffered, and they also reported significantly more psychological and psychosomatic symptoms one month after the previous treatment terminated. No differences in outcome were found between those involved with therapists or with other health care practitioners, and 20 (95%) out of the 21 patients involved with any of these professionals reported the impact to be entirely negative. The variables found to be most predictive of greater severity of outcome were prior sexual victimization as a child or adult, and involvement with a therapist who was married, the latter perhaps being attributable to the guilt and anxiety this entails for the victim.

Thus, the results of these and other empirical investigations together with case studies (e.g. Bates & Brodsky, 1989; Freeman & Roy, 1976; Plaisil, 1985;

Walker & Young, 1986) indicate that the consequences of sexual involvement with therapists are predominantly negative for most victims who subsequently re-enter therapy (Bouhoutsos et al, 1983; Pope & Vetter, 1991; Gartrell et al, 1986) or volunteer as subjects for research (Feldman-Summers & Jones, 1984). Unfortunately, nothing is known about the effects on victimized patients who do not re-enter therapy or volunteer for research. It is possible that they do not do so because they are not experiencing any problems, or on the other hand they may have been so traumatized by their previous victimization that they will not risk further contact with professionals. For these or other reasons selection biases are introduced into samples of victims about whom information is currently available. This may not be regarded as a vital limitation for practitioners since it is those patients who do seek further treatment that subsequent therapists are called upon to help. Another difficulty is that, by definition, patients are people who have sought and entered treatment because they are experiencing psychological problems. Consequently, it may not be easy to distinguish the persistence of these problems after the original treatment has ended from the specific effects of sexual involvement with the therapist. In general, it seems plausible that such involvement can originate, precipitate, exacerbate and maintain a variety of psychological problems, but its aetiological role in individual patients may be difficult to identify with any certainty. Again for practitioners, it may be argued that this is not important because it is existing problems that subsequent therapists have to address, often without precise knowledge of their origins. These problems among previously victimized patients can be categorized broadly and somewhat arbitrarily as post-traumatic stress reactions, mood disturbances, self-damaging behaviour, sexual dysfunction, psychosomatic complaints and personality problems. They are discussed in the following sections.

Post-traumatic stress reactions

The findings and sources cited above indicate that sexual abuse by a therapist is often a traumatic event in the sense that it is psychologically distressing to the patient concerned. In response to this trauma some of these victims experience stress reactions such as those shown in Table 8.1 and reviewed below. Thus, Vinson (1984) found that 64% of 21 female victims met the then current criteria for post-traumatic stress disorder (American Psychiatric Association, 1980). Similarly, these criteria were met by 92% of 12 women who were victims of incest in childhood and of therapist abuse as adults (Kluft, 1990). This finding perhaps reflects the strong association between childhood sexual abuse and post-traumatic stress in later life (Jehu, 1991b). For instance, 62% of 97 adult female victims of incest met the criteria for post-traumatic stress disorder (American Psychiatric Association, 1987), compared to none of 65 matched controls who had not experienced incest (Albach & Everaerd, 1992).

Table 8.1: Post-Traumatic Stress Reactions among Patients Abused by Therapists

Persistent re-experiencing of abuse
1. Recurrent and intrusive recollections of abuse
2. Recurrent distressing dreams related to the abuse
3. Sense of reliving the abuse
4. Distress at exposure to events resembling the abuse

Persistent avoidance of features related to abuse
1. Avoidance of activities or situations
2. Avoidance of thoughts and feelings: (a) denial, (b) minimization, (c) rationalization, (d) numbing, (e) inability to recall, (f) dissociation (disengagement, depersonalization, multiple personality)

Persistent increased arousal
1. Sleep disturbances
2. Irritability/anger/aggression
3. Hypervigilance
4. Physiological reactions to events resembling abuse

Re-experiencing

Victims are very likely to re-experience the abuse by their therapists in the ways shown in Table 8.1. Often they report being unable to stop thinking about the abuse, so that however hard they try to suppress the memories they still force their way through into consciousness. Vinson (1984) found that 67% of her subjects experienced upsetting, recurring thoughts about their relationships with their therapists. The abuse may also be re-experienced in dreams that are either direct recapitulations of the event or symbolic representations such as threatening figures, attacks by animals, frightening chases or bodily injuries. Repeated bad dreams about the relationship with the therapist were reported by 14% of Vinsons's (1984) subjects, but this prevalence rate might be in respect of direct recapitulations only, excluding symbolic representations. Victims may experience a sense that they are reliving the abuse at the present time, perhaps in the form of flashbacks. These may be in any sensory modality; for example, a victim may see the offender's face, hear him asking her to touch his penis, feel his hand on her body, smell his alcoholic breath or aftershave, or taste his semen. Thus, 67% of Vinson's (1984) subjects reported sudden feelings that the abuse was happening again. Finally, victims may re-experience the abuse in the form of distress when they are exposed to events that in some way resemble the abusive situation. These might include sexual activity with other partners, especially if the victim perceives this as a demand or obligation; revictimization of any kind, such as experiencing a crime of violence or spouse abuse; meeting with another therapist, particularly in circumstances that relate to the abusive situation such as the absence of other people in the clinical setting; and media coverage of sexual abuse or aggressive acts. Among Vinsons's (1984) subjects, 52% reported feeling upset when reminded of their abusive relationships with their therapists.

Avoidance

These reactions may be of a behavioural or cognitive-affective nature. Victims may engage in behaviour that enables them to avoid physically any activities or situations that in some way relate to the abuse by their therapists, such as sexual activities or therapeutic situations. These reactions sometimes generalize into a marked and chronic lack of interest in relevant activities; for instance, 57% of Vinson's (1984) subjects reported loss of sexual interest. As discussed below, many forms of addiction, including gambling, overeating, substance abuse and workaholism, as well as self-damaging behaviour, such as self-mutilation and attempted suicide, can serve an avoidance function by distracting victims from distressing activities and situations. This may contribute to the reports of taking more pills, drugs or alcohol by 43% of Vinson's (1984) subjects.

Other coping strategies listed in Table 8.1 are of a cognitive-affective nature in that they influence victims' perceptions of and feelings about the abuse, and such defences may be deployed with varying degrees of awareness by the victims. They may deny the abuse in statements such as: "It wasn't really abuse", "I'm not sure if it really happened, I might have made it up, fantasized it or dreamed it" or "I try not to think about it".

Victims may also minimize or play down the abuse in statements such as: "It happened but it didn't bother me", "It wasn't all that bad", "Many people have been abused far worse than me", "It was only petting, not sex" or "I left it behind a long time ago, it doesn't affect me now".

Another way of reducing the emotional pain of the abuse is to rationalize it by excusing the offender on grounds such as: "He was helping me to overcome my sexual problems", "I must have been so sexy that he couldn't stop himself", "We were in love" or "His wife was frigid".

Some victims are so disturbed by the abuse that they numb their feelings and may even be unaware of them. This is sometimes referred to as "dread of affect" and it can generalize so that victims distrust and fear any expression of emotion by themselves or other people. Thus, 76% of Vinson's (1984) subjects reported feeling emotionally dead or numb.

Victims are very commonly unable to recall their abuse experiences in some degree. Sometimes whole periods of time during which the abuse occurred cannot be recalled. As far as the abuse itself is concerned sometimes it cannot be recalled at all; in other cases specific features may be recalled but not other features (e.g. petting, but not intercourse), or the facts of the abuse may be recalled but not the feelings accompanying it (e.g. disgust or pleasure). Clearly, such psychogenic amnesia, motivated forgetting or repression can serve as a defence against distressing memories of the abuse experience.

Because victims often cannot escape from sexual abuse situations physically they commonly detach themselves mentally through various dissociative reactions, which then tend to persist as responses to subsequent abuse-related situations. Thus, Putnam (1989, p. 53) suggests that these reactions may serve the purposes of:

1. Escape from the constraints of reality.
2. Containment of traumatic memories and affects outside of normal conscious awareness.
3. Alteration or detachment of sense of self (so that the trauma happens to someone else or to a depersonalized self).
4. Analgesia.

One such dissociative reaction is disengagement or "spacing out", by which survivors cognitively withdraw themselves from abuse-related situations so that in effect the distressing events are not happening. For example:

> If any associations to the abuse experience occur ... it is an immediate stop ... I can't allow myself to think, see or feel. Sex is something that is being done to me ... I remove myself mentally from the situation—I'm not there, I'm mentally numb—if I think, I'll freak out.

Another form of dissociation is depersonalization, in which the victim in some way feels different from her usual self so that in effect it is not really she who is experiencing the distressing event. Often feelings of having left her body, of floating outside it and of watching the event as an observer are reported, as in the following example:

> It's like I actually rise up out of my body. I could feel myself sitting in a chair, and I could feel myself floating up out of my body. That's exactly what it is, like being suspended in midair. I know that my body is in the chair, but the rest of me is out of my body.
>
> (Bass & Davis, 1988, p. 210)

The last form of dissociation to be discussed is multiple personality disorder (MPD). As reported in Chapter 7 on vulnerability, very large proportions of patients with this diagnosis have histories of childhood sexual abuse, usually accompanied by physical abuse. For instance, Ross (1989) reports that in a series of 236 MPD patients studied by himself and his associates, 79% had a history of sexual abuse, and 74% a history of physical abuse; 88% had experienced either or both sexual or physical abuse. Ross goes so far as to write, "What is MPD? MPD is a little girl imagining that the abuse is happening to someone else" (1989, p. 72), although he is clear that the diagnosis also applies to males. Among his MPD patients, 86% exhibited one or more child alter personalities, which were usually the repository of abuse memories and often frightened and untrusting. They may represent a dissociation from the host personality, which exhibits unconflicted positive feelings for the offender and complete amnesia for the abuse, while memories of this and reactions to it are features of the alter personality. Thus, the aetiological role of events related to later abuse by a therapist may be to precipitate, and perhaps to maintain or exacerbate, dissociation into an alter personality which originated much earlier in the victim's childhood.

Arousal

A third group of post-traumatic stress reactions shown in Table 8.1 consists of various symptoms of persistent increased arousal. Victims may have difficulty in falling or staying asleep and they may be very restless during sleep. Thus, 48% of Vinson's (1984) subjects reported difficulty in getting to sleep or staying asleep.

Victims may be chronically irritable and prone to outbursts of anger and perhaps aggression. For instance, irritability was reported by 57% of Vinson's (1984) subjects, and Feldman-Summers & Jones (1984) found that subjects who had been abused by their therapists were significantly more angry than those who had not been so abused. It is readily understandable that victims feel angry towards those who have abused them as well as to people more generally. Often, however, these feelings are very threatening to victims, perhaps because they believe that they do not have any right to be angry, that it is wrong to feel angry towards one's therapist, that their anger might become overwhelming and out of control, or that it may bring retaliation, harm or disapproval from others. Victims may attempt to cope with such threats by totally suppressing or denying their angry feelings, which may adversely affect their self-esteem, psychological stability and lifestyle.

Hypervigilance is another common reaction among survivors. They may be fearful of people or of certain events or situations and extremely alert and on guard against any possible hurt or harm from these sources. This chronic perception of impending danger is understandable in the light of previous abuse experiences and the victim's attempts to avoid them.

Finally, victims commonly react to events resembling the abuse with various physiological signs of autonomic arousal such as muscle tension, sweating, rapid breathing, palpitations, dizziness/fainting and nausea/retching/vomiting.

Conclusion

There appear to be certain advantages in conceptualizing some of the problems experienced by victims of therapist abuse within the general diagnosis of post-traumatic stress disorder (American Psychiatric Association, 1987). To do so provides links between them and the victims of many other forms of trauma such as child sexual abuse, rape, violence, medical and surgical procedures, road traffic accidents, terrorism, war experiences and civilian disasters. Such integration contributes to the understanding and treatment of stress reactions among victims of therapist abuse. A particular benefit is that it depathologizes these patients, in that they can be assured that their reactions are normal responses to an abnormal situation, that many people respond similarly to such events and to do so does not imply some weakness or defect in the victim, and that often frightening and seemingly bizarre reactions such as flashbacks and dissociation do not signify that the victim is going crazy. Such normalization can be enormously reassuring to victims and is likely to reduce the pathogenic influence of the abuse.

On the other hand, some limitations on the application of a post-traumatic stress framework to the problems of victims of therapist abuse need to be recognized. Not all the problems they commonly present, such as those discussed below, can be accounted for adequately or most appropriately as post-traumatic stress reactions. Finally, not all victims necessarily experience such reactions (as far as our present knowledge goes) but they are common among those who seek further treatment.

Mood disturbances

Among patients who were sexually abused by their therapists these disturbances commonly include the three overlapping conditions of depression, grief and guilt.

Depression

The victims of therapist abuse studied by Vinson (1984) reported several indicators of depression; 86% were "blue" and depressed, 81% felt hopeless about the future and 67% had less interest in activities that they previously enjoyed. As many patients enter treatment for depression it may well be that this in many cases was exacerbated by therapist abuse. Alternatively, such abuse may originate depressive reactions in patients not hitherto affected. In either case, it may be grief and/or guilt associated with the abuse that are pathogenic, and these are discussed next.

Grief

Paradoxical as it may seem, many victims grieve for the loss of their relationships with the therapists who abused them. Often these relationships have included positive components such as support and help for victims. They may also have experienced genuine or transferential feelings of love for the therapists. Associated with these feelings may have been an expectation or hope that a long-term intimate relationship would develop. Thus, losses of support, help, love and expectations may evoke grief reactions in victims, perhaps accompanied by depression.

Guilt

Feelings of guilt or shame about their relationships with their therapists were reported by 67% of Vinson's (1984) subjects. Often such feelings arise because victims blame themselves for these sexual relationships. They may believe that they were responsible because they were not forced to have sex, they did not tell anyone or take other action to end the abuse, they must have been seductive and provocative, they experienced sexual pleasure and gratification, or they complied with the therapists' demands because they wanted to be "special" to him. Victims may also be ashamed of their poor judgement in accepting the persuasive communications used by the therapist to overcome their resistance (Chapter 5), such as that sex is a necessary and appropriate part of their treatment, that it is all right to have sex outside sessions or after they have ended, or that the therapist is in love with her. In addition to self-blame for the abuse other sources of guilt include the perceived betrayal of the therapist by disclosing his abuse and perhaps instigating legal or disciplinary proceedings, infidelity to a regular partner and engagement in sexual acts with the therapist that would normally be unacceptable to the victim. As indicated above, whatever the sources of victims' guilt it may be accompanied by depression.

Self-damaging behaviour

This category of problems among victimized patients includes suicidal behaviour, self-mutilation and substance abuse.

Suicidal behaviour

As mentioned above, among victimized patients prevalence rates of 14% have been reported for attempted suicide (Pope & Vetter, 1991) and 1% for committed suicide (Bouhoutsos et al, 1983; Pope & Vetter, 1991), while 33% of Vinson's (1984) subjects had thoughts of ending their lives. Victims may engage in suicidal behaviour as a relief from intolerable distress, including depression, as a cry for help, as a means to exercise some control in their lives, as a punishment for being such a guilty person, as an inward-directed expression of anger and as a form of revenge on the abusing therapist.

Self-mutilation

This type of self-damaging behaviour commonly includes the victim cutting and burning her own body, and it is perhaps most likely to occur among those with a history of childhood sexual abuse (Briere, 1992; Van der Kolk, Perry & Herman, 1991; Walsh & Rosen, 1988). In addition to sharing the motives for suicidal behaviour cited above, self-mutilation can function as an attempt to prevent further abuse by making the body unattractive, a demonstration of control and ownership over the victim's own body, an infliction of pain on one part of her body to distract from the pain experienced in the abused organs, a means of relieving tension or of terminating dissociative episodes, and an addictive behaviour used to regulate intense affect.

Substance abuse

Bouhoutsos et al (1983) found increased alcohol and drug use by victimized patients, and 43% of Vinson's (1984) subjects reported taking more pills, drugs or alcohol than usual. Briere (1992) refers to these substances as "immediate painkillers" and lists their acute effects as "temporary attenuation or elimination of dysphoria, inducement of some level of euphoria or relative well-being, interference with memory of painful events, [and] for some individuals, provision of an opportunity to express painful affect (e.g. sadness, rage) that might otherwise be inhibited" (p. 59).

Sexual dysfunctions

Some victimized patients suffer from various sexual dysfunctions, particularly negative reactions to sex such as phobias, aversions, impaired motivation and dissatisfaction. For instance, among Vinson's (1984) subjects 57% experienced loss of sexual interest at the time their abusive relationships with their therapists ended, and 38% reported sexual difficulties two years later. Many of the other psychological problems discussed in this section may contribute to sexual dysfunctions (see, for example, Bancroft, 1989; Hawton, 1985; Jehu, 1979; Spence, 1991). Post-traumatic stress reactions, such as flashbacks, distress, avoidance behaviour, numbing, dissociation and autonomic changes may disrupt and impair sexual response. It is well known that depression, grief and guilt are often accompanied by lack of sexual desire and interest. Substance abuse can have both short- and long-term adverse effects on sexual performance. Psychosomatic complaints such as chronic pelvic pain are associated with sexual difficulties, including vaginismus and dyspareunia. Finally, it is clear that sexual dysfunctions can arise from personality problems concerning personal safety, trust in other people and the victim's own judgements, self-esteem, control of the victim's own behaviour and that of others, and the victim's intimate relationships with other people.

Psychosomatic complaints

There does not appear to be any direct evidence on psychosomatic complaints among victimized patients generally, but these complaints are associated with childhood sexual abuse, which many such patients have also experienced. The complaints reported to occur significantly more frequently among victims of child sexual abuse include chronic pelvic pain, stomach pain, spastic colitis, nausea, asthma, shortness of breath, heart palpitations, headaches, hypoglycaemia, hypertension and chronic muscle tension (Cunningham, Pearce & Pearce, 1988; Domino & Haber, 1987; Morrison, 1989).

The evidence of an association between child sexual abuse and chronic pelvic pain is perhaps the strongest. For example, 64% of 25 pelvic pain patients with little pelvic pathology were sexually abused before the age of 14 compared to 23% of 30 pain-free women undergoing tubal ligation or investigation for fertility problems (Harrop-Griffiths et al, 1988). Similarly, 48% of 106 idiopathic pelvic pain patients were sexually abused before the age of 16, compared to 6% of 92 matched pain-free patients presenting for routine annual examination (Reiter & Grambone, 1990). Many hypotheses have been advanced to explain this association, including that pelvic pain may be a reflection of the physiological components of post-traumatic stress such as muscle tension, a conversion of psychological distress into a physical complaint as a substitute for emotional pain the victim cannot tolerate, a means of avoiding social or sexual encounters that are stressful for the victim, a symptom of depression, a consequence of the victim's disregard and neglect of her own body (as she was taught to do during the abuse), an expression of self-hatred directed at the body or a means of obtaining and retaining the attention of the physician. These hypotheses are likely to be equally applicable to other psychosomatic complaints in addition to chronic pelvic pain.

Personality problems

According to the American Psychiatric Association Diagnostic and Statistical Manual (1987, p. 335):

> Personality traits are enduring patterns of perceiving, relating to, and thinking about the environment and oneself, and are exhibited in a wide range of important social and personal contexts. It is only when personality traits are inflexible and maladaptive and cause either significant functional impairment or subjective distress that they constitute *Personality Disorders*.

Although victimized patients often have such difficulties these do not always meet the specific criteria for the personality disorders in the manual. Therefore, I am using the term "problems" rather than "disorders"; otherwise, this definition applies. Among such victims these problems commonly concern personal safety, trust in others and one's own judgements, self-esteem, control of one's own behaviour and one's environment, and intimacy with other people. Before describing each of these categories I shall outline how schema theory may cast light on their aetiology.

Aetiology

To recapitulate from Chapter 6, schemas are cognitive structures that organize experience and behaviour. They contain certain core beliefs about oneself, other people and the world in which one lives. These beliefs influence one's thoughts, feelings and actions. More particularly, they interpret and attach meaning to events. Schema concepts have a relatively long history in psychology (e.g. Bartlett, 1932; Head, 1920; Kelly, 1955; Piaget, 1926, 1970, 1971; Rotter, 1954) and there has been a revival of interest in them recently (Beck & Freeman, 1990; McCann & Pearlman, 1990; Roth & Newman, 1991; Young, 1990).

Whether a schema is adaptive or maladaptive can only be judged in the light of an individual's current circumstances. It may have been adaptive and functional for a victim to have been mistrustful and suspicious of others when abuse was likely in childhood, but this mistrust and suspicion might be maladaptive and dysfunctional in adulthood with a partner who would not harm or distress the victim.

Establishment and maintenance of schemas   It is postulated that schemas originate and develop mainly in response to life experiences. In particular, traumatic experiences early in life, especially those of an ongoing and cumulative nature, are alleged to be important in the establishment of maladaptive schemas that are lasting. Therefore, the schemas contributing to personality problems in victimized patients may have originated in childhood and perhaps been activated, maintained and exacerbated by therapist abuse.

The very long-term nature of schemas may result from certain cognitive, behavioural and affective processes. Cognitively, the perception of events is influenced by schemas and this may contribute to their maintenance. Input from these events is selected and interpreted in ways that are consistent with existing schemas, so that input that confirms a schema is likely to be emphasized and exaggerated, while input that is discrepant with a schema tends to be denied, minimized or rationalized.

Behaviourally, individuals may act in ways that confirm their existing schemas. For instance, victims who believe and expect that they will be unable to protect themselves may fail to mobilize coping resources to deal with real threats—such as sexual abuse by a therapist—and therefore suffer harm, which confirms the schema that they are unable to protect themselves. Furthermore, such self-defeating behaviour may evoke responses from others which confirm the victim's schemas. Thus, a victim who does not trust others may act towards them with suspicion, so that in turn they respond to the victim with rejection and hostility, which serves to confirm the victim's lack of trust in people.

Affectively, schemas may be maintained because to change or relinquish well-established and familiar beliefs can be very threatening and anxiety evoking ("What will it be like to be different?" "Will I get hurt or distressed?" "Will my partner still love me if I'm different?"). Schemas have been likened to an old shoe, too comfortable to throw away. Furthermore, individuals often feel hopeless about changing their schemas, which they perceive as being inextricably part of themselves ("This is how I have always been", "This is who I am").

Thus, it is hypothesized that traumatic experiences early in life such as being sexually abused are likely to establish maladaptive schemas, which are maintained over long periods by cognitive distortions, self-defeating behaviour patterns and feelings of anxiety and hopelessness about changing schemas.

Activation of schemas   Schemas are activated when individuals are confronted by life events that they perceive as relevant to a particular schema. Thus, subsequent treatment with a non-abusive therapist might be perceived as threatening by a victimized patient, with consequent activation of safety schemas. Once activated, maladaptive schemas are accompanied by automatic thoughts such as "sex is dangerous", and by emotional reactions such as fear, guilt or disgust. These reactions are usually intense and painful, and to avoid or ameliorate such unpleasant feelings one or more of four major processes may occur.

Individuals may attempt to find a match between input from life events and schemas by interpreting the input in a way that is consistent with their schemas. For instance, victims may minimize their abuse or rationalize the offender's behaviour. Unfortunately, such *assimilation* tends to support and strengthen maladaptive schemas rather than exposing them to reality-testing and possible modification.

Schemas may be modified so that they are more consistent with input from life events. For example, "All men cannot be trusted" might be modified to "Some men cannot be trusted". The adaptiveness of such *accommodation* depends on its appropriateness and extent.

As discussed above, victimized patients may *avoid* events, thoughts or feelings that activate or accompany maladaptive schemas. Behaviourally, they may physically avoid such events. Cognitively, disturbing thoughts or images may be blocked by processes such as suppression, denial, repression, dissociation or distraction by addictions. Affectively, unpleasant feelings might be avoided by numbing or restricting them or even by self-mutilation so that physical pain blocks emotional pain. Thus, behavioural, cognitive and affective avoidance processes may enable individuals to evade or reduce the distress associated with the activation of maladaptive schemas. The price of such avoidance, however, is that these schemas may never be exposed and checked out, and life experiences that might invalidate them are precluded.

Finally, individuals may *overcompensate* for maladaptive schemas by thinking, feeling and acting in ways that seem to be the opposite of what one would expect from knowing their schemas. For instance, an individual whose schemas reflect concern about personal safety may act in extremely reckless and risky ways. Such compensation processes may be viewed as attempts to challenge maladaptive schemas which are not completely successful in that they disadvantage the individual in various ways. For example, someone whose schemas demand total personal control may reject help from others and be unable to ask for it even when necessary and appropriate, or someone with low self-esteem schemas may deny the validity of any criticism and thus lose the benefit of constructive feedback. Furthermore, compensation may mask an underlying vulnerability and therefore leave the individual unprepared for distress if it fails and the schemas are activated. Finally, overcompensation may infringe on the rights of others and lead to adverse reactions from them. Thus, an individual whose schemas concern emotional deprivation in relationships may be so demanding of other people that they respond with rejection and alienation and thus maintain the deprivation.

Conclusion It is suggested that traumatic experiences—especially in childhood—might contribute to personality problems through the establishment and maintenance of lasting maladaptive schemas, which are subsequently activated by relevant events with accompanying automatic thoughts, emotional arousal, assimilation, accommodation, avoidance and compensation. The nature of these problems among victimized patients and the schemas contributing to them are considered in the next section.

Safety

Personality problems concerning safety may be manifested in several ways. Victims may have a sense of unique vulnerability to future harm or distress. There may be an increased probability of events being perceived and reacted to as threatening even when this is not so. Self-defeating behaviour may occur, in that the schema that one is unable to protect oneself may result in failure to take steps necessary to do this and thus enhance the risk of harm or distress, which will then confirm the schema. Finally, post-traumatic stress reactions— especially hypervigilance—are likely to occur, as well as generalized anxiety, and phobic and panic disorders in some cases.

Typical schemas contributing to these personality problems include: "Other people are dangerous and can be expected to harm or distress me", "I am incapable of protecting myself from harm or distress" and "I am uniquely vulnerable to being harmed or distressed".

Trust

Often closely related to safety problems are those concerning the abilities to trust and depend on other people and to rely on one's own perceptions and judgements. These may be manifested in many ways. There may be an overgeneralized and inappropriate distrust of others. They may be regarded with disappointment, disillusionment, suspiciousness, resentment and anger. There may be an unwillingness to depend on others and an avoidance of close relationships, with consequent loneliness. Because of self-doubt about the validity of their own judgements, victims may exhibit excessive caution, confusion and paralysis in decision making. They may also make disadvantageous choices in life and fail to protect themselves because of a difficulty in judging when it is appropriate to trust or distrust others.

Typical schemas contributing to personality problems concerning trust include: "Other people cannot be relied upon to provide my necessary care and support, and they will hurt, betray, exploit or disappoint me", "I cannot trust my own perceptions and judgements" and "I cannot discriminate when it is appropriate to trust or distrust other people or myself".

Self-esteem

A range of problems may be associated with low self-esteem. There may be mood disturbances such as dysphoria, depression, guilt or shame. Victims may engage in self-damaging behaviour, perhaps as an expression of their hatred of themselves. In an attempt to boost their self-esteem they may strive relentlessly for achievement at the expense of their pleasure, health and relationships. Fearing negative evaluation, they may physically avoid other people and thus isolate and alienate themselves. To mitigate or evade recognition of their own transgressions they may cognitively or affectively avoid them by means such as denial, minimization, rationalization, numbing, inability to recall or dissociation.

Typical schemas contributing to personality problems concerning self-esteem include: "I am bad, evil or destructive", "I deserve to suffer and be punished", "I'm basically flawed, defective, and damaged", "I'm not a worthy person in that I am not lovable, competent or acceptable and desirable to others, and do not deserve their attention, love and respect" and "I can never achieve enough to earn the love and respect of others".

Control

The powerlessness of victims of sexual abuse often leaves them with a profound sense of helplessness, to which one type of response is to abandon any attempt to control events and become passive, submissive and unassertive. In psychological theory such reactions have been referred to as learned helplessness (Abramson, Seligman & Teasdale, 1978; Seligman, 1975) and impaired perceived self-efficacy (Bandura, 1977, 1982). Associated problems include vulnerability to exploitation and revictimization; dread of being weak, inadequate, powerless or dependent on others; devaluation of oneself for exhibiting these qualities; and dysphoria and depression.

Perhaps to compensate for their perceived helplessness and lack of control, victims very commonly attempt to exercise excessive control over themselves and other people. They may avoid recognition or expression of their own feelings, needs, interests, wishes, preferences and opinions, and be reluctant to ask for support and help. Other people may be manipulated, exploited or victimized.

Schemas that typically contribute to problems involving control include: "I am weak and powerless if I fail to control myself and others", "I must be in control of my actions and my life", "I must be in control of other people and my environment", "I cannot tolerate and must control my own strong feelings otherwise I will be overwhelmed and perhaps experience adverse reactions from others", "If I express my own needs, desires, interests, preferences and opinions, I will suffer disapproval, rejection or punishment by others", "I should be able to rely on myself and not need to seek support or help from others" and "I must be free from restrictions and be able to do or to have what I want regardless of others".

Intimacy

Some victims are isolated and fear getting close to anyone in case this results in further suffering. They may be unable to experience intimacy even with those who genuinely care for and love them. There may be emotional numbing and emotional detachment from others, together with a pervasive sense of loneliness and alienation. Because of an inability to establish and maintain intimate relationships clients may experience inner emptiness, meaninglessness, futility and despair.

Examples of schemas that typically contribute to personality problems concerning intimacy with others include: "I cannot connect with other people in a stable, enduring, and trusting manner", "It is dangerous to have close and intimate emotional relationships with others, even those who genuinely care for and love me", "I no longer care for other people", "I am isolated and different from other people", "I cannot belong to, and fit into, any group of family, friends or community" and "Other people will not meet my needs for understanding, support, nurturance and protection, or they will not continue to be available to do so because they are unreliable, unpredictable or liable to abandon me".

Intimacy appears to be the only personality problem on which there is some quantitative evidence on prevalence among victimized patients, although other such problems are frequently cited in clinical reports. Among Vinson's (1984) subjects, at the end of the abusive relationships 81% were less close to friends and family. Two years later, 43% reported much more arguing with spouse or lover, and much less participation in social activities, 38% reported that their friends and family had become more distant, and marital separation due to conflict had occurred in 19% of cases. The worsening of sexual, marital and intimate relationships was reported by 29% of another series of victimized patients (Bouhoutsos et al, 1983).

An important implication of such findings and of other problems among victimized patients is that their abuse is likely to have adverse consequences not only for themselves but also for their partners, families, friends and colleagues who, because of this ripple effect, may well become "vicarious victims" meriting treatment in their own right.

Conclusion

The results of several studies indicate that sexual abuse by therapists is followed by predominantly adverse consequences among those victimized patients who subsequently re-enter treatment or volunteer as research subjects. These consequences can be categorized as post-traumatic stress reactions, mood disturbances, self-damaging behaviour, sexual dysfunctions, psychosomatic complaints and personality problems. The treatment of victims presenting with certain of these problems is considered in Chapter 9.

9　Psychological interventions with victims

In this chapter, the attitudes and reactions to treatment of victimized patients and their subsequent therapists are discussed, some foundations for such treatment are identified, specific treatment approaches to certain problems that are prevalent among victims are described, and some modalities for such interventions are reviewed.

Attitudes and reactions to intervention

Victims

Common attitudes and reactions to subsequent therapy among victimized patients are well summarized by Kluft (1989):

> The assumption that one is entering a benign and helping environment has been shattered, even if the patient superficially expresses feelings to the contrary. Some patients openly express fears that the new therapist will exploit them sexually. . . . Some attempt to suppress their misgivings but clearly share similar concerns. . . . A small number take steps to test the therapist . . . there may be mistrust and misgiving rather than optimism and confidence . . . conversely, such patients may enter treatment with a most unrealistic optimism and expression of faith in the therapist. . . . This would appear to be a fervid and irrational expression of the wish that the new therapy will prove magically safe and efficacious . . . denying the misgivings . . . that would be expected under the circumstances.
>
> (Kluft, 1989, pp. 490–491).

Therapists

Sonne & Pope (1991) discuss several common attitudes and reactions among subsequent therapists faced with the disclosure that a patient was sexually abused by a previous therapist.

For any of several reasons, subsequent therapists may disbelieve or deny such disclosures. They may hold a naive view that such things do not happen in therapy, or it may be too distressing to contemplate the possibility that therapists like themselves could engage in such behaviour. They may find it hard to accept the word of a disturbed patient against that of a well-qualified and sometimes respected and prestigious colleague. Mistakenly, they may believe that sex with patients is legitimate because it was said to be part of treatment, the patient consented, the participants were in love or it occurred only after termination. The sexual activities described by the patient may seem too bizarre to be probable. Many victimized patients anticipate such disbelief and rejection by subsequent therapists and consequently are hesitant to seek further treatment or to disclose the previous abuse. Unfortunately, these fears are sometimes well founded and, as discussed further below, it is vital that disclosures are received in an open-minded and sensitive manner. They may well be true, although a small number of false complaints are made.

Subsequent therapists may believe that abuse occurred but minimize the harm this entailed for the patient. This defence may mitigate the behaviour of the abuser and its implications for the reputations of the therapeutic professions. It may also reduce the degree of threat involved in the prospect of having to undertake the complex and difficult treatment of a previously victimized patient.

Perhaps in an attempt to reduce the complexity of victims' experiences and to understand them, subsequent therapists may make assumptions about what happened in the abusive encounters and their consequences for the patients. Such stereotyping involves the imposition of the therapist's preconceived ideas rather than openness to the uniqueness of each patient's experiences and an ability to empathize with them. Victims need to be allowed to tell their own stories in their own ways and to express the whole range of their feelings with acceptance and support from the therapist. In this regard it is especially important that subsequent therapists accept and empathize with the ambivalent feelings that victims may have towards their abusers. It may be assumed too readily that victims will experience only undiluted rage and hatred, together with a wish to avenge themselves. In fact, in many victims such negative reactions are accompanied by respect, dependence, affection, love, gratitude and other positive feelings, together with a wish to protect their abusers. If these positive reactions are not recognized and accepted by subsequent therapists, who ignore or reject them, then the victims concerned are unlikely to be able to resolve their contradictory feelings and some may drop out of therapy.

Subsequent therapists may blame victims for having been abused, perhaps for behaving in a provocative and seductive manner or at least cooperating with the sexual approaches. This may be seen as mitigation for the abusive behaviour in that, while admittedly inappropriate, it was perpetrated by a colleague who is generally ethical and competent but who was unreasonably tempted and provoked by the patient in this instance. An opposing view attributing complete ethical responsibility for the abuse to the therapist is reiterated throughout this book.

It is quite likely that subsequent therapists will experience sexual attraction towards, and sexual fantasies involving, certain of their patients, including some of those who were victimized by previous therapists. These reactions may evoke anxiety, guilt and confusion, perhaps especially if they cause the subsequent therapist to see similarities between himself and the abuser. As discussed in Chapter 1, however, sexual attraction and fantasies are not in themselves unusual or unethical providing they are not acted out.

If victimized patients instigate disciplinary or legal proceedings in respect of their abuse then subsequent therapists may be required to hand over their notes and to give evidence at hearings, which is subject to cross-examination. It may be disturbing and distressing for them to experience such transgressions of the privacy and confidentiality to which they are accustomed, and the conflict may be especially acute if they have not forewarned their patients of the legal limitations on confidentiality.

The obverse may occur also. If patients do not consent to the release of information or if this is not legally mandated then subsequent therapists must not breach confidentiality. This can be difficult for them if they are outraged by the abuse and concerned to protect the public and the profession from the abuser's behaviour.

These reactions may lead subsequent therapists to pressure victims into making formal complaints about their abuse, and it may be argued that this would be therapeutic for them and that they should do so in order to stop the abuser practising and to protect other potential victims. Alternatively, the opposite may occur, in that subsequent therapists may guide and perhaps pressure victims against complaining. Therapists may not wish to suffer the discomfort of involvement in legal or disciplinary proceedings as discussed above, and they may argue that victims should forget what happened in the past, that such proceedings would not be helpful to them, or that the abuser did not intend harm and does not deserve sanctions. To push victims either towards or against making a complaint has been termed "intrusive advocacy" (Sonne & Pope, 1991), and these decisions should more appropriately be left to the victim to make at her own pace and without undue influence from the therapist.

If she does decide to make a complaint then her subsequent therapist may experience a sense of "vicarious helplessness" (Sonne & Pope, 1991) at his inability to protect her adequately from the vicissitudes of the legal or disciplinary processes and decisions, as discussed in Chapters 10 and 11.

Finally, Sonne & Pope (1991) point out that feelings of rage, neediness, loss and ambivalence arising from abuse by previous therapists are likely to be directed at subsequent therapists. Consequently, these therapists may experience, anxiety, guilt and feelings of inadequacy, which they may be tempted to avoid by withdrawing from treating the victim.

Conclusion

Thus, victimized patients may approach subsequent therapy with attitudes and reactions that include fear of further sexual exploitation, distrust of therapists and lack of confidence in psychological treatment, or alternatively they may have an unrealistic sense of optimism that a "magic" cure will be provided together with excessive faith in the abilities of subsequent therapists.

Among such therapists certain common attitudes and reactions include disbelief or denial of the abuse, minimization of its harmful effects, assuming knowledge of what happened in the abuse and of its consequences, blaming victims for being abused, feeling sexually attracted to victims and fantasizing about them, discomfort over involvement in legal or disciplinary proceedings, difficulty in maintaining confidentiality, intrusive advocacy, vicarious helplessness, and distress at being the object of negative emotional reactions originating with the previous therapist.

Clearly, these attitudes and reactions among both victims and subsequent therapists need to be recognized and addressed in the planning and implementation of psychological interventions.

Foundations of intervention

Certain fundamental components and processes in interventions with victimized patients constitute a foundation for the deployment of more specific procedures with particular categories of problems. These foundations include the relationship between patient and therapist, the promotion of a positive prognostic expectancy, the disclosure and exploration of the abuse and its associated problems, the therapist's acceptance and support of the patient, his empathic understanding of her experiences, the formulation of a causal explanation for her problems, providing her with relevant information and empowerment of the victim.

Relationship

At the core of these foundations is a relationship between patient and therapist that is characterized by mutual liking, respect and trust. *Inter alia*, this is likely to decrease the patient's defensiveness and to increase her openness to influence from the therapist toward the achievement of her chosen goals. In addition, her maladaptive interpersonal relationship patterns may be replicated in her interactions with the therapist, whose responses can constitute new learning experiences, through which she may acquire more appropriate ways of relating to others, as discussed in the section "Treatment of personality problems".

It is particularly important that relationships with victimized patients are characterized by clarity, openness and honesty of communication. Because of their previous exploitation and probable distrust of subsequent therapists, such patients need to be clearly informed about what is happening in their therapy and to have complete access to their records. Similarly, because of the boundary violations in the previous abuse and the distrust these engendered, it is important that proper limits are set and communicated to victimized patients entering subsequent therapy. For example, such limits might include the avoidance of all touching, holding sessions only when other people are present in the clinical setting, no outside meetings, discussion of sexual matters only when therapeutically appropriate and with the permission of the patient, and certainly the total exclusion of any form of sexual activity with the therapist should be clearly stated to the patient.

Prognostic expectancy

A second foundation in therapy is the promotion of a positive prognostic expectancy. Many victimized patients lack confidence in treatment and have feelings of hopelessness when they present for subsequent therapy, and it is important to communicate to them that while the effects of abuse can be long term and very distressing this does not mean necessarily that they are irremediable and permanent. Victims are assured that they can reasonably expect to receive effective help, but at the same time they are warned that treatment is unlikely to follow a completely smooth course or to produce an extremely rapid improvement, thus countering any unrealistic optimism, as mentioned above.

Disclosure

On the basis of a therapeutic relationship and the prospect of effective help, victims are likely to enter the painful process of disclosing and exploring their abuse experiences and associated problems, as well as expressing their often intense accompanying emotional reactions. More specifically, for some victims this is the first time that they have shared the secret of the abuse with anyone, while the attempted revelations of other victims have been met with disbelief, blame or anger. Consequently, it can be an enormous relief for a patient to unburden herself to a therapist who responds in positive ways.

Acceptance and support

The victim's disclosure of her abuse and associated problems are often accompanied by intense feelings of shame, and perhaps by fear that the subsequent therapist will not be willing or able to deal with these issues. It is therefore very important that she is accepted and supported. Thus, a therapist who is respectful, non-judgemental and immune to shock or embarrassment offers a non-threatening, safe and trusting relationship in which the victim is free to explore her experiences without restraint or restriction, which enhances her self-esteem. Associated with such acceptance is the therapist's genuine concern for the patient's welfare and his deep commitment to helping her. This can be very supportive to the patient, who now has a source of aid and is no longer alone in attempting to cope with her problems. She is, moreover, seeing a therapist who views these problems as understandable and as potentially amenable to treatment.

Empathic understanding

The quality of a therapeutic relationship and the outcome of treatment are both strongly influenced by the level of empathic understanding exhibited by the therapist and perceived by the patient. Such understanding involves the ability to comprehend both the experiences and the feelings of a victim, together with their meaning and significance for her. It is essential also that this comprehension is communicated to the patient so that she feels deeply understood by the therapist. This process is the antithesis of the stereotyping of victims' experiences and reactions discussed above.

Causal explanation

A closely related process is the formulation of a causal explanation for the victim's problems that is shared and negotiated with her. It is based upon an empathic understanding of the individual patient, together with the hypotheses and theoretical conceptualizations advanced as possible reasons for the problems reviewed in Chapter 8. Victims often experience difficulties that seem inexplicable, strange and bizarre; for example, flashbacks and dissociative reactions. It can be very reassuring for them to have a plausible explanation for such difficulties, and the fact that the therapist appears to understand their problems also tends to reduce anxiety and to engender hope for successful treatment. Finally, a causal explanation for the problems which is shared by patient and therapist constitutes a rationale for the more specific procedures to be used in the treatment of particular problems, which is discussed below.

Provision of information

Providing victims with relevant information through reading assignments, audio-visual materials or discussion with other patients who have been abused may help them to understand their own abuse experiences and ensuing problems, as well as reduce feelings of difference, alienation and isolation from other people. According to the motivation and capacity of the victim, such reading assignments might include suitable clinical and research literature as well as autobiographical accounts (e.g. Appendices B and C; Bates & Brodsky, 1989; Freeman & Roy, 1976; Plaisil, 1985; Walker & Young, 1986). Several recent television programmes may be available for viewing, and other victims may be met in self-help groups.

Empowerment

Because of their lack of power and control in the previous abuse victims need to be given maximum opportunity to make choices and decisions in subsequent therapy. This will help to enhance their sense of mastery over what happens to them in life and to boost their self-esteem. For example, victims should be free to choose the gender of their subsequent therapist, in so far as this is practicable. If a suitable therapist of the preferred gender is not available this should be explained to the victim so that she can decide whether she wishes to enter treatment with the non-preferred alternative. At present there is no empirical evidence on the influence of gender of the subsequent therapist *vis-à-vis* that of the abuser on the progress and outcome of treatment, but some general considerations on this issue may be discussed with victims (Mogul, 1982). The pace at which therapy proceeds both within and across sessions should be determined largely by the victim so that she is not overwhelmed or retraumatized by pressure to express and confront disturbing material before she is ready to do so. She should be encouraged to feel completely free to raise questions about any aspect of her treatment at any time. If she wishes to leave treatment—with or without referral elsewhere—then she should be able to do so without criticism but with an open invitation to return whenever she feels ready to resume treatment. Finally, victims should be allowed to make their own decisions on whether to file a formal complaint, as discussed above in relation to intrusive advocacy. These are just a few examples of the many aspects of therapy in which victims should be empowered to choose.

Conclusion

Thus, it is suggested that the components and processes reviewed in this section constitute a foundation for therapy with victimized patients. They guide and permeate the whole intervention and provide a necessary basis for the implementation of more specific procedures for particular categories of problems.

Assessment for intervention

The subsequent treatment of victimized patients needs to be based on a comprehensive assessment process comprising an initial phase, the negotiation of therapeutic objectives, and the assessment and formulation of target problems.

Initial phase

The initial phase comprises two assessment tasks: (i) facilitating the disclosure and exploration of the abuse and its consequences, and (ii) taking a history from the victim and perhaps from other informants.

Disclosure   The occurrence of previous sexual abuse may be presented to the subsequent therapist, either overtly or covertly. Some victims overtly disclose that they have been abused, often make some degree of connection between this experience and their current problems, and to some extent seek treatment related to their abuse.

In contrast to the overt presentations, other victims present in a covert or disguised manner; they do not readily disclose their abuse, often do not connect it in any way with their current problems, and do not seek treatment related to the abuse. There are several common reasons for such non-disclosure. Some victims are to some extent unaware that they were abused because of defences such as denial, repression, suppression or dissociation. Some lack sufficient information about what constitutes abuse so that they do not realize that certain behaviour by the perpetrator is abusive. Victims may still feel subject to the pressure put upon them to keep the abuse secret. Sometimes this pressure is in the form of various threats against them if they disclose. Pressure is also exerted through the intense loyalty that many victims feel towards the abuser, so that disclosure is seen as a betrayal. Many do not disclose because they fear that this will result in stigmatization and rejection by others, and this is not altogether unrealistic because victims may have attempted to disclose in the past only to have had these attempts ignored, rejected or criticized by professionals. Finally, victims may not disclose because of their profound mistrust of other people arising from the abuse and its surrounding circumstances.

This leads to the topic of how subsequent therapists can facilitate the disclosure of abuse by victimized patients. If there is any reason to suspect that it might have happened then patients can be asked directly. After a reassuring statement that sexual activities do sometimes occur between patients and therapists the patient can be asked if anything of this nature happened to her. The fact that the matter is raised specifically signals that the subsequent therapist is comfortable in dealing with such abuse, is knowledgeable about it and regards it as a very relevant issue in therapy. If abuse is not disclosed despite indications of its probable occurrence then the therapist may gently probe further, perhaps by describing what constitutes abusive behaviour and providing appropriate reading material or audio-visual presentations. If direct questioning and further gentle probing does not elicit disclosure then it is usually better not to press the patient to remember and acknowledge the suspected abuse. If it in fact occurred then enhanced recall and willingness to disclose may occur later as the patient becomes less anxious and guilty about the abuse, receives more cues to facilitate remembering, and is more comfortable in the therapeutic situation.

History taking   This second assessment task during the initial phase involves the systematic gathering of information in interviews with the patient and perhaps with other informants. Luepker (1989a) has prepared an extensive protocol for such interviews, which she summarizes as follows (p. 162):

- Current problems, needs, suicide-risk.
- Specific history of therapy abuse (who did what to whom, when and how).
- Meaning of the therapy abuse to the client.
- Neglect/exacerbation of original problems by therapy abuse.
- Previous functioning and earlier life history.
- Relation of earlier life themes to therapy abuse as perceived by client.

Negotiation of objectives

The goals of treatment are chosen mainly by the patient in accordance with her own wishes and values, although in consultation with the therapist. The major contribution of professional treatment *per se* is to provide effective ways of achieving these goals only after they have been selected on personal, social and ethical grounds. The aim is to negotiate a therapeutic contract in which mutually agreeable goals are specified. Apart from the ethical imperative of patients agreeing to the goals of treatment, it should be noted that there is evidence from a number of sources that they are more likely to work towards change when they feel that they have some say in the goals of change (e.g. Kanfer, 1980). This is likely to maximize collaboration and minimize resistance during treatment.

Quite commonly, the assessment reveals that a victim has a number of problems, and this raises the issue of which to treat and in what order of priority. Some guidelines for this selection process include:

1. The values and preferences of the victim.
2. The degree of danger, distress or incapacity that the problem entails for the victim and others; for example, high risk of suicide would necessitate urgent therapeutic attention.
3. The potential benefits that the resolution of the problem entails for the victim and others.
4. Some problems are so closely related to each other that their concurrent treatment is indicated; for example, guilt and low self-esteem associated with sexual victimization.
5. It is preferable to concentrate on a small number of problems at any one time. This focuses the treatment efforts of patient and therapist, and it is likely to expedite demonstrable benefits to the patient, which will serve to promote motivation in treatment.
6. The resolution of certain problems is sometimes a necessary precondition for the successful treatment of other problems; for example, mood disturbances and any serious discord in the current partnership both usually need to be alleviated before specific treatment for sexual dysfunction is implemented.

Finally, although goals are initially selected at this stage in the intervention process, it will often be necessary to revise them during the course of further assessment and treatment, either because the therapist has reformulated the problem in a different way, or because the patient has presented the therapist with new problems.

Assessment and formulation of target problems

Next, the problem(s) selected for the initial intervention are further assessed, as discussed below, and all the information gathered during the assessment stage provides the basis for a clinical formulation of the patient's problems, which includes a precise specification of the nature of the problems, some hypotheses about the current events that evoke and maintain them, any historical or developmental factors that have predisposed the patient to react in these problematic ways, and an appraisal of the resources available for treatment from the patient, significant others and the therapist. This formulation is not regarded as definitive or final; it is open to modification in the light of the feedback that is actively solicited from the patient and is subject to constant revision as treatment proceeds. The formulation is shared with the patient in terms and language that she can understand. In addition, it is personalized to the particular patient's problems rather than being presented as a routinized and didactic description of the therapist's preferred theoretical model. The formulation is likely to be much more credible to the patient if the therapist demonstrates how theory casts light on the patient's own problems, rather than seeming to force her into some abstract theoretical system. A causal explanation that makes sense of problems that previously seemed inexplicable and strange may be very reassuring for a victim. Finally, the shared formulation provides a necessary basis for the planning of treatment and evaluation.

When the therapist and patient agree that sufficient progress has been made in resolving a particular problem, the processes of selecting and assessing target problems are repeated with the remaining problems.

Space precludes discussion of the specific treatment of the multitudinous problems exhibited by victimized patients but therapeutic approaches to post-traumatic stress reactions, mood disturbances and personality problems are indicated below. These are perhaps the most prevalent categories of problems among victims.

Treatment of post-traumatic stress reactions

These reactions among victimized patients are discussed in Chapter 8, and a useful instrument for their assessment is the Trauma Symptom Checklist-40 (Elliot & Briere, 1992). The treatment of these reactions can be conceptualized as involving three concurrent processes, as shown in Table 9.1: exposure to stressful features related to the abuse in safe therapeutic conditions, training in skills that will help the patient to cope better with these stressful features, and changing the meaning of the abuse so that it is less stressful for the patient. Each of these processes may involve a number of specific procedures, which are also indicated in Table 9.1. For reasons of space and their familiarity to some readers these procedures are outlined only very briefly below.

Table 9.1: Interventive Processes and Procedures for Post-Traumatic Stress Reactions

Exposure to stressors
1. Discussion in therapy
2. Writing assignments
3. Imaginal desensitization
4. Imaginal flooding
5. Role play
6. *In vivo* assignments

Training in coping skills
1. Relaxation
2. Withdrawal
3. Thought and image stopping
4. Guided self-dialogue
5. Coping plans
6. Imagery rehearsal
7. Role play
8. *In vivo* assignments

Changing meaning of trauma
1. Cost–benefit analysis
2. Corrective therapeutic relationship
3. Provision of information
4. Logical analysis
5. Decatastrophizing
6. Distancing
7. Reattribution
8. Guided imagery
9. Assigned activities

Therapeutic exposure to features related to the abuse

There is now general consensus that in order to alleviate stress reactions it is necessary for patients to be exposed to the threatening features that elicit these reactions while in safe circumstances where actual harm will not result (Foa & Kozak, 1985, 1986; Marks, 1981).

One way in which such exposure can be provided is by discussion of stressful features related to the abuse in the safety of treatment sessions. This helps victims to recall traumatic memories and to express the emotions associated with them. Such recall and expression can often be facilitated by appropriate bibliographical and audio-visual materials, such as autobiographical accounts of abuse. It is important that victims recall not only relevant facts but also that they experience the accompanying feelings. As mentioned earlier these feelings are commonly very threatening to victims and this dread of affect needs to be reduced. Clearly, discussion continues throughout therapy until the victim can recall and tolerate memories and feelings associated with the abuse, although most therapists who are experienced with victims agree that total recall is not essential for recovery, and that victims need not be pressured to achieve this. Moreover, during this process it is important for therapists to help patients to pace themselves so that they are not overwhelmed by intense traumatic memories and feelings that are too threatening and beyond their capacity to cope with at that particular point in time. In other words it is necessary to respect their "affect tolerance".

Another relatively safe method of exposure is for victims to write about their experiences and reactions. There are many formats for such writing, including a journal, an autobiography, preferably with accompanying photographs, and letters to the abuser, which may or may not be sent.

In imaginal desensitization patients are exposed to stressful features related to the abuse in a graded manner and in imagination. More specifically, the procedure consists of training patients in muscle relaxation, preparing with them a hierarchy or hierarchies of stressful features from the least to the most disturbing, and relaxing them and asking them to imagine the least disturbing item in the hierarchy for short periods until they can do so without distress, at which point the procedure is repeated for the next most disturbing item, and so on up the hierarchy.

Imaginal flooding is similar to desensitization except that patients are asked to imagine each item in the hierarchy repeatedly and for prolonged periods until the distress it evokes is significantly reduced, and muscle relaxation may not be employed specifically during this process.

When feasible and ethical, abuse-related situations may be re-enacted in role plays. The literature on psychodrama and Gestalt techniques such as the empty chair or hitting pillows provides useful sources of ideas for the conduct of role plays.

Finally, victims may be exposed to stressful features by undertaking therapeutically prescribed assignments in real life. These are usually prescribed in a graded manner from the less to more distressing tasks. For example, they might involve progressing through the process of re-entering therapy entailing the tasks of inquiry, discussion, exploratory meetings and the initial phase of therapy.

Training in coping skills

Skills can be taught to victims to enable them to cope better with stressful features related to the abuse. Breath control and/or deep muscle relaxation can help them to cope with stress in several ways, including reducing bodily tension which is a common reaction to stress, producing a state of psychological calmness, distracting the attention of clients from their stress reactions, and enabling them to exercise some control and mastery in stressful situations.

When victims feel that they are confronted by an abuse-related feature that is beyond their coping capacity at that point in time then it may be appropriate for them to withdraw from the situation. For example, some victims may need a period of celibacy when faced with sexual demands that are stressful for them. Similarly, leaving a provocative situation may be appropriate if victims feel that their anger may lead them to become violent or result in retaliation from another person.

As discussed in Chapter 8, victims are often troubled by intrusive recollections of their abuse, flashbacks and dissociative reactions, in which they disengage or depersonalize in their thought processes. One way in which such thoughts and images can be disrupted and reduced is termed "grounding" or "reality orientation". Victims are taught to focus on the "here and now" by means such as concentrating on and describing their immediate environment, touching objects around them, attending to their own bodies by touching, deep breathing or other sensations, and talking to someone else who is present. In such ways victims can learn to discriminate between past and present experiences and to prevent themselves from dissociating from the current situation. Another way of reducing intrusive thoughts from the past is termed "tape recognition" (Briere, 1989). First, in discussion victims are helped to increase their awareness and recognition of such thoughts, some examples of which are "I was to blame for what happened to me in therapy and when things go wrong it is always my fault" and "Other people can exploit and take advantage of me because I don't count, I'm not worthy of respect or consideration". Next, victims are introduced to the idea of regarding such learned thoughts as tapes that were recorded in the past—often originally in childhood—when their knowledge and judgement were limited but that are still running at the present time. The victims are encouraged to spot when these tapes are playing, and later to try to ignore them rather than believing them or fighting them. As victims become better at recognizing that the tapes are derived from past rather than current experiences and at ignoring them then they are gradually erased. A third way of disrupting troublesome thoughts and images is for victims to distract themselves by activities such as physical exercise, listening to music, reading or hobbies.

The procedure of guided self-dialogue is based on the principle that their thoughts can influence how victims react to and cope with stressful features related to their abuse. Therefore, it is useful for them to have prepared with their therapist suitable statements that they can say to themselves when faced with such features. If a victim became worried that sex might occur in subsequent therapy she might use statements such as "my current therapist has never made any kind of sexual approach", "there are plenty of people just outside the door", "I can leave the session whenever I want to" and "I always have the option of suspending or terminating therapy".

The coping skills reviewed above are often combined into a coping plan prepared by victims and their therapists and implemented by the former in situations that are stressful for them. For example, the following is a plan used by a victim to help her to cope with discussion of her abuse experiences: "If you get unpleasant feelings and become upset during therapy (i) stop discussing your abuse, (ii) take several short deep breaths to fill your chest and relax as you breathe out, (iii) open your eyes, look around and remember where you are *now*, (iv) relax and calm yourself and (v) when you have calmed down either resume discussion again on this occasion or try again at another time".

The procedure of imagery rehearsal consists of victims imagining themselves confronting and coping with situations that are stressful for them. Thus, they are able to rehearse and practise in imagination the implementation of the coping skills they have learned, as a bridge to doing this in real life. This procedure is derived from imaginal desensitization but it contains variations so that coping with stress is emphasized, rather than counterconditioning.

Role playing is another way of rehearsing and practising coping skills in preparation for their implementation in real-life stressful situations. This procedure tends to reduce stress reactions and to increase the probability of coping skills being used when required.

Finally, victims may undertake a graded series of *in vivo* assignments in which they confront and cope with a hierarchy of stressful situations in real life, as discussed above.

Changing meaning of abuse

The meaning of the abuse for individual victims can influence considerably their reactions to the trauma. Typically, victims hold certain distorted beliefs derived from the abuse that are likely to have later adverse effects on their feelings and behaviour (Beck & Emery, 1985; Chemtob et al, 1988; Foa, Steketee & Olasov-Rothbaum, 1989; Janoff-Bulman, 1992; Litz & Keane, 1989; McCann & Pearlman, 1990; Taylor, 1983). If these beliefs signal some kind of threat then post-traumatic stress reactions are likely to be precipitated. It follows that the therapeutic correction of such beliefs is likely to be accompanied by an alleviation of these reactions. Cognitive restructuring is one such approach. This was introduced in Chapter 6 and is discussed further below. Some specific procedures deployed in this approach are listed in Table 9.1, and an example of its application is shown in Table 9.2.

Table 9.2: Example of Cognitive Restructuring in Treatment of Post-Traumatic Stress Reactions

Distorted beliefs	Alternative beliefs
Like my previous therapist, my new therapist will want to have sex with me.	My new therapist has not done or said anything that might indicate that he is interested in having sex with me.
	We have discussed the ground rules for therapy, which totally exclude sex.
	Because one therapist demanded sex with me, this does not mean that all therapists will do so.
	I can protect myself by leaving therapy at any time.
Because he knows I had sex with my previous therapist, my new therapist will think I am trying to seduce him.	I have not done or said anything of a seductive nature and my new therapist has not shown any sign that he regards me as seductive.
Like all men, my new therapist will expect something in return for what he does for me.	There are men who can care for me without expecting sex in return.

Treatment of mood disturbances

The mood disturbances of depression, grief and guilt among victimized patients are described in Chapter 8. To the extent that sexual abuse in therapy contributes to these disturbances it is hypothesized that this association is mediated by certain distorted beliefs concerning the abuse that are held by victims. Such distorted or unrealistic beliefs are postulated to lead to distressing feelings and inappropriate actions, and in so far as mood disturbances are a function of these beliefs then it follows that their therapeutic correction is likely to be accompanied by an alleviation of the disturbances. This cognitive model and the cognitive restructuring intervention discussed below are derived from the work of Aaron Beck and his associates (Beck, 1976; Beck & Emery, 1985; Beck et al, 1979). The role assigned to distorted beliefs associated with sexual abuse in the aetiology of mood disturbances among victims does not exclude other possible contributory factors to these disturbances, such as organic causes of depression, discordant relationships or self-destructive lifestyles. These and any other contributory factors need to be addressed by other components in treatment.

Assessment procedures

The nature of mood disturbances and the existence of distorted beliefs and other factors that may contribute to them are often revealed during interviews; for example, those conducted in accordance with the initial assessment protocol discussed above.

In order to identify such sources of distress, certain events and thought processes can be reconstructed during therapeutic sessions by means of instant replay, remote recall, role play or induced imagery. In the first of these techniques if a victim becomes distressed but cannot pinpoint the thoughts and beliefs that preceded these feelings, she then immediately reviews the sequence during which they occurred in an attempt to identify the relevant cognitions on the second occasion. Similarly, in remote recall when a victim recalls an occasion in the past when distress was experienced but the accompanying thoughts and beliefs cannot be remembered, she reviews the past events in slow motion in an attempt to revive the relevant cognitions. Alternatively, a recent or past event that evoked distress can be re-enacted in a role play, perhaps with the therapist assuming the role of another person in the interaction, so that the thoughts that evoked the distress can be repeated and identified. Finally, in the induced imagery technique the victim is asked to relax, close her eyes and to imagine vividly and clearly an event during which distress was experienced so that the thoughts that evoked this can be recaptured.

Very commonly victims are asked to self-monitor their thoughts and feelings in certain situations and to maintain a written record of these experiences in notes, letters, diary entries, essays or on various forms.

The Beck Depression Inventory (Beck et al, 1979; Beck, Steer & Garbin, 1988) covers all the major symptoms in this syndrome. An alternative is the Center for Epidemiologic Studies Depressed Mood Scale (Radloff, 1977).

Treatment procedures

Cognitive restructuring is based on the premise mentioned above that the correction of distorted beliefs is likely to be accompanied by the alleviation of the associated mood disturbance. These aims are pursued through the therapist exploring with the victim some more accurate and realistic beliefs as alternatives to the distorted beliefs that were identified earlier. A variety of techniques is used to explore alternative beliefs with patients, including those outlined next.

Provision of information   The therapist may provide factual data to correct any inaccurate information that may be contributing to a victim's distorted beliefs.

For example, information about the prevalence of sexual abuse in therapy often serves to reduce her feelings of guilt. As well as disseminating information verbally, it is very useful for the therapist to prescribe appropriate reading materials for victims, and some suitable sources are recommended in the section "Foundations of intervention", above.

Logical analysis   The victim's logic is reviewed to determine whether the evidence necessarily entails the conclusion that she has drawn and what alternative conclusions there might be. One instance is the victim who concludes that, "I must have been to blame, because I did not complain". Clearly, another possible conclusion is that she did not do so because of the power exerted over her by the abuser.

Decatastrophizing   Victims often predict the direst consequences for themselves. For example, "I will never be able to find another therapist to help me, or another person to love". In such circumstances the therapist may be able to decatastrophize the situation by widening the victim's perspective so that she takes all the relevant information into account when she makes her predictions. Thus, a victim may benefit from knowing that many victimized patients do progress in subsequent therapy and that they can establish new loving relationships.

Distancing   This term refers to the process of a victim shifting from a subjective to an objective perception of her own beliefs, so that they are no longer regarded as self-evident truths but rather as hypotheses that may or may not be valid. Let us take as an example a woman who "knows" that she was responsible for her sexual abuse. If she is exposed vicariously to the abuse experiences of other women then she may strongly deny that they were to blame for being abused and consequently begin to shift to a more objective view of her own responsibility for what happened to her. Such vicarious exposure might be arranged through participation in group therapy with other abused women, by reading their personal accounts of sexual abuse or by viewing equivalent audio-visual presentations.

Reattribution   This procedure is designed to correct a victim's tendency to assume total responsibility for her abuse and not to take into account factors that were beyond her control. The therapist and victim review the circumstances of the abuse to arrive at a more appropriate assignment of responsibility by showing that the facts do not support the victim's complete acceptance of blame, as discussed further below.

Conclusion   The deployment of these and other cognitive restructuring procedures in the treatment of mood disturbances is described in greater detail elsewhere (e.g. Beck et al, 1979; Burns, 1980; Hawton et al, 1989; Freeman et al, 1989). As noted in Chapter 8, depression among victimized patients may well arise from grief and/or guilt associated with the abuse, and the treatment of these reactions is outlined next.

Grief reactions

Separation from a therapist who was sexually abusive but on whom the victim was emotionally dependent can be a very traumatic and distressing experience for her. Understandably, therefore, some grief reactions to such losses have much in common with the post-traumatic stress reactions discussed in Chapter 8 (Bowlby, 1980; Lindemann, 1944; Parkes, 1972; Raphael, 1983). Thus, victims may re-experience the loss in intrusive recollections and dreams about the absent therapist, and having to confront the separation may evoke intense distress in the forms of anxiety, panic, sadness and a sense of helplessness and hopelessness at the thought of life without him. Attempts may be made to avoid the loss and the feelings accompanying it by cognitive-affective mechanisms such as denial, impaired memories and numbing. Increased arousal may be exhibited as anger at having to suffer the loss and towards those perceived as responsible for it, and in various physiological reactions such as breathing difficulties, palpitations, feelings of weakness, gastrointestinal reactions and agitated restlessness.

It follows that many of the treatment procedures for post-traumatic stress discussed above are likely to be applicable with grief reactions. In particular, exposure to the trauma of the loss (often referred to as "working through" or "emotional processing" in the grief literature) and decatastrophizing the perceived adverse consequences of the loss may be especially efficacious. Similarly, among the foundations of intervention discussed above, promoting a positive prognostic expectancy, acceptance and support, and empowerment of the victim are likely to counteract her feelings of helplessness and hopelessness.

Guilt reactions

Some sources of these reactions are discussed in Chapter 8. Perhaps especially potent among them are certain self-blaming beliefs which lead victims to assume responsibility for having been abused, and appropriate alternatives to such beliefs need to be explored by cognitive restructuring procedures in order to alleviate the associated guilt reactions. Some examples of self-blaming beliefs and alternatives to them are shown in Table 9.3.

Table 9.3:   Example of Cognitive Restructuring in the Treatment of Guilt Reactions

Distorted beliefs	Alternative beliefs
I must have been to blame for having sex with my therapist because I wasn't forced into it.	The power I felt my therapist had over me made it difficult for me to say "No", and to be a "good" patient I was supposed to trust my therapist and to comply with his instructions.
It must have been my fault because I didn't tell anyone.	I kept the abuse secret because I was afraid of what might happen if I spoke out, e.g. being disbelieved or blamed by others, my therapist being angry with me, betraying and damaging him, and losing his therapeutic help.
I must have been seductive and provocative.	Even if I was, this is irrelevant because it was my therapist's responsibility to ensure that nothing unethical occurred rather than to exploit me for his own gratification.
I was aroused during the sex, therefore I must have wanted it, therefore it was my fault.	Sexual arousal is a normal, automatic, reflex response to sexual stimulation and it does not mean that I wanted it to happen.
I went along with my therapist's sexual demands because I wanted his attention and affection and to be "special" to him.	My therapist should make me feel worthwhile and cared for as an individual without me having to buy his attention and affection with sex. This was an unfair price for him to impose on me.
I am to blame because I should have known better than to believe my therapist when he said that sex would be good for me/that sex was ethical as long as it occurred outside sessions or after termination/that he was in love with me.	I could not give an informed consent to sex because I did not fully understand that it was inappropriate and could distress and damage me, and my therapist held such power over me that I was not really free to resist his influence.

Treatment of personality problems

In Chapter 8, personality problems are defined; those involving issues of safety, trust, self-esteem, control and intimacy among victimized patients are described; and the role of schemas in their aetiology is discussed.

Typically, these patients complain to subsequent therapists about relatively acute and specific problems such as sexual dysfunctions, marital difficulties, anxiety disorders, depression, attempted suicide, self-mutilation or substance misuse, rather than more chronic and pervasive personality problems. Such acute problems may be separate and apart from any personality problems that co-exist, or they may be derived from and motivated by such a personality problem. Some victims come seeking treatment only for their acute problems, and they are resistant to working on any co-existing personality problem, perhaps for the reasons discussed in Chapter 8 in the section on maintenance of schemas. When their acute problems are relieved such victims may resume their problematic mode of personality functioning based on maladaptive schemas. It is essential that victims agree the goals of therapy but if these do include ameliorating personality problems then schema-focused cognitive therapy is likely to be the treatment approach of choice, although it should be emphasized that this "characterological" phase of treatment is likely to be long and complicated (Beck & Freeman, 1990; Janoff-Bulman, 1992; McCann & Pearlman, 1990; Young, 1990). The positive side of this considerable effort is that it may be more productive to modify one or more schemas that are assumed to underlie a broad range of a victim's problems rather than to address each of these problems separately.

Identifying schemas

There are now at least three questionnaires available to assist in the identification of victims' schemas: the McPearl Belief Scale (Pearlman, McCann & Johnson, 1993), the Schema Questionnaire (Young, 1990) and the World Assumptions Scale (Janoff-Bulman, 1989). There are also several techniques that can be used to activate schemas so that they can be identified in therapy. Victims can be asked to discuss current events in their lives that are distressing or that arouse strong feelings, and by enquiring about the meaning of these events for the patient the therapist can get information about relevant schemas. Similarly, memories of distressing experiences in the past or repeated dreams can be used for this purpose. Schemas can be activated also by relevant bibliographical and audio-visual materials, by interaction with others in group therapy, or by prescribed assignments for the victim to be undertaken between sessions. Finally, schemas may be elicited in the victim's relationship with the subsequent therapist or by guided imagery, as discussed below.

Changing schemas

The basic aim of the treatment procedures used in schema-focused cognitive therapy is to weaken maladaptive schemas and to strengthen more adaptive alternatives. A corrective therapeutic relationship and guided imagery are generally considered to be particularly important means of pursuing this aim, and they are discussed below. Other relevant therapeutic techniques include cost–benefit analysis of retaining or changing schemas, provision of information, logical analysis, decatastrophizing, distancing, reattribution, guided self-dialogue, role play and assigned activities, as discussed above.

Among these techniques, cost–benefit analysis may be a useful means of enhancing motivation in those victims who are resistant to addressing their personality problems. This technique is illustrated in Table 9.4, together with some background information summarized in Tables 9.5 and 9.6, which was discussed with the victim.

Table 9.4:   Cost–Benefit Analysis of Trust Issues

Options Open

1. Trust most people, most of the time.
2. Mistrust most people, most of the time.
3. Defer judgement/check out trustworthiness/protect myself

1. Trust most people, most of the time.

	Advantages		Disadvantages
(a)	None	(a)	Will be let down or hurt in various ways.

2. Mistrust most people, most of the time.

	Advantages		Disadvantages
(a)	Don't get let down or hurt as much	(a)	Being lonely/isolated
		(b)	Feeling anxious/threatened
		(c)	Feeling angry
		(d)	Not seeing positive things
		(e)	Being rejected by others
		(f)	Potential contribution by others to a relationship is limited because they are not trusted.

3. Defer judgement/check out trustworthiness/protect myself

	Advantages		Disadvantages
(a)	Avoid disadvantages of 2 above	(a)	Some risk of being let down or hurt

Corrective therapeutic relationship   Maladaptive schemas are likely to be activated in the subsequent treatment situation, thus providing opportunities for their identification and modification. For instance, safety schemas may be activated by the victim's uncertainty about access to exits if required; the absence of other people in the clinical setting; being alone with the therapist;

Table 9.5:   Introduction to Trust Issues

1.   People are usually neither completely trustworthy nor completely untrustworthy but somewhere in between. Trust is not an all-or-none thing—either black or white—it is usually in a grey area in between.

2.   Trust is something that builds up between people over time—a process— rather than an instant judgement. All new relationships go through a period of testing, during which the participants risk more and more and increase or decrease their trust according to the results.

3.   Few people can or should be trusted with absolutely everything. One would trust a tradesman, a professional advisor, a friend, a relative, a spouse, to do what is appropriate according to their expertise or role. For example, you might trust a mechanic to service your car but not to resolve your personal problems.

Table 9.6:   Indicators of Trustworthiness/Untrustworthiness

Indications from other people
Extent to which:
1.   They are reliable
2.   They are supportive/helpful when needed
3.   They usually meet reasonable requests
4.   They relate to me and make me feel that I belong and am wanted
5.   They make me feel able to confide appropriately in them
6.   They do not harm or distress me
7.   They do not attempt to deceive me
8.   They do not attempt to control or manipulate me
9.   They do not attempt to exploit me
10.   They do not put me down or humiliate me
11.   They do not discriminate against me in favour of others

Indications from myself
Extent to which other people make me feel:
1.   Angry/resentful
2.   Anxious/threatened
3.   Suspicious/on guard

the perception of the therapist or the therapeutic procedures as threatening for some reason; or boundary violations such as the victim being flirtatious to test the therapist, the therapist touching or holding the client, the therapist and victim being seated too closely, the therapist asking too many questions prematurely, or the therapist being too directive. Therefore, in order to facilitate the modification of safety schemas it is important *inter alia* that the physical setting in which therapy is conducted be made "safe" from the victim's point of view, and that her boundaries are respected and not intruded upon or violated in any way.

Trust schemas may be activated if victims are afraid of being misused, exploited, betrayed or abandoned by the subsequent therapist, if they fear becoming dependent on a therapist who may not be trustworthy or reliable, or if their sense of vulnerability is heightened by the premature encouragement of trust in and closeness to the therapist. The provision of a therapeutic relationship in which victims can begin to risk trusting another person and to learn that not everybody is untrustworthy may go some way towards modifying such maladaptive trust schemas. During this process it is important for therapists "to recognize and to accept the client's distrust. Efforts to win the client's trust are ill-advised and usually unnecessary ... we commend a client for being appropriately guarded and note that distrust of us is no problem. We make it clear that we do not have sex with clients or try to run their lives or make their decisions for them, but that does not mean that we, or any other helpers, should be trusted completely" (Schoener, Milgrom & Gonsiorek, 1989, p. 104).

Among the therapeutic circumstances that may activate self-esteem schemas are fear of being disliked, rejected, humiliated or blamed by the subsequent therapist, doubts that he could ever truly be concerned about and care for such an unworthy person as the victim, or fear that he will in some way be contaminated or harmed by the perceived malignancy, badness and destructiveness of the victim. Therapists can help to modify maladaptive self-esteem schemas by, *inter alia*, abstaining from any remarks or actions that victims might construe as demeaning or rejecting, and demonstrating by the provision of consistent care and concern that clients are worthy of such positive attention.

Maladaptive control schemas may be activated if victims fear that the subsequent therapist will dominate or otherwise control them against their will, if they feel helpless in relation to him or if they feel dependent on him. Signs that he cares for and is concerned about the victim may be interpreted by her as threats to her control over her own life. Therapists can contribute to the modification of control schemas by promoting, encouraging and respecting the victim's decisions and choices at all stages in treatment, and by avoiding behaviour that might be construed by her as too intrusive, directive or controlling. It is very important that the need to empower victims during therapy is observed constantly in order to counteract the schemas developed or strengthened by their lack of power in the abuse situation.

Perceived threats of being betrayed or abandoned if the victim enters into a relationship with the subsequent therapist are one reason for the activation in treatment of maladaptive schemas concerning intimacy with others. At least to some extent, these threats can be reduced by the therapist being especially careful to adhere to the arrangements for treatment made with the victim, including the punctuality and regularity of appointments and the duration of therapy. If any real circumstances necessitate changes in these arrangements then this should be discussed with the victim to reduce the risk of the changes being misinterpreted as betrayal or abandonment. Maladaptive intimacy schemas may be activated also if the victim exhibits signs of a wish for a deeper attachment to the therapist and these are rejected or responded to unsympathetically. Within appropriate practical and ethical limits the therapist can respond to this wish and over time demonstrate the acceptability and advantages to the victim of meaningful relationships with others.

In conclusion, subsequent therapists need to be alert to indications that maladaptive schemas are being activated in therapy. If they are not recognized and addressed they may continue to disrupt the process of therapy and a valuable opportunity for understanding and helping victims may be lost. One aspect of this opportunity is the information that activated schemas can provide on victims' interpretations of events and habitual beliefs, which can then be examined, tested and perhaps restructured in the light of what is really happening in therapy. Furthermore, therapeutic relationships can serve to weaken maladaptive schemas and strengthen more adaptive alternatives. Clearly, therapists need to ensure that they are not behaving in any way that might inadvertently reinforce maladaptive schemas, and they can also provide the kind of relationship that will counteract such schemas.

Guided imagery (Edwards, 1989, 1990) Schemas that originated early in life before the acquisition of mature language skills are encoded in memory in the form of visual, aural, tactile or olfactory images rather than words. Thus, one reason for the alleged importance of guided imagery in schema-focused therapy is that it provides access to early, pre-verbal, core beliefs. Another reason is that emotion is strongly linked to the imagery system of memory, therefore the evocation of images is often accompanied by powerful emotional states; in fact, imagery has been described as the "gateway to emotion". Consequently, patients are exposed to the affective components of their traumatic memories and these become accessible to therapeutic change. Often a memory of a traumatic experience such as sexual abuse is fragmented. The victim may have access only to a partial image, a thought or a feeling that is inexplicable in the current situation. These fragments can be very distressing to the victim, who cannot understand what a particular recurring image or thought means or who experiences overwhelming emotions for no understandable reason. Similarly, a victim may "remember" the facts of the abuse as represented in verbal memory but not the associated imagery and feelings. The therapeutic process includes integrating the verbal, imagery and emotional fragments into whole memories. Once these are constituted they are available for schematic interpretation and, if necessary, restructuring. Guided imagery appears to be a particularly important means of pursuing these therapeutic tasks.

In this procedure there are several ways of evoking images. Victims may be asked to visualize a specific event, such as some aspect of their sexual abuse, or to focus on a specific theme of therapeutic relevance and to let an image arise spontaneously, to reinstate an image that has arisen previously in a dream, fantasy or earlier session of guided imagery, or to focus on an emotion being experienced in a session and to let an image arise from the feeling. When imagery is vague victims can be requested to focus on the image through different senses in an attempt to sharpen the detail.

Once an image has been evoked its meaning for the victim is explored. She may take the role of a person in the image, such as herself being sexually abused by her previous therapist, while the subsequent therapist asks questions of this person; for example: "What were you thinking?", "What were you feeling?", "What was the meaning of this event for you?" and "What did you expect to happen in future because of this event?". Another exploratory technique is for the victim to take the role of a person in the image and to address another person in the image. For example, the subsequent therapist might say "Be the abused patient and tell your therapist how you feel when he does that to you". The effect of this on the client, particularly affectively, is carefully tracked in an attempt to understand the idiosyncratic meanings of the imagery.

The next step is to scrutinize and challenge these meanings. A major method of this restructuring is to ask the victim to take the role of one of the imagery figures and to speak certain lines dictated by the subsequent therapist; for example, to take the role of the abused patient and say to her abuser, "You are so powerful and frightening that there is nothing I can do when you do that to me", which may lessen her tendency towards persistent self-blame. Such dysfunctional beliefs can also be challenged and contradicted. For instance, the abused patient might be asked to say to her abuser "Although I'm helpless with you now, this does not mean that I will be helpless when I get treatment from someone else". As restructuring proceeds, instead of the subsequent therapist dictating what the victim should say, more general directions may be given, such as "Tell your previous therapist how you are going to act differently in future", or "What do you need to say to him?".

Thus, it is suggested that the evocation, exploration and restructuring of images in schema-focused cognitive therapy is an important complementary process to the evocation, exploration and restructuring of thoughts and beliefs expressed in words, which has been standard in traditional cognitive therapy and is also a component of schema-focused cognitive therapy.

Conclusion

To the extent that personality problems do arise from maladaptive schemas then it follows that the resolution of such problems is likely to involve the modification of the underlying schemas, and schema-focused cognitive therapy appears to be the treatment of choice for this task in the present state of knowledge. This is a relatively recent form of therapy, and only scant evidence is currently available on its effectiveness and on the roles of its alleged crucial ingredients such as a corrective therapeutic relationship and guided imagery (Beck & Freeman, 1990). Clinical experience indicates quite strongly that the treatment of long-standing and pervasive personality problems is difficult and protracted, so rapid or complete resolution is unlikely to be a frequent outcome.

Modalities of intervention

Although individual psychotherapy is likely to be the most usual format for the subsequent treatment of victimized patients, they may also be treated in groups or in couple therapy, and the possible contributions of these modalities are indicated below.

Group therapy

There are several descriptions of group programmes for victimized patients in the literature (Kaufman & Harrison, 1986; List, 1989; Luepker, 1989b; Milgrom, 1989a; Pope & Bouhoutsos, 1986; Sonne, 1986; Sonne et al, 1985), and some potential benefits of group treatment are listed in Table 9.7.

Table 9.7:   Potential Therapeutic Benefits of Group Treatment

1.	Feelings of difference, alienation, isolation and loneliness are likely to be mitigated.
2.	In the understanding and supportive environment of the group, the members can extend their disclosure and exploration of the abuse experience and related problems beyond their individual therapist or other confidants.
3.	Through the shared experience of other participants a victim may gain a better understanding of her own reactions to the abuse and of its subsequent consequences.
4.	Effective methods of coping with problems may be disseminated between members.
5.	There is an opportunity to develop trust in other participants as a possible basis for trusting people on a wider basis.
6.	Ability to help others in the group may increase self-respect and self-confidence in social relationships.
7.	The group may provide a springboard for social action concerning, for example, public education about therapist abuse or the provision of resources for victims.

This form of treatment might be provided as an alternative or as an adjunct to individual or couple therapy. Some victims are unsuitable or unwilling to participate in a group, and there may not be enough victims available to constitute a group at a particular point in time, therefore it is important to keep open the options of individual or couple therapy for those who need or prefer them. There is also the question of whether some victims can obtain sufficient attention and support to meet their individual needs in a group context, which has led some clinicians to advocate an adjunctive role for group treatment. On the other hand, to the extent that group treatment can replace individual or couple therapy, then this may conserve scarce professional resources. For reasons of space, only professionally led groups are addressed here, but there are also self-help groups conducted by and for victimized patients in the U.S.A. (Pope & Bouhoutsos, 1986; Schoener, 1989d) and in the U.K. (e.g. Prevention of Professional Abuse Network (POPAN), Flat 1, 20 Daleham Gardens, Hampstead, London NW3 5DA).

Couple therapy

As mentioned above, abuse experiences and their associated problems among victims have considerable implications for their significant others, particularly partners (Luepker & O'Brien, 1989; Milgrom, 1989b). If a victim is in an established relationship then it may be desirable and perhaps essential to offer at least part of her subsequent treatment in a couple format with her partner, and a rationale for this proposal is summarized in Table 9.8.

Table 9.8: Rationale for Couple Therapy

1.	Helps partner to understand victim's problems and how they relate to her earlier abuse.
2.	Facilitates partner's acceptance and adaptation to therapeutic changes in victim (e.g. enhanced self-esteem and assertiveness) that are altering the nature of their relationship.
3.	Resolution of marital and sexual problems requires participation of both spouses.
4.	Meets partner's need for help with the implications of the victim's problems for himself, e.g. (a) feeling a vicarious victim (e.g. because of victim's instability and their lack of satisfactory sexual relationship) (b) feeling deprived and confused in his relationship with the victim (e.g. her mistrust of all men) (c) feelings of anger and hostility towards the offender (d) feelings of low self-esteem and depression (e.g. over why he married victim and his inability to resolve her problems himself).

Conclusion

In summary, certain attitudes and reactions to subsequent treatment among both victimized patients and their new therapists need to be recognized and addressed in such treatment programmes.

These programmes are rooted in certain fundamental components and processes that provide a necessary foundation for the deployment of more specific procedures with particular categories of problems.

Prior to the implementation of treatment it is necessary to conduct a comprehensive assessment, which includes an initial phase of disclosure and history taking, the negotiation of therapeutic objectives, and the assessment and formulation of target problems.

On the basis of this assessment, treatment is planned and implemented for these target problems. Possible approaches to post-traumatic stress reactions, mood disturbances and personality problems were proposed in this chapter,

As an adjunct or alternative to individual psychotherapy, it may be desirable and perhaps necessary to deliver subsequent treatment through the modalities of group or couple therapy.

While there is outcome data on the interventions discussed in this chapter in the references cited, none of this data is derived specifically from the subsequent treatment of patients who were sexually abused by previous therapists. At present there does not appear to be any systematic information available on the efficacy of various psychological interventions with this particular patient group. Thus, the feasibility, acceptability and effectiveness of treatment for the wide range of problems presenting among these victims remains to be demonstrated.

Part V

REGULATION AND PREVENTION

10   Regulation in the U.S.A.

Linda Mabus Jorgenson and Gary Richard Schoener

Psychotherapists' sexual contact with their patients has been the subject of increasingly close scrutiny over the past 20 years. Studies documenting the prevalence of sexual misconduct in the profession and the harm caused to patients by such behaviour have caused a public outcry, as well as a search for solutions by each of the psychotherapy professions (Gabbard, 1989). Estimates of therapists who become sexually involved with their patients are as high as 10% or more; the damage which may be caused by this breach of trust includes depression, post-traumatic stress disorder, increased suicidality, decreased self-esteem and inability to trust (Schoener et al, 1989).

In response, a patchwork of options for taking action has developed across the United States: common law remedies; criminal, civil and regulatory statutes; professional licensing boards and disciplinary procedures; ethics committees and complaint procedures; and some informal options such as complaints to employers, processing sessions and mediation (Table 10.1).

"Common law" refers to the flexible body of law that emerges from cases tried in the courts, and includes decisions in lawsuits filed by the patient (known as the plaintiff) to recover monetary damages resulting from negligence (or malpractice), breach of fiduciary duty, breach of contract, or intentional torts such as assault, battery, fraud and infliction of emotional distress. Civil statutes typically codify common law actions and provide monetary damages for victims of therapist–patient abuse, while criminal statutes impose fines and/or imprisonment on the convicted offender but generally provide no compensation for victims. Statutes regulating professional practice and licensing boards provide disciplinary sanctions for the offender, including revocation of the offender's licence to practise psychotherapy. Ethical codes and ethics committees

Table 10.1: Psychotherapist–Patient Sexual Contact: Differences between Criminal, Civil, Board and Professional Society Remedies

Criminal	Civil	Licensing board	Professional society
Who presents the patient's case?			
District attorney	Private attorney	Board Prosecutor	Patient and/or an advocate
What result may a patient expect from a successful case?			
Prison term or probation for perpetrator	Monetary damages paid to patient (by insurance company and/or personal assets)	Disciplinary sanctions, including licence revocation for perpetrator	Most severe sanction for perpetrator may be revocation of professional society membership
What is the sexual contact that is prohibited?			
Specifically defined	Usually broader than the criminal definition	Usually broader than the criminal and civil definitions, i.e. unprofessional conduct	Unethical conduct as defined by society's ethics code

are developed by professional associations to provide self-regulation for the professions. In addition, employers and individual professionals themselves may provide informal avenues for resolutions of complaints.

This chapter presents an overview of options for patients seeking redress for their psychotherapists' sexual misconduct. These options are not exclusive; several may be used in the same case. To best illustrate these points, the hypothetical case study of a patient, Sara Doe, is presented.

Hypothetical case study

Shortly after reaching the age of thirty, Sara Doe, married and the mother of two children, began to have difficulty sleeping. When she did sleep, her rest was interrupted by nightmares, the memory of which disturbed her waking hours and began to interfere with her duties as a social worker as well as with her enjoyment of life. Doe's physician, Dr Mary Smith, finding no physical source for Doe's complaints, recommended that she consult John Jones, PhD, a licensed clinical psychologist who shared office space and secretarial support with Dr Smith.

Doe reports that Dr Jones diagnosed her condition after two or three sessions as post-traumatic stress disorder resulting from serious emotional abuse in her childhood. He recommended that she seek long-term therapy and severely limit her consumption of alcoholic beverages, which she admitted relying upon for stress relief. Jones suggested that Doe take Valium whenever she felt tempted to take a drink and requested that Doe obtain the prescription from Dr Smith. Doe complied with Dr Jones's recommendations, relieved and grateful that at last someone had given her sense of unease a name, a treatment regimen and a prognosis.

Two years later, Doe was still in therapy with Dr Jones. Sam Doe, Sara Doe's husband, sometimes complained that the cost of therapy sapped nearly all of the family's discretionary income. Since his wife seemed to have recovered from her insomnia and nightmares, however, he did not question the time commitment her therapy with Dr Jones seemed to require.

About a year after therapy began, Dr Jones began to make sexual overtures to Doe, which led to sexual contact between them. On occasion, they had intercourse at his suburban office or, when he was in town, at his office at St Perpetua Hospital; more frequently, she simply went to his house late in the day, since she was often last on his daily patient schedule. Three years after she became Jones's patient, Doe came to his office for her weekly appointment and found that Jones had closed his practice and departed. Jones had never discussed terminating therapy with Doe, and he had not made any efforts for her continued care.

Sara Doe left Dr Jones's office that day and stopped at a liquor store on her way home. For the next two years, Doe became increasingly alienated from her husband and her children. She often considered suicide, but managed to drag herself through each day with help from alcohol. She was consumed with guilt over her role in the sexual relationship with Dr Jones and believed that it was her fault that it had happened.

Then, two years after her last office appointment, Doe encountered Dr Jones at a Grand Rounds presentation at St Perpetua. They spent the night together at a nearby hotel. Jones left the next morning, promising to keep in touch. Doe attempted suicide later that day. Now, six months later, and two and a half years after the termination of her therapy, Doe has inquired whether there is anything she can do to:

1. Prevent Dr Jones from harming others as he harmed her.
2. Obtain financial compensation from him for her pain and suffering and for costs associated with her therapy, lost income and future ameliorative therapy.
3. Obtain some form of vindication of the inappropriateness of Dr Jones's "treatment".

Sam Doe has asked whether there is any claim he and the couple's children can bring to recover the cost of three years of "therapy" and to compensate them for the damage Dr Jones did to their marriage and family.

Common law causes of action

Negligence/malpractice

In malpractice lawsuits against therapists, sexual exploitation of patients is a leading complaint. "Malpractice" is the term for professional negligence, and is recognized under the common law in most of the fifty states of the United States. The common law is the body of law that is created out of the decisions rendered by the courts. A patient who wishes to pursue a lawsuit for monetary damages must retain a lawyer and must establish that the therapist's conduct was negligent and caused them harm. To establish the negligence, the patient (referred to as the "plaintiff") must prove the existence of a therapist–patient relationship, the actual negligence or breach of the duties owed by the therapist to the patient, and the harm that was caused by the therapist's negligence. Negligence is proven through testimony that the therapist's conduct was in violation of the standard of care owed to the patient. This is usually done through expert testimony. One of the earliest reported opinions to sustain a malpractice verdict in a case of therapist sexual misconduct was *Zipkin* v. *Freeman* (436 S.W.2d 753, Mo. 1969).

Like the hypothetical Sara Doe, Mrs Zipkin sought treatment from Dr Freeman, a psychiatrist, for physical symptoms—headaches and a gastric complaint that had eluded diagnosis by her regular physician. Mrs Zipkin testified at the trial that (p. 759):

> "I did exactly as [Dr Freeman] told me to do, because he told me that this was what I needed and should be doing in order to overcome my illness." She testified that she loved the doctor, put her faith and trust in him and did or said anything he told her was good treatment for her; that he told her all he had her do was for the purpose of ridding her of her character disorder and the other things she needed to be cured of.

During the course of treatment, Dr Freeman invited his patient to parties at his home, and took her skating, swimming in the nude at a rock quarry and on out-of-town vacations. Dr Freeman also induced Mrs Zipkin to engage in a sexual relationship with him.

Dr Freeman's treatment of Mrs Zipkin was found to be negligent. Mrs Zipkin's expert trial witness opined that a "psychiatrist should no more take an overnight trip with a patient than shoot her", (p. 761) because such conduct constituted mishandling of the transference that routinely takes place in psychotherapy. The court agreed (p. 761):

> Once Dr Freeman started to mishandle the transference phenomenon . . . it was inevitable that trouble was ahead. It is pretty clear from the medical evidence that the damage would have been done to Mrs Zipkin even if the trips outside the state were carefully chaperoned, the swimming done with suits on, and if there had been ballroom dancing instead of sexual relations.

In support of its analysis, the court cited the English case of *Landau* v. *Werner* (105 Sol. J. 1008, 1961) for the proposition that social relations with patients constituted inappropriate treatment even when, as in *Landau*, they were confined to meetings for tea and dinner. Boundary violations, such as social relations or sexual contact between therapist and patient, represent the therapist's negligent mishandling of the patient's transference and the therapist's own countertransference (Simon & Sadoff, 1993; Gutheil & Gabbard, 1993).

Thus, Sara Doe, in most jurisdictions in the United States, would be able to pursue a common law negligence action against Dr Jones for malpractice for negligently mishandling the transference.

Negligent breach of fiduciary duty

Other common law causes of action may also be available to Doe. Liability was premised upon negligent breach of fiduciary duty in *Roy* v. *Hartogs* (81 Misc.

2d 350, 366 N.Y.S. 2d 297, 1975), a 1975 therapist–patient sexual misconduct case that received broad public attention and is described in the book *Betrayal* (Freeman & Roy, 1976).

The patient, Roy, sought treatment from a psychiatrist, Dr Hartogs. Hartogs told Roy that in order for her to "recover" from her lesbianism, she had to have sexual relations with him. The court characterized Roy's malpractice claim as an allegation "for deceit and assault" by a "person in a position of overpowering influence and trust" who stood in a fiduciary relationship with her. The court noted that (p. 301):

> there is a public policy to protect a patient from the deliberate and malicious abuse of power and breach of trust by a psychiatrist when that patient entrusts to him her body and mind in the hope that he will use his best efforts to effect a cure. That right is best protected by permitting the victim to pursue civil remedies, not only to vindicate a wrong against her but to vindicate the public interest as well.

The court in *Roy* also found that, due to the "fiduciary" nature of the therapist–patient relationship, the patient was unable to "consent" to her therapist's sexual contact with her. This opened the door to patients' claims of intentional torts—battery, assault, intentional infliction of emotional distress and fraud—caused by their therapists' sexual misconduct (Jorgenson, Randles & Strasburger, 1991).

Post-termination sexual contact

The issue of post-termination sexual contact between therapist and former patient has arisen in the context of therapists' attempts to avoid liability by terminating the therapeutic relationship with the patient before beginning a sexual relationship (Appelbaum & Jorgenson, 1991). In *Noto* v. *St Vincent's Hospital and Medical Center* (142 Misc. 292, 537 N.Y.S. 2d 446, Supreme Court 1988), a New York court held that the psychiatrist could still be found liable for sexual misconduct even when the contact took place after the patient was discharged from his care at the hospital. However, there is as yet no consensus against post-termination sexual relations; the results of lawsuits seeking recovery on this ground will vary from state to state, and may depend on distinctions between professions that make little difference to the patient who has suffered emotional damages as a result of a professional's misconduct.

Statute of limitations

Another issue patients face when pursing a malpractice claim against a therapist for sexual abuse is the statute of limitations. The statute of limitations is the time period within which any lawsuit must be filed. The time period varies from state to state, with some states setting the period at one year after the last office visit, and others allowing patients to file lawsuits only when they "discover" that they were harmed and that their therapists' misconduct caused the harm (Jorgenson & Appelbaum, 1991; Jorgenson & Randles, 1991).

Malpractice insurance

Doe clearly has the right to bring a legal action against Dr Jones in most states. The issue of whether she will actually recover money on her claim is less certain. Most licensed therapists have malpractice insurance which would cover any judgment against them. Malpractice insurers have attempted to avoid paying money on claims of sexual misconduct. In *Zipkin*, for example, Dr Freeman's malpractice insurer argued that it was not liable to pay the jury's monetary award to Zipkin because Freeman's conduct went so far beyond the pale of professional standards that the insurer ought not be obliged to compensate his victim. The court concluded, however, that Freeman's malpractice consisted of negligence in his mishandling of Zipkin's transference, and thus fell squarely within the bounds of his professional liability coverage (Jorgenson, Bisbing & Sutherland, 1992).

Recently, malpractice insurance companies have begun specifically excluding or limiting coverage for sexual misconduct claims. However, it is possible to avoid these limitations by focusing on the other acts of negligence committed by the therapist (Jorgenson & Sutherland, 1993). In our example, Doe could also bring claims for:

1. Misuse of drugs in treatment, based on Jones's suggestion that she take Valium when there were grounds to suspect she had a pre-existing substance abuse problem.
2. Failure to treat the patient's presenting problems, also involving Doe's possible substance abuse.
3. Termination of the patient's therapy without appropriate follow-up or referral as a result of Jones's abrupt disappearance.
4. Failure to obtain appropriate consultation and referral, since Jones had no training to evaluate the medical necessity of providing Doe with Valium.
5. Failure to warn Doe of the potential adverse consequences of Jones's "treatment".

Other victims of Dr Jones's misconduct include Sara Doe's husband and their children. Mr Doe and the couple's children may have actions for loss of consortium arising out of Sara Doe's inability (as a result of Jones's treatment) to function as their wife and mother. Mr Doe may also have a claim for negligent infliction of emotional distress, an action to recoup any fees paid and perhaps an action for alienation of affection or criminal conversation. In general, however, it has been held that a therapist has no special duty to patients' spouses, even if the spouse employed the therapist and was paying the fees (See *Homer* v. *Long*, 90 Md.App. 1, 599 A.2d 1193, 1198, 1992).

Litigation stresses

Patients harmed by their therapists' sexual misconduct may file a lawsuit against the therapist in most states. Whether the lawsuit will be framed as "negligent mishandling of transference" or some other cause of action will vary from state to state. Regardless of the legal theory chosen, patients pursuing malpractice actions face stresses caused by the litigation. These include:

1. Personal exposure if the case becomes public.
2. The expense of retaining an attorney (although most attorneys working in this area will agree to accept a fee equal to a percentage of the patient's monetary recovery).
3. Loss of privacy concerning personal and sexual history.
4. Past and present therapy records opened to scrutiny.
5. Needing to undergo a psychiatric examination by both plaintiff's and defendant's experts.
6. Personal vilification and attack on both motives and sanity.
7. Intrusion in family life by others being involved in lawsuit.

Furthermore, civil suits and appeals that follow may last for years, making it difficult for victims to put the matter behind them and go on with their lives. Books describing such lawsuits graphically depict these challenges (Bates & Brodsky, 1989; Walker & Young, 1986). In some states, a few of these issues have been addressed by the state legislature's enactment of statutory remedies.

Civil statutes

The problem of therapist sexual abuse has drawn some amount of legislative attention in recent years, resulting in the enactment of mostly "victim-friendly" legislation intended to codify patients' rights to a safe therapeutic environment.

To date, five states have enacted civil statutes governing patients' suits against sexually abusive therapists (Table 10.2). The legislation generally eases plaintiffs' route to recovery of damages by eliminating the need for plaintiffs

Table 10.2: Psychotherapist–Patient Sexual Contact: Civil Statutes in Five American States

	Minnesota	Wisconsin	California	Illinois	Texas
Citation	Minn. Stat. Ann. § 148A (West 1993)	Wis. Stat. Ann. §895.70 (West 1992)	Cal. Civ. Code §43.93 (West 1993)	740 ILCS 140/1-140/2 (Smith-Hurd 1993)	Senate Bill 210, Enacted May 22, 1993
Class of therapist covered	All who perform or purport to perform psychotherapy, whether licensed or not	Same as Minnesota	Specific list of therapists	Same as Minnesota	Same as Minnesota
Sexual contact	Intercourse, oral sex, sodomy, intended touching of intimate parts or clothing covering such parts, plus requests for the above	"Bikini Rule"	"Bikini Rule"	Same as Minnesota	Same as Minnesota plus patterns, practices or schemes of conduct for sexual arousal, gratification or abuse
When covered	During any ongoing professional relationship, in or out of therapy session	Same as Minnesota	Same as Minnesota	Same as Minnesota	Same as Minnesota
Former patient	Prohibited for 2 years if the patient is emotionally dependent or if there is proof of therapeutic deception	Prohibited for 6 months	Prohibited for 2 years; thereafter if proof of therapeutic deception	Prohibited for 1 year if patient emotionally dependent or therapeutic deception	Prohibited for 2 years; prohibited thereafter with proof of emotional dependence or therapeutic deception

to establish at trial that their therapists' sexual contact constituted malpractice. Under the statutes, malpractice is assumed once the fact of the sexual contact is established. The statutes also acknowledge plaintiffs' legitimate needs for legal redress in the face of humiliating injuries.

The enactment of statutes creating a specific cause of action for psychotherapist sexual abuse also provides an opportunity for legislatures to revisit policy issues arising out of pre-existing statutes of limitations, and to extend time periods where equity justifies a change. Civil statutes address reporting requirements for therapists and employer liability. All statutes incorporate "victim shield" provisions, barring the introduction of the victim's sexual history because the burden of avoiding a sexual relationship falls squarely on the therapist. This prohibition may encourage more victims to come forward. All states have included provisions for post-termination liability, with prohibitions on sexual contact between therapist and former patient ranging from six months after termination (Wisconsin) to two years in Minnesota and California.

Civil statutes, while easing some of the stresses of the litigation, still require the pursuit of a lawsuit that may take years and may be at great expense to the patient. Some state legislatures have examined whether sexual misconduct by therapists should be criminalized. To date, twelve states have enacted legislation making therapist–patient sexual misconduct a crime.

Criminal statutes

Sara Doe would also like to seek criminal sanctions against her abuser, both because she feels she was victimized and because she hopes to protect other women. Dr Jones's abuse affected her and her family and was more than merely professional misconduct. State legislators addressing this issue have agreed, and thus have enacted statutes that impose prison sentences for sexual abuse by professionals. In a criminal prosecution, the patient is a witness in the government's lawsuit against the therapist. The attorney prosecuting the case is either a district attorney or a prosecuting attorney and the patient is not responsible for legal fees. However, in most jurisdictions, the patient will not be able to recover any monetary damages from a successful criminal prosecution.

Criminal statutes may be particularly tailored to address psychotherapist sexual abuse, or may have been originally enacted to punish "generic" sexual assault and have been construed by the courts to apply to cases such as that of Doe.

Sexual contact under the pretext of medical treatment is defined as sexual assault in five states. This approach addressed the need to remove "consent" as a defence in cases where the patient's trust in the therapist left him or her vulnerable to non-violent yet undeniably coercive behaviour on the part of the medical professional. The New Hampshire statute has been interpreted to apply to a psychologist who assaulted his patient during counselling, and it is fair to presume that similar statutes may be similarly construed. In Alabama and Michigan, a physician's misrepresentation that leads to sexual contact is actionable. Wyoming criminalizes sexual contact resulting from coercion by a person occupying a position of authority with respect to the victim (Jorgenson, Randles & Strasburger, 1991).

More therapist-specific statutes have been enacted since 1984, when Wisconsin became the first state to criminalize therapist–patient sexual exploitation. Minnesota enacted such law in 1985; a North Dakota criminal statute was passed in 1987; Colorado's followed in 1988. As of 1993, a total of twelve states have addressed psychotherapist–patient sexual contact in the context of their criminal statutes. As with the civil statutes previously discussed, *definitions* of the conduct proscribed, by whom and with whom it is proscribed are as important as the proscriptions themselves (Table 10.3). A broad definition of psychotherapy such as Minnesota's ("treatment, assessment or counseling of a mental or emotional illness, symptom or condition") will ultimately protect a larger class of patients than a narrower definition. Statutes such as Minnesota's can readily be interpreted to apply to both licensed and unlicensed therapists. Maine's statute, on the other hand, limits its application to psychiatrists, psychologists and social workers, thus leaving a substantial class of "therapists" unregulated (Jorgenson, Randles & Strasburger, 1991).

Likewise, the type of sexual contact prohibited under a criminal statute will be limited to only the acts or conduct specifically articulated by the statute. North Dakota, for example, has enacted a broad definition prohibiting "any touching of the sexual or other intimate parts of the person for the purpose of arousing or satisfying sexual or aggressive desires." (N.D. Cent. Code sec. 12.1-20-02[4], 1991). Maine and Florida have adopted a much more restrictive definition of sexual contact, prohibiting specific acts such as intercourse, fellatio, cunnilingus and sodomy. To a certain extent, precise definitions of the conduct proscribed are necessary in order to avoid constitutional challenges on the ground that the statute fails to provide sufficient notice to possible offenders (Strasburger, Jorgenson & Randles, 1991; Hoge et al, 1993).

All but Maine's statute remove the consent of the victim as a defence. The availability of this defence in prosecutions under general rape laws rendered these laws generally unavailable to therapist sexual abuse victims because it could rarely be shown that the victims had not "consented" within the meaning of the existing law, with its focus on acts of physical violence rather than guile. If consent were an issue under the new statutes, juries would have

Table 10.3: Psychotherapist–Patient Sexual Contact: Criminal Statutes in Twelve American States

	Minnesota	Wisconsin	North Dakota	Colorado	California	Maine
Citation	Minn. Stat. Ann. §609.341 et seq. (West 1993)	Wis. Stat. Ann. §940.22 (2) (West 1992)	N. D. Cent. Code §12.1-20-06.1 (1991)	Colo. Rev. Stat. §18-3-405.5 (1992)	Cal. Bus. & Prof. Code §729 (West 1993)	Me. Rev. Stat. Ann. tit. 17-A, §253 (I) (1992)
Class of therapist covered	All who perform or purport to perform psychotherapy, whether licensed or not	Nearly identical to Minnesota	Nearly identical to Minnesota	Nearly identical to Minnesota	Specific list of licensed therapists or one who holds himself/herself out as one	Psychiatrist, psychologist, social worker or purports to be
Sexual contact	Intercourse, oral sex, sodomy, intended touching of intimate parts or clothing covering such parts	Nearly identical to Minnesota	Nearly identical to Minnesota	Nearly identical to Minnesota	Nearly identical to Minnesota	Intercourse oral sex, sodomy
When covered	During any ongoing professional relationship, in or out of therapy session	Identical to Minnesota	Only during therapy session	Identical to Minnesota	Identical to Minnesota	Identical to Minnesota

	Minnesota	Wisconsin	North Dakota	Colorado	California	Maine
Citation	Minn. Stat. Ann. §609.341 et seq. (West 1993)	Wis. Stat. Ann. §940.22 (2)	N. D. Cent. Code §12.1-20-06.1 (1991)	Colo. Rev. Stat. §18-3-405.5 (1992)	Cal. Bus. & Prof. Code §729 (West 1993)	Me. Rev. Stat. Ann. tit. 17-A, §253 (2) (I) (1992)
Former Patients	Yes, forever, if emotionally dependent on therapist or therapeutic deception	No	No	No	Yes, when terminated to engage in sex; UNLESS refer to therapist recommended by third party therapist	No
Consent	Not a defense	Not a defense	Not a defense	Not a defense	Not a defense	Victim to prove intimate relationship, trust, dependence, substantial potential for vulnerability and abuse
Maximum Penalty	10 years and/or $20 000 for sexual penetration; 5 years and/or $10 000 for sexual contact	Felony with up to 5 years or $10 000 or both	Felony with up to 5 years or $5000 or both	Felony with 2–8 years, $2000–500 000 or both	Misdemeanour for first offense; other offenses are "wobblers" with maximum penalty of 1 year and/or fine	Felony with 3–5 years

Table 10.3 *continued*

	Florida	Iowa	Georgia	Texas	South Dakota	New Mexico
Citation	Fla. Stat. Ann. §§491.0111-491.0112 (West 1993)	Iowa Code Ann. §709.15 (West 1992)	Ga. Code Ann. §16-6-5.1 (1992)	Texas Senate Bill 210 Enacted May 22, 1993	Senate Bill 236 (Enacted 1993)	N.M. Stat. Ann. §§30-9-10 through 30-9-16 (effective 1993)
Class of therapist covered	Nearly identical to Minnesota	Nearly identical to Minnesota	Nearly identical to Minnesota	Nearly identical to Minnesota	Nearly identical to Minnesota	Specific list of psychotherapists or one who purports to be a psychotherapist
Sexual contact	Oral, anal, vaginal penetration	Nearly identical to Minnesota, plus kissing	Genital area, groin, inner thighs, buttocks, or breasts of a person	Intercourse, oral sex, sodomy, intended touching of intimate parts; schemes of conduct intended to sexually arouse, gratify or abuse any person	Nearly identical to Minnesota	Intercourse, oral sex, sodomy, intended touching of intimate parts
When covered	Identical to Minnesota	Identical to Minnesota	Identical to Minnesota	Identical to Minnesota	During any ongoing therapy relationship, in or out of therapy session if patient is emotionally dependent	Identical to Minnesota

	Florida	Iowa	Georgia	Texas	South Dakota	New Mexico
Citation	Fla. Stat. Ann. §§491.0111-491.0112 (West 1993)	Iowa Code Ann. §709.15 (West 1992)	Ga. Code Ann. §16-6-5.1 (1992)	Texas Senate Bill 210 Enacted May 22, 1993	Senate Bill 236 (Enacted 1993)	N.M. Stat. Ann. §§30-9-10 through 30-9-16 (effective 1993)
Former patients	Yes, when terminated primarily to engage in sexual contact	Nearly identical to Minnesota plus emotional dependency presumed for 1 year after termination	No	Yes, 2 years; thereafter with proof of emotional dependence or therapeutic deception	No	Yes, for 1 year after termination
Consent	Not a defense	Statute is silent on issue of patient's consent as a defense	Not a defense	Not a defense	Not a defense	Not a defense
Maximum penalty	Felony for first offense, no more than 5 years and $5000; for second offense, felony with no more than 15 years and $10 000	With two or more patients or former patients, felony with 5 years or $7500 or both; with patient, misdemeanour with 2 years or $5000 or both; with former patient, misdemeanour with 1 year or $1000 or both	Felony with not less than 1 or more than 3 years	First offense, felony with 1–10 years and $10 000; second offense, 2–20 years and $10 000	Felony with up to 10 years and $10 000 for sexual penetration; 5 years and $5000 for sexual contact	Felony with up to 18 years and $15 000 for sexual penetration

difficulty understanding why patients would continue—unconsenting—to make themselves available to their therapist's abusive conduct. Most psychotherapeutic professionals now believe that the victim's consent (or lack of consent) is irrelevant to the characterization of the therapist's conduct as criminal because of the fiduciary nature of the relationship and the harm that results from the sexualization of the relationship.

Six states have also enacted prohibitions against post-termination sexual contact. In Florida, post-termination relationships are prohibited if the therapist terminates the therapeutic relationship primarily for the purpose of engaging in sexual contact. In California, subsequent sexual contact is not criminalized if the therapist terminates for sexual purposes, but a second therapist refers the patient to another therapist. New Mexico absolutely prohibits post-termination sex for six months; the prohibition in Iowa extends for one year, and in Texas for two years or for longer if emotional dependency can be shown. Minnesota has enacted legislation criminalizing forever sexual contact between a former therapist and patient if the patient's "emotional dependence" on the former therapist rendered the client unable to resist the sexual advances or if the therapist has engaged in therapeutic deception, leading the client to believe that the sexual contact is a part of therapy.

Constitutional challenges to statutes enacted to address therapist misconduct have generally been unsuccessful. Challenges are usually grounded in the Fourteenth Amendment Due Process Clause, asserting that the statute (i) is vague and fails to define sufficiently the criminal behaviour, or (ii) infringes on other Constitutional rights because its proscription on behaviour is too broad, or (iii) deprives the defendant of his or her right to insist that the government prove all elements of the alleged criminal behaviour beyond a reasonable doubt before guilt is established.

In *People* v. *West* (724 P.2d 623, Colo. 1986), the defendant argued that the provisions of a Colorado statute should be found "void for vagueness" on the ground that (p. 626):

> the statute forbids the doing of an act in terms so vague that persons of ordinary intelligence must necessarily guess as to its meaning and differ as to its application.

At issue was the language that proscribed:

> knowingly touching . . . the victim's intimate parts by the actor, or . . . the actor's intimate parts by the victim, or . . . knowingly touching . . . the clothing covering the immediate area of the victim's or actor's intimate parts if that sexual contact can reasonably be construed as being for the purposes of sexual arousal, gratification, or abuse.
>
> (Colo.Rev.Stat. sec. 18-3-401[4] 1986)

The defendant argued that the phrase "can reasonably be construed as being for the purposes of sexual arousal, gratification, or abuse" was unconstitutionally vague; the court disagreed. The defendant also asserted that the same phrase improperly abrogated the prosecution's burden of proving culpable intent beyond a reasonable doubt because the term "can reasonably be construed" could permit the jury to ascribe criminal intent solely from the defendant's behaviour on the theory that "he did it, hence he must have meant to do it". The court rejected this argument as well, noting that at trial the judge had instructed the jury that the state must prove criminal intent beyond a reasonable doubt (Jorgenson, Randles & Strasburger, 1991).

In *Ferguson* v. *People* (824 P.2d 803, Colo. 1992), a psychotherapist challenged the Colorado criminal statute on several grounds, including that (p. 806):

the criminal proscription against sexual assault on a client by a psychotherapist is constitutionally overbroad and, hence, violative of substantive due process rights guaranteed by the Fourteenth Amendment because it infringes on the fundamental privacy and associational rights of psychotherapists and clients to engage in a consensual act of sexual intercourse [and also because] it irrationally deprives psychotherapists of the consent defense when no such limitation is imposed on other health-care professionals.

Both arguments were dismissed by the reviewing court because (i) there is no fundamental constitutional right to have sex with whomever one chooses, and (ii) it is permissible for the legislature to regulate the behaviour of one branch of a profession without imposing the same restrictions on the entire profession, even though they may be warranted.

While these laws have survived constitutional challenges, there have not been a large number of prosecutions. As of 1993, there have been seventeen criminal prosecutions under Minnesota's statute, resulting in four acquittals, one dismissal prior to trial, eight guilty pleas and three jury trials resulting in convictions (one case is currently undecided) (Theisen, 1993). Wisconsin, which criminalized earlier than Minnesota, has also had a number of prosecutions, with mixed results (Kane, 1992). In both states a large percentage of the prosecutions involved unlicensed therapists and clergy acting in counselling roles.

Civil lawsuits and criminal actions both utilize the court system—civil lawsuits result in monetary awards to the patient, and criminal actions result in criminal confinement and possibly fines for the therapist. Other options exist that do not require the involvement of attorneys and the court system. A complaint to the applicable licensing board is one such option.

Administrative statutes and regulations

Psychiatrists, who must be licensed as physicians, and psychologists, are licensed in all fifty states. Social workers are also now licensed in all fifty states, but only thirty states license or regulate marriage and family therapists. A few states license professional counsellors. In all fifty states it is possible to practise some forms of psychotherapy without a license if one calls oneself a "therapist."

Licensure boards are government agencies that are often located within departments of health in state governments. Boards themselves are dominated by members of the regulated profession, although limited consumer representation is usually required. Board members are typically appointed by a public official, usually the state governor, who receives nominations from a variety of sources, including professional associations. Boards create methods for determining who should be licensed, usually relying on a national examination, plus some other criteria. When a board is in the process of evaluating a complaint against a professional, it is usually represented by a prosecuting attorney (Hall, 1986).

Although licensure laws vary from state to state, as well as between professions (and even within the same profession), sexual involvement with patients is explicitly prohibited virtually everywhere. Most state licensure laws require the practitioner to follow the accepted code of ethics for the profession, and all codes of ethics for mental health professionals prohibit sexual contact between therapist and patient (Jorgenson, Randles & Strasburger, 1991).

In our hypothetical case study, Doe may ask that her jurisdiction's licensing authority for psychologists sanction Dr Jones for his unprofessional conduct. This may represent a particularly good option if Doe's primary goal is to protect other clients or to see Dr Jones's practice limited. It is also chosen at times by clients who are seeking assistance for a practitioner they believe is impaired. Sanctions available through such administrative proceedings include licence suspension or revocation, published or unpublished reprimands, and limitations on or supervision of the therapist's practice or counselling with respect to the problem presented by the complaining party. In general, no damage payments to victims are available either through or as a consequence of disciplinary board actions.

Doe might also choose the licensure complaint option because it does not require that she employ an attorney—as with a criminal complaint, the legal work will be done by a prosecutor. In board actions, the prosecutor is employed by the licensing board. Proceedings in front of administrative boards are generally less financially burdensome to clients than lawsuits, in large measure because boards operate under more relaxed evidentiary and procedural standards (Jorgenson, Randles & Strasburger, 1991). Doe may also choose this option because the act of bringing a complaint and triggering an investigation is generally confidential.

Furthermore, in most jurisdictions, there is no statute of limitations, so a complaint can be filed long after the deadline for filing a malpractice suit has passed. The vast majority of complaints are eventually settled without a formal hearing or trial through a negotiation between the practitioner and the licensing board which leads to a stipulation and agreement. Both sides are usually seeking to avoid the expense of a hearing, and for the accused practitioner there is a reality that the board has considerable power (the power to deprive the therapist of his or her livelihood), even though its decisions can be appealed against through the court system.

If the practitioner wishes to contest the allegation or is not willing to comply with the consequences demanded by the board, a formal hearing is held. The board itself may hear the case, or it may be heard by an administrative law judge in a quasi-judicial proceeding. Under these circumstances Doe will face cross-examination from a defence attorney. There is considerable variability as to whether such proceedings are open to the public and the press. Hall (1986) notes that of the 50 states, 8 Canadian provinces, the District of Columbia and Puerto Rico, 21 have open hearings, 14 have open hearings which can be closed to protect the privacy of the complainant or the psychologist, 15 have closed hearings which can be opened and 10 do not specify. So, in a number of states Doe might have the same exposure of her privacy that can occur if she files a criminal or civil action.

Although in a number of jurisdictions it is possible for a licensure board to suspend a licence on an emergency basis, this is very rarely done. In fact, as a general rule, the process of investigation is often quite lengthy, and many boards lack sufficient staff to function efficiently, so it is not uncommon for there to be delays of a year or more before action is taken. One Minnesota case took nearly four years. This sort of delay and the typical lack of communications between the board and the patient during the process may prove quite frustrating to Doe.

Periodic negative news stories in the United States and Canada have focused on particularly egregious examples of the failure of boards properly to sanction misconduct, reducing consumer confidence and leading to legislative efforts to "sunset" licensure laws. Throughout Canada, professional self-regulation through a system of professional colleges (e.g. the College of Physicians and Surgeons of Ontario) has come under scrutiny because of a perceived failure to handle properly sexual misconduct complaints. A recent study of the disciplinary actions undertaken by state medical boards suggested that the internal mission of these administrative bodies (to rehabilitate impaired practitioners) may in fact be different from the public's perception of their role (to protect the public from practitioners unable—for whatever reason—to deliver good care). The interplay between these competing interests could result in a frustrating experience for Doe if she is seeking a punitive result from the licensing board. Nevertheless, in the absence of civil or criminal remedies having a more immediate impact, the administrative remedies available through licensing boards are important remedial tools.

Ethics complaint

If Dr Jones is a member of a state, provincial (in Canada) or national professional organization, Doe has the option of filing a complaint with the ethics committee of the organization. There is no requirement that a therapist belong to a professional organization; among licensed medical doctors, for example, less than 50% belong to the professional association for doctors, the American Medical Association. Membership of a professional organization generally requires that the practitioner has appropriate credentials and pays annual dues.

In Doe's case, she might contact the ethics committee of the state Psychological Association or the American Psychological Association. As a general rule, if Dr Jones belongs to both, the matter will be handled by the state association, except in cases where he has moved to another state so that jurisdiction is confusing or when other factors create a conflict-of-interest situation. For example, if he is an officer of the state association or a member of its ethics committee the matter will probably be handled nationally. In the case of psychiatry, the actions of a state District Branch can be appealed against to the American Psychiatric Association, and in the case of social work the actions of a state Committee of Inquiry can also be appealed against to the national organization.

Although most state committees follow a general procedure which was developed nationally, there is considerable variability from state to state within the same profession as to how such committees function. They typically lack the legal consultation and expertise available to the licensure boards and are handicapped in their ability to investigate cases. They lack clarity about standards of proof and at times appear to utilize a very high standard, equivalent to the "matter of reasonable doubt" test used in criminal cases. It is not uncommon for consumers to find the outcome of their work to be quite disappointing.

While professional associations are sometimes able to move more quickly than licensure boards, this is not always the case. The likelihood is that Doe will end up telling her story in front of the committee and will be cross-examined by an attorney for Dr Jones. She will then leave and Dr Jones will be able to give his version of events unchallenged. If Jones appeals against the decision of the committee, Doe will have no voice in the appeals process and will probably not know that it is happening. The final results will probably be communicated to her, but otherwise be private save for a brief notice in a professional newsletter if Dr Jones is sanctioned.

Typically, ethics committees have only limited sanctions. They can recommend suspension of membership in the organization; they can reprimand, either formally or informally; and they can request some form of rehabilitation or voluntary practice limitations. In many instances, professionals have been able to resign from the professional organization to avoid discipline, although there has been some effort to make this more difficult. However, beyond some professional embarrassment, the loss of membership carries with it one penalty often overlooked—the inability to obtain malpractice coverage through the organizational policy. It has also become more common for insurance carriers to ask, in the application process, whether the applicant has ever been sanctioned by a professional body, and this may also be a question on a job application. The Committee on Inquiry of the National Association of Social Workers has the power to request restitution from the practitioner, and state chapters have done so in some cases. In addition, it can remove the "A.C.S.W.", a national credential from the Academy of Certified Social Workers.

Doe might choose this option because it generally is quicker than a complaint to a licensure board, or because it is highly confidential. Typically, however, an ethics complaint, given its limitations, is made in conjunction with other remedies, assuming that they exist. If a profession is not licensed, if there is no criminal statute that is applicable, and if there either are not major damages or the client does not wish to sue, then this may be the only option.

Two final notes are in order concerning professional ethics committees. First, in recent years there has been considerable debate concerning their role in some states. In the case of the Minnesota Psychological Association, for example, the Ethics Committee has begun offering a consultation service to its members, encouraging people to phone for advice on ethical dilemmas. This service, plus an ongoing programme of newsletter articles and other educational efforts, has been undertaken in the hopes of the Ethics Committee being more proactive, rather than just serving a disciplinary role after unethical conduct has occurred. In addition, the Committee has broadened its range of disciplinary responses, allowing for a determination that conduct was unwise, rather than just having the option of declaring it ethical or unethical. Secondly, some state ethics committees have at times refused to investigate or adjudicate complaints, fearing lawsuits from angry members who are disciplined. The California Psychological Association, for example, stopped hearing cases for a period of time for this reason (Pope, 1987b). Many have had to examine the insurance coverage carried by the state associations to determine if it would protect them in such an instance.

Complaint to an employer

If Dr Jones is employed by a mental health centre, clinic or hospital, Doe has the option of reporting the misconduct to his employer. This has the advantage of being typically quite confidential and of allowing for a prompt response. If Doe is contemplating a malpractice suit, she may be less likely to do this, but sometimes clients try the direct approach first and only sue when the employer fails to take action.

Employers, like others, vary in their ability to investigate properly such complaints. The employer may not have a defined procedure for handling such complaints and may be unwilling to devote significant resources to investigating them. A complaint to Dr Jones's employer would possibly result in putting him on probation and requiring close supervision of his work, or compelling him to undergo an independent evaluation to determine what risks there are to clients, or firing him. The employer may require that he undergo some form of rehabilitation before returning to work (Schoener & Gonsiorek, 1989).

While, historically, employers often tended to protect the accused professional, over the past ten years there has been a great increase in the degree to which employers will conduct a thorough investigation and take strong action. Although in the past, it was not uncommon for there to be a private agreement for a resignation accompanied by an agreement to keep the matter secret, this has begun to change as employers are facing more aggressive background checks from those evaluating the professional's credentials. Minnesota Statute 148.A obligates employers to pass on such information when it is requested or face liability for future damages. Mandatory reporting rules and statutes also require employers to report such conduct to licensure boards.

Beyond the problem of possible ineptness in the handling of such a complaint, there is also the reality that the employer's action does not prevent Dr Jones from going into private practice, being hired by a friend or being hired by an employer who does not do careful reference checks. (A model for doing such reference checks can be found in Schoener et al, 1989.) Furthermore, if Dr Jones is in private practice there may be no employer.

Mediation and processing sessions

If Doe is only concerned with understanding what happened between her and Dr Jones, she might consider a processing session utilizing a consultant who would facilitate a meeting between herself and Dr Jones. Developed at the Walk-In Counseling Center in Minneapolis in response to a client's request, this technique is discussed in depth elsewhere (Schoener et al, 1989, pp. 345–357). The sole purpose of such a session is to provide the client, or both parties, with an understanding about why the conduct occurred. As such it is a quasi-therapeutic undertaking. Its value is in providing an opportunity for inquiry and understanding, which is usually impossible in legal proceedings.

By contrast, mediation, while it seeks to allow for some sharing of feelings and provides the opportunity, for example, for an apology, is focused on providing for some resolution through private compensation. This may be done through the use of a therapist who acts as a consultant (Bouhoutsos & Brodsky, 1985) or through the use of an attorney who negotiates a private contract (Schoener et al, 1989, pp. 327–328). Such agreements can involve the payment of money by the therapist and may even include requirements that he or she participate in a processing session and/or undergo rehabilitation. However, unlike the actions of a licensure board or employer, there can be no guarantee that the rehabilitation will be completed. The principal advantage of mediation for Doe is that it might provide her with compensation for injuries without her having to undergo the lengthy and painful process of a lawsuit. Furthermore, it would be Dr Jones, and not his malpractice insurance carrier, who would be compensating Doe. The incentive to Dr Jones would be that he would avoid the publicity that often accompanies a malpractice suit, and if Doe has not already filed an ethics or licensure complaint he might also avoid those consequences.

There is no way of knowing how frequently these options have been utilized since the literature concerning them is scarce. It is clear, however, that mediation has been used in a number of cases around the United States and is continuing to be seen as an option.

The professional as a reporter or client advocate

There has been considerable discussion in the American literature concerning the failure of psychotherapists to report colleagues who engage in sexual misconduct (Davidson, 1977; Grunebaum, Nadelson & Macht, 1976; Stone, 1983). Estimates of the percentage of cases reported suggest that only a minuscule proportion ever reach licensure boards (Noel, 1988; Vinson, 1984). Some studies have found that in only 5% of the cases did professionals fail to report their colleague because the complaint was disbelieved (Gartrell et al, 1987; Pope & Vetter, 1991). Rationales for failure either to report or to assist or advocate in the reporting process have included (Schoener et al, 1989, p. 316):

1. Lack of belief in the mechanisms.
2. Lack of knowledge about complaint alternatives.
3. Concern about negative impact on the therapy.
4. Unsure of professional boundaries of advocacy role.
5. Concern that the allegations are not true or that they may be exaggerated, or that the complaint may destroy the career of the subject of the complaint.
6. Fear of retaliation by the alleged perpetrator.

In response to the problem of non-reporting, several states have passed statutes aimed at improving reporting. Perhaps the most severe standards exist in Minnesota as part of the licensure laws for the various psychotherapy professions. With the exception of psychology, all of the health care professions require all licensed professionals from all health care fields to report any conduct that might lead to licensing board discipline. This can include a variety of boundary violations, impairments and even the use of sexually demeaning language. Psychologists are required to report any therapist–patient sex, unless the knowledge was gained from the offender while performing professional services for that person (Schoener et al, 1989, pp. 560–565).

Both Texas and Wisconsin have also mandated reporting of sexual misconduct by therapists, although the reporter can withhold the patient's name if the patient wishes anonymity. The Texas law mandates a report to *both* the local district attorney and the licensure board, apparently reflecting legislators' distrust of the professional licensing boards. While a prosecution could not proceed in either the criminal or licensure arenas without the patient willing to testify as a witness, it is possible for prosecutors to contact the patient if other complaints are received. This may be done either directly or through the patient's subsequent therapist. Sometimes if there are other complaints, a patient may decide to come forward and testify.

In California, therapists who interview victims must provide them with a consumer brochure, published by the state, which discusses therapist sexual misconduct and provides information on various complaint mechanisms. Although exact numbers are not available, this brochure had the immediate effect of increasing complaints. The Minnesota licensure boards in psychology and medicine also report a more modest but still substantial increase in complaints due to mandatory reporting.

The special case of post-termination

Suppose in our hypothetical case that Dr Jones had terminated his therapist–patient relationship with Sara Doe before engaging in sexual contact with her. The legal and ethical implications for therapist–patient sexual contact during treatment uniformly prohibit such conduct throughout the fifty states; however, the laws regarding therapist–former patient sexual contact after treatment are less clear.

Debate has raged over the past five years (Appelbaum & Jorgenson, 1991; Gabbard & Pope, 1989; Letters to the Editor, 1992; Schoener et al, 1989). While studies of psychologists and psychiatrists show that virtually all condemn therapist–patient sex, approximately one-third of the profession believes that post-termination sexual relationships may be acceptable (Herman et al, 1987;

Pope, Tabachnick & Keith-Spiegel, 1987). This is consistent with recent data from British Columbia showing that 39% of psychiatrists believe that a post-termination relationship with a former patient may be acceptable (College of Physicians and Surgeons of British Columbia, 1992).

At one end of the spectrum is the perspective that it is never acceptable to engage in sexual contact with a former patient ("once a patient, always a patient"), recently adopted by the American Psychiatric Association. However, there are constitutional concerns for freedom of association and privacy rights: how can restrictions on these fundamental rights be infringed upon without clear evidence that post-termination sexual contact is harmful? Reflecting these constitutional concerns, other professional associations are beginning to set finite time periods: in 1988, the American Association for Marriage and Family Therapy adopted a two-year prohibition on sexual contact with former patients, and in 1992, the two-year prohibition (with some additional requirements) was adopted by the American Psychological Association. The National Association for Social Workers has been silent on the issue.

One of the difficulties in evaluating post-termination restrictions is the lack of a clear standard for proper termination (Gottlieb, Sell & Schoenfeld, 1988). In therapist–patient sexual misconduct cases, it is not uncommon for the therapist to have abruptly terminated the professional relationship in order to engage in sexual contact with the patient. The case against psychiatrist Jason Richter featured in the television program, "My Doctor, My Lover", involved Dr Richter's claims that he had begun a sexual relationship with the plaintiff only after termination of the psychiatrist–patient relationship. The court rejected Dr Richter's allegations that a proper termination had been conducted several days before commencing a sexual relationship, and he was found liable for the harm caused to his patient.

Therapists' liability for post-termination sexual contact was initially recognized in the common law. The primary case in the area is *Noto* v. *St Vincent's Hospital and Medical Center of New York* (537 N.Y.S. 2d 446, Supreme Court 1988), discussed earlier. There are still few recorded cases holding therapists liable for post-termination contact with former patients, so common law liability for therapists will vary from state to state.

Of the five states that have adopted civil statutes, all have addressed post-termination sexual contact (see Table 10.2). The period of prohibition ranges from six months after termination (Wisconsin) to two years (California). Table 10.3 lists the states that have criminalized post-termination sexual contact.

Disciplinary sanctions by licensing boards and administrative agencies similarly vary from state to state. There is also variation from profession to profession. In the case against Dr Jason Richter, the Colorado licensing board for physicians refused to discipline Dr Richter because the sexual contact took place after termination. At that time, there was no specific rule prohibiting post-termination contact at the licensing board for psychiatrists—however, at the licensing board for psychologists in Colorado, post-termination sexual contact was prohibited for six months after termination. Thus if Dr Richter had been a psychologist instead of a psychiatrist, he would have been subject to discipline. Psychologists and psychiatrists in Florida are also treated differently: a psychiatrist who engages in post-termination sexual contact violates no ethical rules (Fla. Admin. Code Ann. r. 21R-19.002(13)) whereas a psychologist would be subject to licence revocation and a $1000 fine (Fla. Admin. Code Ann. r. 21U-18.003(1)(k)).

Where termination has been used as a defence in cases brought before psychology licensing boards, the outcome is often the same as if the sex had occurred during therapy (Gottlieb, Sell & Schoenfeld, 1988). However, in many instances in which considerable time has passed between termination and the sexual contact, licensing boards have failed to take action. One exception is the case of *Leon* v. *Ohio Board of Psychology* (63 Ohio St. 3d 683, 1992), in which the board revoked the licence of a psychologist who had begun a sexual relationship with a former patient seven months after therapy terminated. The court upheld the board's interpretation of "immediate" (as in "immediate ex-client") to be seven months.

In general, where there was really no termination or when the sex occurred within days or weeks of termination, ethics committees and boards have tended to treat the case in the same way as one in which sex occurred prior to termination. The same is true where the therapy was terminated in order to allow for a personal or sexual relationship.

Psychotherapy professions have had more difficulty dealing with relationships that develop a year or more after termination, or where marriage occurs. In one study, therapists rated marriage to a former client far less problematic or objectionable than having sex with a former client (Conte et al, 1989; Schoener et al, 1989). Despite all of the surveys of psychotherapists that have been conducted, we are not aware of any that attempted to learn anything about therapists' marriages to their former patients.

Given the shifting standards within ethics codes and laws concerning post-termination sexual relationships with clients, the adjudication of such cases often brings complaints that therapists are being held to new standards that were not in existence when the relationship occurred. Since client complaints are not infrequently about behaviour that occurred several years previously (and sometimes as many as ten or more years previously), when the case involves a post-termination relationship it is important to determine what standards were in force when the relationship occurred.

As noted above, there is considerable evidence that psychotherapists have widely varying attitudes about post-termination sexual relationships, both as to relative ethics and as to factors that might determine propriety or lack of it (Akamatsu, 1988; Conte et al, 1989). There is also considerable confusion and lack of clarity about what constitutes termination, although the most recent revision of the American Psychological Association's Code of Ethics has attempted to define termination. In our hypothetical case, for example, what if Dr Jones had telephoned Sara Doe for a "follow up", and ended up in a two-hour, quasi-therapeutic phone call about how her life was going? Would this be considered a reinitiation of the professional relationship or would it imply that the professional relationship had not ended? Or, if Doe encountered her therapist and they ended up having a two-hour luncheon conversation which included a discussion of her problems and some supportive advice, could this be construed as a continuation of therapy? What if they met socially again the following day and then ended up having sex? At present, there are no clear standards as to what sort of contact with a former client might challenge the notion that there was a final termination.

Conclusion

Patients who have been sexually exploited by their psychotherapists now have a range of options. In the hypothetical case study, Sara Doe could pursue a common law malpractice action against Dr Jones in almost any state in the United States. There has been a favourable trend among the various states with respect to these claims through the relaxation of statutes of limitations. State governments have become increasingly involved, through the enactment of civil and criminal statutes, in attempting to address the problem of therapist–patient sexual contact. Sara Doe could also petition Dr Jones's licensing board for sanctions limiting his ability to practise psychology. She could file a complaint with the ethics committee of his professional association or with his employer. She might also seek understanding and closure through a processing session, or an apology and compensation for therapy costs through mediation—two informal options.

Patients' choices are not exclusive. Doe could pursue any combination of these options, and in fact it is quite common for clients to pursue more than one avenue of grievance. As the public becomes better informed of its options with respect to therapist sexual misconduct, this patchwork of options can become a comprehensive system of remedies, providing a range of redress for unethical and abusive care. The more options that are available, the more likely it will be that clients will come forward and report. As sanctions are actively used, it is also more likely that these sanctions will serve as deterrents. Furthermore, it is likely that there will be earlier reporting of, and more serious attention paid to, the boundary violation precursors of therapist–client sex (Simon, 1991; Strasburger, Jorgenson, & Sutherland, 1992).

11   Regulation in the U.K.

Legislation and litigation concerning the regulation of psychotherapy specifically are less extensive in the U.K. than in the U.S.A., although there is a substantial body of more general medical law and administration that is potentially applicable to this particular form of intervention (e.g. Brazier, 1992; Kennedy & Grubb, 1989). Thus, the four major channels through which regulation and redress may be pursued are civil suits, criminal prosecutions, professional misconduct proceedings and complaint processes in the National Health Service (N.H.S.), which employs many of the therapists practising in the U.K. These options are reviewed in this chapter, together with the issues of reporting abusive colleagues and false allegations by patients.

Civil suits

Unlike in some U.S. states (Chapter 10), there are no civil statutes in the U.K. governing sexual abuse by therapists specifically, but victimized patients may sue for damages under the common law, most probably for the tort of negligence. Some disadvantages of this remedy for patients are described in the section on litigation stresses in Chapter 10.

Negligence

To establish negligence or malpractice the onus is on the plaintiff to prove that the defendant owed her a duty of care, that he was in breach of that duty in that the standard of care rendered was inadequate, and that this breach caused her to suffer harm.

Duty of care   It is clear that N.H.S. patients are owed a duty of care by all members of staff involved in their treatment. In respect of private patients this duty arises from the contract between them and those responsible for their treatment. In either case the duty of care applies not only to therapists and others who render direct treatment but also to their employers, including health authorities and hospitals.

Standard of care   Secondly, the patient (plaintiff) must prove that the defendant was in breach of the required standard of care, and as far as therapists are concerned this is likely to be judged according to what has become known as the *Bolam* principle:

> A man need not possess the highest expert skill . . . It is well-established law that it is sufficient if he exercises the ordinary skill of an ordinary competent man exercising that particular art . . . in the case of a medical man negligence means failure to act in accordance with the standards of reasonably competent medical men at the time . . . as long as it is remembered that there may be one or more perfectly proper standards: and if a medical man conforms with one of these standards then he is not negligent.
>
> (*Bolam* v. *Friern Hospital Management Committee*
> [1957] 2 All ER 118, 121–122)

Progress in professional practice would stultify if any departure from current approved practice was deemed to be negligent. Thus, it has been held (e.g. *Hunter* v. *Hanley* 1955 SC 200) that such departure is not automatically negligent but the defendant must justify it either by the individual circumstances of a particular case or by demonstrating that the innovation improves or at least equals existing practice.

Clearly, sexual activity between therapists and their patients is not in accordance with accepted practice (part I) and this may be breached also by other events related to such activity (Schoener, 1989e). Some of these events are described in the sections "Impairment of therapeutic process" in Chapters 1 and 2; they include loss of a therapist who becomes a lover, underestimation or exaggeration of a patient's problems, adverse effects on the therapeutic alliance, withholding of appropriate advice or treatment, failure to refer to or to consult with other professionals, and inappropriate termination of therapy. Other possible negligent breaches of accepted practice involve boundary violations such as those described in Chapter 5. One instance of this is the case of *Landau* v. *Werner* (1961) Sol Jo 105), in which the relevant circumstances were that a female patient terminated psychotherapy with her male psychiatrist and told him that this was because she had fallen deeply in love with him. Almost immediately he started to take her out to tea and dinner in restaurants on a number of occasions and visited her once in her bed-sitting room; there were also conversations between them about spending a holiday together. On appeal it was held that (p. 1008):

> the real question was whether the social meetings, and the discussion about a holiday together, were bad and negligent practice in the sphere of medicine in which the doctor worked. ... Here the medical evidence was all one way in condemning social contacts and the doctor had failed to convince the judge that this departure from standard practice was justified and was a reasonable development in this young science. The judge was justified in his view that this unwise treatment had led to the grave deterioration in the plaintiff's health. It was negligent and in breach of the duty of the doctor to his patient.

Turning now to the standard of care expected of an employer of therapists, this has been stated as "(a) to select competent and qualified employees (b) to instruct and supervise them (c) to provide proper facilities and equipment (d) to establish systems for the safe operation of the hospital. Since the other components of tort law apply, the hospital has to carry out these duties as competently as the reasonable hospital in the circumstances" (Kennedy & Grubb, 1989, p. 374). For example, in *Cassidy* v. *Ministry of Health* [1951] 1 All ER 574, CA, it was held that:

> the hospital authorities accepted the plaintiff as a patient for treatment, and it was their duty to treat him with reasonable care. They selected, employed, and paid all the surgeons and nurses who looked after him. ... If those surgeons and nurses did not treat him with proper care and skill, then the hospital authorities must answer for it, for it means that they themselves did not perform their duty to him.

Thus, if an employer appointed a therapist without making proper enquiries that would have revealed a history of court decisions or disciplinary findings concerning the sexual abuse of patients, and this therapist subsequently abused another patient while in their employment then this might be considered a breach of the appropriate standard of care expected of the employer. The same might apply if an employer failed to ensure that a therapist was properly supervised and accountable or that he practised only in clinical settings and circumstances that were safe for patients.

Causation of harm   This third element of negligence is often the most difficult for the plaintiff to prove. As Kennedy & Grubb put it: "It is one thing to show that the defendant doctor owed the plaintiff a duty which was breached and that the plaintiff has been harmed, it is quite another thing to establish that the breach *caused* the harm. But this is what the law requires" (1989, p. 426). The plaintiff must demonstrate that the defendant's breach contributed to her current adverse condition, or alternatively that it deprived her of the chance of full recovery. One example of a relatively clear contribution to a current adverse condition might be a patient who became sexually dysfunctional only after sexual abuse by her therapist and in the absence of any other plausible cause for the onset of this difficulty. Another patient might have sought treatment for a sexual dysfunction from which full recovery might reasonably be expected if the therapist had not sexually abused her under the guise of treatment.

Where a clear and unambiguous contribution by the therapist's breach of duty to the plaintiff's current adverse condition cannot be proved, however, then an action for negligence is not likely to succeed. As Brazier puts it, "Where the scientific evidence is ambivalent or suggests a variety of competing causes for the plaintiff's state, the action for negligence will fail" (1992, p. 132). Thus, a patient who was sexually abused by her therapist and also raped by a different man might have difficulty in proving that her sexual dysfunction, which began after both these events, was caused by the therapist rather than by the rapist.

The therapist's breach of duty does not need to be the sole cause of a plaintiff's current problems if it can be shown that the defendant's acts or omissions worsened her condition. For example, a patient might have presented originally with a personality problem concerning distrust of others but at that time she was able to trust professionals enough to seek their help. After she was abused by her therapist her distrust widened and intensified so that she was no longer willing to enter further treatment. In these circumstances it might be argued that the therapist's breach of duty had contributed to the worsening of her distrust of others.

Expert testimony

In order to satisfy the evidential requirements for negligence it will be necessary to obtain the testimony of appropriate experts on matters such as the existence of the defendant's duty of care, his alleged breach of this duty by non-compliance with current accepted professional practice, and the possible contribution of this breach to the plaintiff's psychological problems.

The role of expert witnesses retained by plaintiffs or defendants is discussed by Schoener (1989e). In brief, expert testimony will be based on pre-trial assessments, which include the plaintiff's current psychological status and her history and functioning before, during and after the alleged abuse. This information may be gathered, *inter alia*, from past and current psychological testing, interviews with the plaintiff and other informants, and written records, including those of the allegedly abusive therapist and others who treated the plaintiff. In the Supreme Court Act 1981 there is power for the court to order the disclosure to the plaintiff's advisors of these and all other relevant documents if they are not handed over voluntarily.

Statute of limitations

The Limitation Act 1980 requires that normally actions must be started within three years of the alleged negligence. If, however, the plaintiff was either unaware that she had suffered significant harm or did not know that it was the alleged negligence that had caused the harm, then the three-year period commences from when she did discover, or reasonably should have discovered, these facts. If she knew these facts but not the legal remedy open to her then the three-year period commences when she was or should have been aware of the facts. In the last resort the judge has discretion to override the three-year limitation where in all the circumstances it is fair to all parties to do so.

Damages

Plaintiffs who succeed in actions for negligence may be awarded damages under two major heads: pecuniary losses, including actual and prospective loss of earnings and the cost of future care and treatment, and non-pecuniary losses, such as pain, suffering, disability and loss of the ordinary experiences and amenities in life. Recovery of damages awarded depends on the resources available to the defendant. Hospital staff in the N.H.S. are indemnified by their employers for any damages awarded against them. In most other cases recovery will depend on the provisions and extent of any professional insurance held by the defendant or on his personal resources.

Costs

If a claim for negligence succeeds the plaintiff may be awarded costs against the defendant. Otherwise, she is responsible for her own costs and perhaps for those of the defendant also if the claim fails. In a decreasing number of cases potential litigants may qualify for legal aid, without which many will be unable to pursue a civil action. The Courts and Legal Services Act 1990 does give the Lord Chancellor power to make regulations permitting English lawyers to provide legal services either for no fee if the claim fails or for an increased fee if it succeeds, and a similar arrangement is operative in Scotland. It is still too soon to judge the effect of such conditional fee arrangements, which are the nearest British approximation to the contingency fees common in the U.S.

Criminal prosecutions

In contrast to recent developments in the U.S. (Chapter 10) there are no criminal offences relating specifically to psychotherapy in the U.K. The nearest similar offence is sexual intercourse with a mentally disordered patient. Other more general offences may be committed in the course of sexual activity between therapists and patients, most probably rape or indecent assault, although many other charges are possible (Rook & Ward, 1990).

Sexual intercourse with mentally disordered patients

A male therapist employed in a hospital who has sex with a patient may be guilty of unlawful sexual intercourse (Mental Health Acts 1959, 1983). The victim may be female or male, and in the case of the latter the term intercourse includes buggery or gross indecency. He or she must be suffering from a "mental disorder" defined as "mental illness, arrested or incomplete development of mind, psychopathic disorder or disability of mind". If the victim is an in-patient the offence is committed whether the intercourse takes place on the hospital premises or elsewhere; in the case of out-patients the offence is committed only if intercourse occurs on hospital premises.

Rape

A therapist who has sexual intercourse with a female patient without her consent may be guilty of rape. In this context, sexual intercourse means penetration of the vagina with the penis, and not anal or oral sex. The prosecution must prove that intercourse occurred without the victim's consent and this is a complex issue in law (Rook & Ward, 1990). Use of force is not an essential ingredient of rape, but any apparent consent is vitiated if it is induced by violence or threat of violence. Similarly, an apparent consent is invalidated if it was obtained by deception, including inducing the victim to consent on the basis of a fraudulent misrepresentation as to the nature of the act. An early leading case on this point is *Flattery* (1877 1 QB 410). The defendant ran a market stall, from which he professed to sell medical and surgical services. He advised a 19-year-old woman that she needed a surgical operation and under the pretence of performing it he had sexual intercourse with her. It was adjudged that she had only consented to an operation, not to intercourse, and the defendant was convicted of rape (see also *Case*, below). Thus, a therapist who induced a patient to have intercourse as a component of her treatment would be doing so without her valid consent and could be charged with rape.

Indecent assault

A male or female therapist may indecently assault a male or female patient. The essential requirements of the assault element of the offence are that the defendant must either have inflicted personal violence on the victim or have caused the victim to apprehend the immediate infliction of such violence. For this purpose even the lightest touching may constitute violence (Rook & Ward, 1990). The element of indecency is more difficult to define but one suggested test is whether "right-minded persons would consider the conduct indecent or not" (*Court* [1989] AC 28). Absence of consent to the assault must also be proved by the prosecution, and any apparent consent is vitiated if it was induced by force, fear of force or fraud (Rook & Ward, 1990). This last invalidating condition is illustrated by *Case* [1981] 3 All ER 443, in which a medical practitioner had sexual intercourse with a female patient on the pretence that he was carrying out a form of medical treatment. He was convicted of indecent assault and one of the judges remarked that, "The prisoner disarmed [the patient] by his fraud. She acquiesced under a misrepresentation that what he was doing was with a view to a cure and that only; whereas it was done solely to gratify the passions of the prisoner. . . . She consented to one thing, he did another materially different, on which she had been prevented by his fraud from exercising her judgement and will".

Conclusion

Criminal prosecutions differ from civil suits in several ways, including the following. The victimized patient is a witness in criminal cases rather than a party to the proceedings as in civil actions. She is not responsible for the costs of the prosecution, which are undertaken by the Crown Prosecution Service, or in Scotland by a Procurator-Fiscal. No monetary damages necessarily accompany criminal convictions, although courts are empowered to make compensation orders (Criminal Justice Acts 1982, 1991) and separate application can be made to the Criminal Injuries Compensation Board. The standard of proof required is more rigorous in criminal than in civil proceedings. In the former, the prosecution must prove the commission of the offence beyond reasonable doubt, whereas in the latter the plaintiff must show that it is more likely than not that negligence occurred.

Particularly in the light of developments in the U.S., the question arises as to whether the sexual abuse of patients in psychotherapy should be made a specific criminal offence in the U.K. Some arguments on both sides are reviewed by Strasburger, Jorgenson & Randles (1991). In favour of criminalization, it might be argued that it would signal clearly the unacceptable nature of such abuse; it might deter some potential offenders, although empirical evidence is lacking on this proposition; it would provide retribution for the distress and harm caused to the victim; it offers an alternative to civil suits, which are not feasible financially for many victims, and professional misconduct proceedings, which may be ineffective in ways discussed below; and finally convictions might facilitate and strengthen subsequent applications to the Criminal Injuries Compensation Board.

On the other hand, it might be argued that specific legislation for psychotherapy would be redundant because prosecution for sexual offences such as rape and indecent assault is already possible and would cover most forms of sexual abuse by therapists, although specific legislation might remove the defence of consent by the victim. Furthermore, the possibility of prosecution might deter some victims and professionals from reporting on an abusive therapist whom they are reluctant to see suffering criminal sanctions. Another argument made against prosecution is that it disempowers victims, who lose control of the proceedings when it is the restoration of power and control in their lives that they most need. In practice, there seems little prospect of offences related specifically to psychotherapy being enacted in the U.K. for this would be contrary to a legal tradition in which there is no special criminal law concerning particularly the doctor–patient relationship (Kennedy & Grubb, 1989).

Professional misconduct

All of the major therapeutic professions in the U.K. provide varying forms of self-regulation for their membership. Thus, patients who are victimized by a member may complain to the professional body concerned with the expectation that an inquiry will be undertaken, that disciplinary proceedings will be instigated in appropriate cases, and that sanctions will be applied if the complaint is found to be valid. Such regulation of psychiatrists, psychologists, nurses, counsellors and social workers is considered next.

Psychiatrists

As registered medical practitioners psychiatrists are subject to regulation by the General Medical Council (G.M.C.). This is a statutory body (Medical Act 1983), which discharges its disciplinary functions primarily through its Professional Conduct and Preliminary Proceedings Committees in accordance with the "Blue Book" (General Medical Council, 1992).

Allegations against practitioners are screened by the President or another medical member of the G.M.C., together with a lay member. If they decide that the case should proceed then it goes to the Preliminary Proceedings Committee, which sits in private and on the basis of written evidence and information determines which cases should be referred to the Professional Conduct Committee, or to the Health Committee which deals with practitioners whose fitness to practise is seriously impaired by a physical or mental condition. If the case is not referred to one of these committees then a letter of warning or advice may be sent to the practitioner or it may be decided that no further action is required.

The Professional Conduct Committee normally sits in public and its procedure is similar to that of a court of law. Witnesses may be subpoenaed and evidence is given on oath. It considers those cases referred to it by the Preliminary Proceedings Committee in which registered practitioners have been convicted of criminal offences or who are alleged to have been guilty of serious professional misconduct.

In respect of a criminal conviction the Professional Conduct Committee is bound to accept the conviction as conclusive evidence that the practitioner was guilty of the offence and the committee is concerned only with its gravity and any mitigating circumstances. For instance, in the Blue Book it is stated that a conviction for indecency would be regarded with particular gravity if the offence were committed in the course of professional duties or against the practitioner's patients.

Serious professional misconduct is defined in Halsbury's *Laws of England* as conduct "reasonably to be regarded as dishonourable by professional brethren of good repute and competency" (Vol. 30, para. 125), and examples of it cited in the Blue Book include the abuse of a practitioner's position in order to pursue a relationship of an emotional or sexual nature with a patient, and indecent assault on a patient in the absence of a criminal conviction for this offence.

If the Professional Conduct Committee finds that a registered practitioner has been convicted of a criminal offence or is guilty of serious professional misconduct it may, if it thinks fit, direct that his name be erased from the register, or that his registration be suspended for not more than 12 months, or that his registration be continued on the condition that he complies with certain requirements imposed for the protection of the public and for the practitioner's own interests. Such conditions may be imposed for a period not exceeding three years and they might include a restriction to practise only in a particular appointment or under supervision, or the remediation of certain deficiencies in knowledge, skills or attitudes. Practitioners have the right of appeal to the Judicial Committee of the Privy Council against any of these dispositions and they may apply for restoration to the register after 10 months from the date of erasure. In addition, it is open to a practitioner to sue the G.M.C. on grounds of breach of natural justice if he thinks that he has not been dealt with fairly (*R. v. GMC ex parte Gee* [1987] 1 WLR 564, HL).

The effect of erasure or suspension from the register is that the psychiatrist cannot represent himself as a registered medical practitioner, indeed it would be a criminal offence for him to do so (Medical Act 1983), and he may not hold certain appointments, most notably those in the N.H.S. He is not precluded, however, from continuing to use the prefix "Doctor", for, as Kennedy & Grubb describe the position in the U.K., "Anyone can call himself a doctor. Curiously, medical practitioners do not ordinarily have doctorates and therefore, the attribution to them of the title 'doctor' is wholly a convention" (1989, p. 95). Moreover, "Surprisingly no law expressly prohibits any unregistered or unqualified person from practising most types of medicine or even surgery! A criminal offence is committed only when such a person deliberately and falsely represents himself as being a registered medical practitioner or having medical qualifications" (Brazier, 1992, p. 10). Thus, an erased or suspended psychiatrist could quite legally continue to use the unprotected title of "doctor" and to practise psychotherapy as long as he did not misrepresent himself as a registered medical practitioner.

Psychologists

Under the terms of its Royal Charter the British Psychological Society (B.P.S.) has authority to establish a Register of Chartered Psychologists and it can prevent anyone not on the Register from describing themselves as Chartered Psychologists. As this is a non-statutory register there is no legal requirement to join the Register in order to work as a psychologist in the U.K. Thus, in the opinion of a Past President of the Society:

> the protection offered by the *Register of Chartered Psychologists* falls far short of that achieved by a statutory register. This is simply because, at present, all we can do is to prevent undesirable practitioners claiming to be "Chartered Psychologists". Anyone is free to set up a plate and claim to be a "psychologist" . . . providing they do not claim to be chartered. This even applies to anyone struck off the *Register* . . . !
>
> (Miller, 1992)

Consequently, it is the intention of the B.P.S. to seek government approval and legislation for the establishment of a statutory register which would, *inter alia*, protect the title of psychologist, but this is likely to take some considerable time to achieve.

To be included in the *Register of Chartered Psychologists*, applicants must be members of the B.P.S., hold specified academic qualifications, meet certain requirements of further study or practice, and sign an undertaking to abide by the Society's Code of Conduct. Registration may be refused or erased if the state, condition or professional conduct of the individual is deemed to render him or her unfit for the practice of psychology, and there is a right of appeal against such decisions to a Disciplinary Committee.

Allegations of misconduct are considered first by the Investigatory Committee. If it decides that no further action is necessary then this must be reported to a non-psychologist representative of the Disciplinary Board, who may endorse or overrule this decision.

If further investigation is to be undertaken either on the decision of the Investigatory Committee or on the direction of the non-psychologist representative of the Disciplinary Board, then an Investigatory Panel is appointed consisting of certain senior psychologists with relevant expertise. Such panels have the tasks of gathering and considering all the available information, including representations from the accused, and of reporting their findings to the Investigatory Committee, which will decide whether the allegation should be referred to a Disciplinary Committee. The report of the Panel and the decision of the Investigatory Committee are sent to a non-psychologist representative of the Disciplinary Board, who may endorse or overrule this decision. In cases that are not being referred to a Disciplinary Committee a letter of advice or warning may be sent to the accused.

The Disciplinary Board oversees the Society's regulatory functions and comprises a Chairman, who is not a psychologist, together with other non-psychologist and psychologist members. Disciplinary Committees are appointed from among these members and must have a non-psychologist Chairman and at least one other non-psychologist member as well as at least one psychologist. Their hearings are held in private and the accused person may present written or oral evidence and may either conduct the case himself or herself or this may be done by someone else, including a lawyer. Witnesses may be called and cross-examined but not subpoenaed, and the Society's statutes do not stipulate whether evidence is to be given on oath.

A Disciplinary Committee is required to determine whether the accused is guilty of misconduct and it is guided in this task by the Code of Conduct, although mention or lack of mention in the Code of a particular act or omission is not to be taken as conclusive on any question of misconduct since no code can anticipate every possible offence. The most specific proscriptions of sexual activity between psychologists and patients in the Code are that psychologists do not exploit this relationship for "improper sexual gain" or to further "the gratification of their own desires" (see Tables 1.1 and 1.2).

If professional misconduct is established then the Committee may reprimand the accused, require him or her to undertake not to continue or repeat the offence, suspend him or her from the Society, the Register or both for not more than two years, or expel him or her from the Society, the Register or both. The names of those so disciplined may be published. Those expelled have the right to seek reinstatement after two years. As mentioned above, expulsion does not preclude a person from describing himself or herself as a psychologist or from continuing to practise psychotherapy, always providing that he or she does not purport to be "Chartered".

Nurses

The United Kingdom Central Council for Nursing, Midwifery and Health Visiting (U.K.C.C.) maintains a statutory register of suitably qualified nurses and has the right to remove them from the register if they are found guilty of professional misconduct (Nurses, Midwives and Health Visitors Act 1979; Nurses, Midwives and Health Visitors (Professional Conduct) Rules 1993). This is defined as "conduct unworthy of a registered nurse" (Nurses, Midwives and Health Visitors (Professional Conduct) Rules 1993, Sec. 1.), and the sexual abuse of patients is one instance of such misconduct that has resulted in removal from the register. The Council's functions in this regard are discharged mainly through its Professional Conduct Committee, with cases in which a practitioner's fitness to practise may be impaired by physical or mental illness being considered by the Health Committee, and in accordance with the 1993 Rules cited above.

Preliminary Proceedings Committees are composed of members of the U.K.C.C. but it is not specified whether they must include non-nurses. When an allegation of misconduct is received such a committee investigates it to decide whether it should be referred to the Professional Conduct or Health Committee, or if a caution as to future conduct should be issued. The investigation may include inquiries by a solicitor before the allegation is considered by a Preliminary Proceedings Committee.

Professional Conduct Committees also consist of members of the U.K.C.C., without non-nurse representation being specified. Cases are referred to them by a Preliminary Proceedings Committee and presented by a solicitor employed by U.K.C.C. The practitioner against whom the allegation is made (the respondent) may also be legally represented. Witnesses may be cross-examined and re-examined. Generally, their evidence must be in a form that would be admissible in criminal proceedings.

During the process of a case through the Preliminary Proceedings and Professional Conduct Committees either committee can direct an interim suspension of the respondent's registration if this is deemed necessary for the protection of the public or in the interests of the practitioner.

Respondents who are found guilty of professional misconduct may be cautioned as to their future conduct or removed from the register, either indefinitely or for a specified period. The effect of removal is that practitioners may not describe themselves as "registered nurses", although the title of "nurse" is not protected and removed practitioners could continue to practise therapy under this or another title.

Counsellors

Counsellors are not registered in the U.K. and persons describing themselves as such are not necessarily members of any professional organization. In the absence of registration or professional membership there are no external controls on misconduct, other than those of a legal or employment nature. Thus, membership of an appropriate professional organization is voluntary but those who do join are required to abide by the organization's code of ethics and membership may be terminated if they breach the code. The principal organization in this field is the British Association for Counselling (B.A.C.), and its complaint procedures are outlined next.

When a complaint alleges either physical or emotional harm or exploitation and is of such a kind that it could result in the expulsion of the member if upheld, then rights of membership may be suspended while an investigation is made. If a member resigns or allows membership to lapse before completion of the complaints procedure then it may not be renewed without special approval, and the resignation or lapse of membership may be published in B.A.C. journals.

One or more conciliators are appointed to investigate the complaint and to make recommendations to the Complaints Sub-Committee on the possibility of resolution, the need for adjudication, or that there is no basis for the complaint to proceed. There are no non-B.A.C. members among conciliators.

Cases referred for adjudication are heard by an Adjudication Panel, which does not include any non-B.A.C. members, and it is not specified whether hearings are to be held in private or public, or whether evidence is to be given on oath. The Panel is required to determine if the complaint constitutes a violation of the B.A.C. Code of Ethics and Practice (1992), which, *inter alia*, proscribes engaging in sexual activity with clients. If the complaint is upheld the Panel has powers to warn that practice must be improved, to require that practice is monitored by a supervisor, to request cessation of practice for a specified or indefinite period, or to suspend or terminate membership. There is a right of appeal to an Appeals Panel against any of these sanctions, which after final determination are published in B.A.C. journals. As mentioned above, because of the voluntary nature of membership and the non-registration of counsellors none of these sanctions can prevent the offender from using the title "counsellor" and of continuing to practise therapy under this or another title.

Social workers

There is nothing to stop any unqualified person using the title "social worker" since it has no legal protection. Those practising under this title—whether qualified or unqualified—do not have to be members of the British Association of Social Workers (B.A.S.W.), but if they do choose to join then they are required to comply with the B.A.S.W. Code of Ethics and to refrain from professional misconduct.

Such misconduct is defined as an act or omission that is likely to be harmful to clients, colleagues or members of the public; or prejudicial to the development or standing of social work practice; or contrary to the Code of Ethics. Included in this definition is the misuse of professional position to further an improper association or relationship, and the commission of any criminal offence involving indecency (British Association of Social Workers, 1991).

On receipt of an allegation of misconduct the General Secretary of the Association will invite and if necessary assist the complainant to submit a written statement, which is sent to the Chair of the Disciplinary Board and the Investigating Committee, which does not include non-members of the Association. When this committee finds *prima facie* evidence of misconduct it will refer the case to the Disciplinary Board, which also does not include non-members of the Association.

Meetings of the Disciplinary Board are held in private. If misconduct is established then the member concerned may be expelled or suspended from the Association, or he or she may be reprimanded or admonished. Re-admission to membership may be applied for three years after expulsion or two years after suspension. There is a right of appeal to the Council of the Association.

Because of the unprotected nature of the title of social worker and the voluntary nature of membership of the Association there is nothing to stop those who do not join or those who are expelled or suspended from continuing to practise therapy under this or another title. Consequently, the protection of the public is quite limited. Together with other organizations, the Association is pressing for the establishment of a statutory General Social Services Council to remedy some of these deficiencies.

Conclusion

It will be apparent from the above review that there is considerable variation in the self-regulation of the major therapeutic professions in the U.K. on matters such as the protection of titles, whether misconduct hearings are held in public or private, and the standard of proof and rules of evidence that are adopted. Not infrequently, the professions do not specify their requirements and practices on some of these important procedural issues in their published material.

A major limitation is the lack of protection afforded to many professional titles used by therapists and against the practice of psychotherapy by unqualified or unsuitable persons. Only the titles of "registered medical practitioner", "chartered psychologist", and "registered nurse" are protected. Anyone may call themselves a doctor, psychologist, nurse, counsellor, social worker, psychotherapist, sexual or marital therapist, or any other therapeutic title, providing that they do not mislead patients by falsely claiming to have certain qualifications. Thus, therapy can be practised by quite unqualified persons as well as by former professionals whose registration, chartering or membership has been cancelled for misconduct. Clearly, the public is inadequately protected in this situation.

There is concern also that in their misconduct procedures the professions may be overprotective towards their members to the detriment of complainants, who may feel that insufficient recognition is given to the distress they have suffered and that justice has not been done to them. The inclusion of lay persons who are not members of the profession concerned may reduce the risk of bias towards the rights and interests of accused therapists and ensure that justice is seen to be done, but it appears that the participation of lay persons in misconduct proceedings is not required by all the therapeutic professions in the U.K.

In May 1993, the United Kingdom Council for Psychotherapy (U.K.C.P.) was launched as an umbrella for 71 therapeutic organizations. Membership is voluntary and it is for organizations rather than for individual therapists. Those therapists who belong to a member organization are listed in a National Register of Psychotherapists and are required to comply with the ethical code of their own organization as well as with that of the U.K.C.P. Any alleged breaches of these codes are dealt with by the organization to which the accused therapist belongs and its handling of such complaints is monitored by the U.K.C.P., which may remove a disciplined therapist's name from its Register. It is too early to know how this new umbrella organization will operate or the influence it will have on the regulation of therapeutic practice.

N.H.S. complaints

A fourth and final regulatory channel is by way of complaint to the employer of the accused therapist, which in the U.K. is frequently the N.H.S. The Hospital Complaints Procedures Act 1985 and the Ministerial directions made under it require hospitals to make arrangements for dealing with patients' complaints and to ensure that adequate publicity is given to these arrangements.

They include the appointment of a designated officer to receive and handle complaints in the first place. With the agreement of the patient this officer will attempt conciliation, but if agreement is withheld or conciliation fails then the complaint is investigated further. If it is of a minor nature this will be undertaken by the designated officer but if the complainant is dissatisfied with his or her report or if the complaint is of a more serious nature then it is referred to senior management, sometimes at Regional Health Authority (R.H.A.) level.

At this level complaints may be considered by one or more members of the R.H.A. or in serious cases an independent inquiry may be set up. This will be conducted by a legally qualified chairperson and two members, usually from the profession of the accused therapist. Both the complainant and the accused may be legally represented and witnesses may be cross-examined. No one, however, can be compelled to attend or give evidence and accused professionals have refused to do so, sometimes on the advice of their insurers.

Therapists found guilty of a disciplinary offence during these complaint procedures may be sanctioned in various ways, including the suspension or termination of their employment or the imposition of requirements to undergo remediation or to practise under supervision. When appropriate, cases are referred to the police with a view to criminal prosecution or to professional organizations for possible misconduct proceedings. Findings against the accused therapist in hospital complaints proceedings are sometimes followed by out-of-court settlements to pay compensation to complainants, thus avoiding the need to pursue a civil suit.

Reporting colleagues

As shown in Table 11.1, in the U.K. psychiatrists, psychologists and counsellors are ethically mandated to report members of their professions who may be guilty of misconduct, while there does not appear to be any such requirement for nurses or social workers. I am unaware of any data on the extent to which these requirements are complied with or on the attitudes of British therapists towards them. There is some information from the U.S. on these topics and on the legal mandating of reporting in certain States, as indicated in the discussion of intrusive advocacy in Chapter 9 and the section on the professional as a reporter or client advocate in Chapter 10 (see also Gartrell et al, 1987; Jorgenson, Randles & Strasburger, 1991; Levenson, 1986; Noel, 1988; Schoener, 1989f; Stone, 1983; Strasburger, Jorgenson & Randles, 1990).

False allegations

I am not aware of any data on the proportion of allegations of sexual misconduct found to be false in the U.K., but false allegations are thought to be rare in the U.S. (Schoener & Milgrom, 1989). As with other forms of sexual abuse, it is important not to prejudge allegations as always true or always false rather than

Table 11.1:   Ethical Requirements to Report Colleagues for Professional Misconduct

Organization	Requirement
General Medical Council	It is any doctor's duty . . . to inform an appropriate person or authority about a colleague whose professional conduct or fitness to practise may be called into question . . .
British Psychological Society	Psychologists . . . shall . . . where they suspect misconduct by a professional colleague which cannot be resolved or remedied after discussion with the colleague concerned, take steps to bring that misconduct to the attention of those charged with the responsibility to investigate it . . .
British Association for Counselling	If a counsellor suspects misconduct by another counsellor which cannot be resolved or remedied after discussion with the counsellor concerned, they should implement the complaints procedure, ...

evaluating the evidence on an individual basis. Schoener & Milgrom (1989) suggest several sources of evidence that may tend to validate allegations. The therapist may admit that all or some of the allegations are true. Several patients may independently give similar accounts of what happened between them and the therapist. The patient may be able to demonstrate knowledge of the therapist's body or of the setting in which the abuse occurred which could only have been acquired in conditions of intimacy. Another person may have been aware of the abuse when it was taking place. The same authors also indicate some ways in which false allegations may be challenged, including admission of exaggeration or fabrication by the patient, or evidence from witnesses, treatment notes or other written sources.

Conclusion

The four regulatory options of civil suits, criminal prosecutions, professional misconduct proceedings and complaints to employers are not mutually exclusive, and it is quite possible for more than one course of action to be pursued in the same case. Each option has its particular merits as well as some limitations. The primary advantage of civil suits is that they may enable victims to recover damages, but there may be some procedural problems, as noted above. Criminal prosecutions are designed to punish abusive therapists and perhaps to deter other potential offenders, but they do not in themselves provide compensation for victims. While misconduct proceedings offer some control over therapists who are registered, chartered or members of professional organizations, they can provide no protection from other therapists who are outside their jurisdiction and perhaps practising under a non-protected title. Complaints to employers can result in sanctions against abusive therapists, which may include loss of employment, although not infrequently re-employment as a therapist is obtained elsewhere.

The choice of options to be pursued and the legal requirements involved in doing so are such that victims should obtain expert advice from qualified lawyers. Thus, Pope & Bouhoutsos (1986, p. 87) enjoin therapists not to practise law:

> In the same way that therapists are obligated to have their patients' medical needs assessed and treated by a qualified and licensed physician, they are obligated to have their patients' legal needs . . . assessed (and . . . legal courses of action . . . recommended) by a qualified and duly authorized attorney.

The same authors offer advice to victims considering what action to take, which, although based in the U.S. system, has much relevance for those in the U.K. (Pope & Bouhoutsos, 1986, pp. 110–115).

12   Primary prevention of abuse

The primary prevention of sexual abuse in therapy may be mediated through therapists, employers and patients, and their respective potential contributions are discussed in this chapter.

Prevention through therapists

Some therapist-mediated preventive measures have been mentioned previously in this book. The possibility of incurring the regulatory sanctions described in Chapters 10 and 11 may deter "at risk" therapists from abusing their patients, and the self-regulation and consultative processes discussed in Chapter 6 may enable potential abusers to control their behaviour. It remains to consider the professional education of therapists and the supervision of their clinical practice as means of preventing abuse.

Professional education

It might be predicted that higher levels of professional education will be associated with lower rates of sexual abuse in therapy, but the limited evidence available does not support this hypothesis. For example, among psychiatrists in the U.S. it was found that offenders were more likely than non-offenders to have completed an accredited residency and to have undergone personal psychotherapy or psychoanalysis (Gartrell et al, 1986). Similarly, a survey of social workers in the U.S. showed that personal therapy was not associated with lower rates of sexual abuse by therapists and that offenders were more likely than non-offenders to have fulfilled the additional requirements for membership of the National Academy of Certified Social Workers (Gechtman, 1989). It is not clear why more highly qualified therapists may be more likely to abuse patients but it is possible that their professional status and prestige could help them to avoid detection (Lanyon, 1986) and/or they may hold the elitist belief that they are above the rules applicable to more run-of-the-mill therapists (Pope & Bajt, 1988).

A more general question is why professional education fails to prevent some therapists from abusing their patients. One answer may be that certain characteristics which put therapists at risk of offending (Chapter 5), such as personal distress; tendencies towards professional isolation, grandiosity or domination; or an antisocial personality disorder, are likely to be relatively impervious to educational influences. Ideally, persons exhibiting such characteristics should not be selected for the mental health professions or at least should be identified and excluded from training before completion. In practice, this is difficult to achieve. Selection procedures are not usually sufficiently sensitive or rigorous in the difficult task of screening out candidates with risk characteristics, and once training is commenced there is often a reluctance to terminate it, perhaps because of the perceived subjectivity of the judgements involved, compassion for the trainee concerned or the risk of having to defend the decision in the face of litigation.

Another reason for the apparent shortfall of professional education in preventing sexual abuse is that this topic area is inadequately addressed in training. For example, Pope, Keith-Spiegel & Tabachnick (1986), in a survey of U.S. psychologists, found that only 9% believed that the issue of sexual attraction to patients had been given adequate coverage in their training, and 55% indicated that they had received no education about such matters. Similar deficiencies are reported in the training of U.S. psychiatrists (Gartrell et al, 1986, 1988; Rieker & Carmen, 1983). Thus, there is considerable room for improvement in the professional education of therapists, perhaps along the lines discussed below, and there is some encouraging evidence that this may have beneficial effects for it has been found that psychologists who had studied ethics courses were more aware of impaired or burned-out colleagues, and more likely to seek help themselves or to help an impaired colleague, and to report such a colleague to a regulatory agency (Wood et al, 1985).

Curriculum   Professional education for therapy could be improved, and abuse, perhaps, reduced by adequate coverage of many of the topics discussed in this and similar books (e.g. Edelwich & Brodsky, 1991; Gabbard, 1989; Pope & Bouhoutsos, 1986), including:

1. Ethical issues and codes of conduct (part I).
2. Epidemiology of sexual abuse in therapy (part II).

3. Psychological characteristics that put therapists "at risk" of offending (Chapter 5).
4. Factors that motivate therapists to abuse, including the nature and management of sexual attraction to patients (Chapter 5).
5. Ways in which therapists overcome internal inhibitions, external constraints and patient resistance to abuse, including boundary violations (Chapter 5).
6. Self-regulation and consultation as means of controlling potential abusive behaviour (Chapter 6).
7. Psychological characteristics that render patients vulnerable to abuse, including the nature and management of sexual attraction to therapists (Chapter 7).
8. Psychological problems experienced by patients abused in therapy (Chapter 8).
9. Treatment of victimized patients (Chapter 9).
10. Regulatory provisions and sanctions (Chapters 10 and 11), together with the practical issues of dealing with allegations by victimized patients, confronting and, if appropriate, reporting offending colleagues.
11. Ways of reducing the prevalence of sexual abuse in therapy (Chapter 12).

Presentation Rather than being presented in a purely didactic manner, it is important that there are opportunities for the sensitive issues in such a curriculum to be discussed in small groups, and for victim empathy training, as described for offenders in Chapter 6 and suitably modified for trainees. Pope, Keith-Spiegel & Tabachnick (1986) make the additional valuable points that coverage of topics such as sexual attraction to patients "must not be limited to a one-hour lecture, set apart from the 'normal' curriculum. Education regarding this topic can be an appropriate part of almost all clinical . . . coursework and training" (p. 156), and that "programs must provide a safe environment in which therapists in training can acknowledge, explore, and discuss feelings of sexual attraction. If students find or suspect that their teachers are critical and rejecting of such feelings and that such feelings are treated as a sign of an impaired or erring therapist, then effective education is unlikely" (p. 157).

Role models There is some indication that trainees who have been sexually involved with their educators, including clinical supervisors (Bartell & Rubin, 1990), may be more likely to enter into sexual relationships with patients. As shown in Table 12.1, sexual contact between educators and trainees is not infrequent, and it may have increased in recent years (Glaser & Thorpe, 1986; Pope, Levenson & Schover, 1979). In the survey of psychologists conducted by Pope, Levenson & Schover (1979), 23% of the women who as students had sexual contact with educators reported later sexual contact in their roles as professionals (although the extent to which this was with patients is not specified), in contrast to 6% of those women who had not been sexually involved with educators. The number of men who had been sexually involved with educators was too small to test for a similar significant difference. The sexualization of relationships between educators and trainees may have the additional adverse effect of inhibiting the discussion of matters such as sexual feelings in therapy. Trainees may fear that raising such matters might be construed as provocative or seductive by educators. An association between educator–trainee sex and therapist–patient sex is not necessarily causal; both might arise from third factors such as personality characteristics or lifestyles. To the extent, however, that educator–trainee sexual relationships do contribute to the subsequent abuse of patients by these trainees, then it follows that any decrease in educator–trainee relationships that can be attained might serve to prevent the occurrence of some abuse of patients.

Table 12.1:   Sexual Contact Between Educators and Graduate Students of Clinical Psychology

Source	Gender of informants	Proportion reporting contact (%)
Students reporting contact		
Pope, Levenson & Schover (1979)	Female	16
	Male	3
Glaser & Thorpe (1986)	Female	17
Educators reporting contact		
Pope, Levenson & Schover (1979)	Female	8
	Male	19

Clinical supervision

Effective clinical supervision of trainees and practitioners can help to prevent the sexual abuse of patients by identifying and responding to the risk characteristics and preconditions discussed in Chapter 5 (see also Schoener, 1989c; Schoener & Conroe, 1989), including:

1. Personal distress.
2. Misuse of drugs or alcohol.
3. Sexual or emotional attraction to patients.
4. Distorted perceptions and feelings about the sexual abuse of patients.
5. Violation of boundaries.
6. Personality problems involving narcissism, power or antisocial behaviour.

Appropriate supervisory responses to signs of such problems range through confrontation, discussion, advice, intensifying supervision, remedial education, treatment, restricting or "counselling out" of therapeutic practice, termination of employment and reporting to regulatory bodies.

Prevention through employers

Schoener (1989g) has identified several ways in which employers can help to prevent the sexual abuse of patients, which are incorporated into an Administrative Safeguards Checklist on which this section is based.

Appointment of therapists

Because of the appreciable risk of serial offending (part II), it is particularly important that employers ensure that their selection processes enable them to identify applicants who have been the subject of any form of regulatory action (Chapters 10, 11) or who have resigned or been dismissed prior to the resolution of such actions (Gonsiorek, 1989c). This information can then be taken into account when the current job application is being considered so that unsuitable therapists are not appointed.

Sexual conduct of therapists

Employers should have clear written policies on the standards of sexual conduct required of therapists in matters such as sexual or romantic relationships with patients and former patients and the sexual harassment of other members of staff. This responsibility might be discharged by employers requiring therapists to undertake to comply with the codes of conduct of the professions of which they are members, always providing that the code concerned is sufficiently explicit on the relevant requirements.

Education of therapists

Copies of written policies concerning sexual conduct and other matters discussed below should be given to each therapist; new employees will need to be orientated to these policies, and there should be regular periodic training sessions to support their implementation, as well as special sessions to consider what can be learned from any incidents of misconduct that have occurred.

Supervision of therapists

Particularly for the reasons discussed above, clinical supervision can help to prevent the sexual abuse of patients, and employers should ensure that it is available to therapists and operating effectively.

Feedback from patients

Another way in which employers may contribute to the prevention of sexual abuse in therapy is by routinely obtaining feedback from current and former patients on the satisfactoriness of their treatment experiences. Such inquiries might facilitate complaints of misconduct from some patients who would not otherwise disclose.

Complaints by patients

Finally, in case the above preventive measures fail and a patient is sexually abused, employers need to ensure that written policies and procedures are in place so that complaints are received and properly handled. These need to cover thanking, reassuring and supporting patients, regardless of the apparent validity of their complaints; helping them to obtain independent advice and resources; when necessary the suspension of therapists until cases are resolved; investigatory procedures; referral to prosecuting or professional bodies if appropriate; and keeping patients informed about the progress and outcome of their complaints.

Prevention through patients

Finally, consumer education has an important preventive function. Patients may be able to avoid being abused if they are sufficiently well informed. Commonly, however, they do not know whether their therapist is behaving appropriately, they are not aware of warning signs that could alert them to the risk of abuse, and if this materializes they are unfamiliar with the responses, including the complaint options, open to them.

Content of consumer education

What constitutes abuse?   Many patients do not know what behaviour by their therapists is inappropriate and sexually abusive. Thus, the information on this topic in part I needs to be communicated to patients in readily understandable ways, as is attempted in several of the sources of consumer education reviewed below.

Warning signs   If patients are made aware of these signs they could be alerted to the risk of abuse and perhaps implement some action to avoid it, as discussed below. The nature of the signs is indicated in Chapter 5 in the section on how therapists overcome the resistance of patients by means of boundary violations, persuasive communications, exploitation of the therapeutic relationship and encouraging the misuse of drugs or alcohol. They have also been incorporated in checklists for patients, for example by Pope & Bouhoutsos (1986, appendix B) and Schoener et al (1989, appendix Z). Often warning signs will evoke feelings of confusion, discomfort, apprehension or guilt in patients, and such feelings are important indicators to them that something is amiss in their treatment.

Response options   Finally, patients need to know the options available to them in response to potential or actual abuse by their therapists, including:

1. Asking the therapist to explain his behaviour.
2. Checking this out with someone else, perhaps a friend, self-help group (see below), another therapist or professional organization.
3. Confronting the therapist and ending the sexual activity.
4. Suspending or terminating therapy.
5. Changing to another therapist.
6. Instigating some form of regulatory action (Chapters 10 and 11).

It must be recognized, however, that knowledge of these options will not in itself enable all patients to exercise them. They may well find it difficult to do so because they blame themselves for the abuse, believing that they must have been provocative and seductive, they may feel helpless and quite incapable of resisting victimization, or they may be sorry for the therapist and not wish to cause him distress or damage.

Sources of consumer education

The above content can be communicated to patients in ways which include consumer guides, self-help groups and the media.

Consumer guides   The literature on such guides to therapy generally and more specifically to sexual relationships between therapists and patients is reviewed by Schoener (1989d). The latter includes leaflets prepared for patients in the

U.S. (e.g. Committee on Women in Psychology, 1989; Schoener et al, 1989, appendix Z) and the U.K. (e.g. MIND, n.d.). The topics covered in the most comprehensive of these (Committee on Women in Psychology, 1989) are:

1. Is it ethical for a therapist to have sexual contact with a patient?
2. Why is sexual contact bad for a therapy relationship?
3. What is sexual contact in therapy?
4. What about your falling in love with your therapist?
5. Should you end therapy in order to have a sexual relationship with your therapist?
6. What can you do if you feel uneasy about your therapist's sexually orientated behaviour toward you?
7. What are your options if you feel that your therapist has not acted appropriately?
8. What can you do to resolve your emotional concerns about taking action against your former therapist?
9. What can you do to resolve your emotional concerns about your experience?

The provision of such a consumer guide to all new patients might well help to prevent some incidents of abuse in therapy.

Self-help groups   Groups of and for victims have a valuable preventive role in so far as they inform patients about sexual abuse in therapy and support their efforts to respond to it effectively. In the U.S. there are groups such as the Association of Psychologically Abused Patients (APAP, PO Box 9682, Fort Worth, Texas 76147, Tel: 817-732-6565), which, together with several others, is reviewed by Schoener (1989d). The major self-help group for victimized patients in the U.K. is the Prevention of Professional Abuse Network (POPAN, Flat 1, 20 Daleham Gardens, Hampstead, London NW3 5DA, Tel: 071-794-3177).

Media sources   Finally, a contribution to consumer education and hopefully to the prevention of abuse is made through the media in the form of articles and advice columns in newspapers and magazines (Schoener, 1989d) and radio and television programmes. The attention given to sexual abuse in therapy by these media sources has increased very considerably in recent years.

Conclusion

The primary prevention of sexual abuse in therapy may be mediated through therapists, employers and patients. Some contribution to prevention is likely to be made through therapists by the threat of regulatory sanctions, use of self-regulation and consultative processes, improvements in selection and training in professional education, and effective clinical supervision.

Employers may help to prevent abuse by arranging suitable selection processes to appoint therapists, having clear policies on the sexual conduct required of them, ensuring that they receive adequate education and clinical supervision, and instituting appropriate procedures to elicit feedback from patients on their treatment and for handling any complaints from them.

Patients themselves may prevent abuse if they receive adequate consumer education on what constitutes abuse, its warning signs and the response options available to them. This information may be provided in consumer guides, self-help groups and media sources.

It is not known how effective these measures might be in preventing abuse but their face validity is such that they are certainly worth implementing and evaluating.

Appendix A
Questionnaire mailed to respondents

Today's date . . . .

Please attempt to answer *all* questions (but
see covering letter)

SECTION ONE

1. Please give your sex (Tick one box)   ☐ MALE   ☐ FEMALE

2. Please give your age   . . YEARS

3. Are you (Tick as many boxes as apply)
   ☐ SINGLE
   ☐ IN A STABLE RELATIONSHIP
   ☐ MARRIED
   ☐ SEPARATED/DIVORCED
   ☐ WIDOWED

4. How would you identify your sexual
   orientation? (Tick one box)
   ☐ HETEROSEXUAL
   ☐ HOMOSEXUAL
   ☐ BISEXUAL

5. In *total*, how many years have you   . . YEARS
   practised as a Clinical Psychologist since
   qualifying?

6. How would you describe your therapeutic
   orientation? (Please indicate the 3
   orientations which *most influence* your
   practice, where 1 = most influence, 2 =
   moderate influence, 3 = least influence, by
   numbering 3 boxes).
   ☐ BEHAVIOURAL
   ☐ COGNITIVE
   ☐ PSYCHODYNAMIC/ANALYTIC
   ☐ SYSTEMIC
   ☐ HUMANISTIC
   ☐ OTHER (Please specify) . . . .

7. What is your *main* area of clinical work?
   (Tick one box)
   ☐ ADULTS
   ☐ CHILDREN AND YOUNG PEOPLE
   ☐ LEARNING DIFFICULTIES
   ☐ ELDERLY
   ☐ PHYSICAL HEALTH
   ☐ NEUROPSYCHOLOGY
   ☐ OTHER (Please specify) . . . .

8. How many hours per week on average do   . . . . hrs
   you spend in face to face patient contact?

9. With what proportion of your patients do   . . . . . %
   you have *long term* therapeutic contact
   (i.e. over 50 sessions)?

10. With what proportion of your patients do   . . . . . %
    you have *brief* therapeutic contact (i.e.
    less than 20 sessions)?

11. What is your *main* work setting? (Tick one
    box)
    ☐ NATIONAL HEALTH SERVICE
    ☐ PRIVATE PRACTICE
    ☐ SOCIAL SERVICES
    ☐ VOLUNTARY AGENCY
    ☐ OTHER (Please specify) . . . .

12. Have you in the past undertaken, or   ☐ YES   ☐ NO
    are you currently undertaking, personal
    therapy? (Tick one box)

SECTION TWO

1. Have you ever engaged in the following
    types of physical contact with any of your
    patients? (Tick as many boxes as apply)

    MALE PATIENTS   ☐ HANDSHAKE
                                                 ☐ PATTING ON ARM
                                                 ☐ HOLDING HAND(S)
                                                 ☐ TOUCHING ARM/SHOULDER ETC.
                                                 ☐ HUGGING
                                                 ☐ OTHER (Please specify) . . . .

    FEMALE PATIENTS   ☐ HANDSHAKE
                                                 ☐ PATTING ON ARM
                                                 ☐ HOLDING HAND(S)
                                                 ☐ TOUCHING ARM/SHOULDER,
                                                   ETC.
                                                 ☐ HUGGING
                                                 ☐ OTHER (Please specify) . . . .

2. Have you ever felt sexually attracted to   ☐ YES   ☐ NO
    one of your patients? (Tick one box)

3. If YES, go to Q4

    If NO, why not?   . . . .

Now go to *SECTION THREE*

4. Please recall the last occasion when you   . . . .
    were sexually attracted to one of your
    patients

    a) How do you feel *NOW* about this   ☐ CONCERNED
    attraction? (Tick one box)   ☐ UNCONCERNED

    b) How, if at all, do you think this   ☐ MAINLY ADVERSE EFFECTS
    attraction affected/is affecting the therapy ☐ LITTLE OR NO EFFECT
    process? (Tick one box)   ☐ MAINLY POSITIVE EFFECTS

SECTION THREE

1. Do you believe that patients can ever   ☐ YES   ☐ NO
    benefit from sexual contact with a
    therapist? (Tick one box)

2. Have you ever had what you regard as   ☐ YES   ☐ NO
    sexual contact with one of your patients,
    no matter whether *current* or *discharged*?
    (Tick one box)

3. If YES, go to Q4

    If NO, what has stopped you?   . . . .
                                                 . . . .

Now go to *SECTION FOUR*

4. a) With approximately how many patients
    have you had sexual contact?

    . . . .

    b) Aggregating all the patients with whom
    you have had sexual contact (if more than
    one), please estimate the total number of
    occasions on which you have had sexual
    contact with patients in your lifetime

    . . . . . OCCASIONS

    c) With how many patients have you had
    sexual contact that commenced after you
    had discharged the patient?

    . . . .

    d) With how many patients have you had
    sexual contact that commenced while the
    patient was in therapy with you?

    . . . .

    e) When have sexual contacts with
    patients who were/are *current* occurred?
    (Tick one box)

    ☐ ONLY WITHIN THERAPY
       SESSIONS
    ☐ ONLY OUTSIDE THERAPY
       SESSIONS
    ☐ BOTH WITHIN AND OUTSIDE
       THERAPY SESSIONS
    ☐ NO SUCH CONTACTS

    f) Prior to completing this questionnaire,
    have you ever disclosed a sexual contact
    with a patient to any of the following?
    (Tick as many boxes as apply)

    ☐ COLLEAGUE
    ☐ MANAGER
    ☐ SUPERVISOR
    ☐ FRIEND/PARTNER
    ☐ ANOTHER PATIENT
    ☐ PERSONAL THERAPIST
    ☐ OTHER (Please specify) . . . .
    ☐ NO SUCH DISCLOSURE

    g) Please consider your most recent
    sexual contact with a patient (if there has
    been more than one)

    i) Please specify this patient's sex (Tick
    one box)

    ☐ MALE   ☐ FEMALE

    ii) Please specify this patient's age

    . . . . . . YRS

    iii) Please specify what forms of sexual
    contact have occurred between you
    and the patient (Tick as many boxes
    as apply)

    ☐ KISSING
    ☐ NON-GENITAL
       TOUCHING/HOLDING/FONDLING
    ☐ HAND–GENITAL CONTACT
    ☐ VAGINAL INTERCOURSE
    ☐ ORAL–GENITAL CONTACT
    ☐ ANAL PENETRATION
    ☐ OTHER (Please specify) . . . .

    iv) Did/does the patient give full consent
    to these contacts? (Tick one box)

    ☐ YES ☐ NO ☐ SOMETIMES

    v) Did/does the contact involve an aim of
    inflicting physical pain on the patient?
    (Tick one box)

    ☐ YES ☐ NO ☐ SOMETIMES

vi) Please specify the length of your
sexual involvement with this patient (Tick
one box)

- ☐ ONE SEXUAL ENCOUNTER
- ☐ LESS THAN 3 MONTHS
- ☐ 3–11 MONTHS
- ☐ 1–5 YEARS
- ☐ MORE THAN 5 YEARS

vii) What is the current status of your
involvement with this patient? (Tick one
box)

- ☐ NO CONTACT WHATSOEVER
- ☐ CONTINUED THERAPEUTIC
  CONTACT, NO SEXUAL CONTACT
- ☐ CONTINUED SEXUAL CONTACT,
  NO THERAPEUTIC CONTACT
- ☐ CONTINUED SOCIAL CONTACT,
  BUT NO SEXUAL OR
  THERAPEUTIC CONTACT
- ☐ CONTINUED THERAPEUTIC
  AND SEXUAL CONTACT WITH
  THE PATIENT
- ☐ MARRIED TO, OR IN A
  COMMITTED RELATIONSHIP
  WITH THE PATIENT

viii) How did you come to be sexually
involved with this patient?

. . . .
. . . .

ix) What effects do you think this sexual
involvement had/is having on the patient?

. . . .

x) How do you feel *NOW* about this
sexual involvement? (Tick one box)

- ☐ CONCERNED
- ☐ UNCONCERNED

xi) Who initiated this sexual involvement?
(Tick one box)

☐ SELF   ☐ PATIENT   ☐ MUTUAL

xii) What steps, if any, did you take to
dissuade this patient from reporting or
disclosing their sexual contact with you?

. . . .
. . . .

SECTION FOUR

1. Do you believe that a student/trainee
   psychologist can ever benefit from sexual
   contact with a lecturer/supervisor? (Tick
   one box)

   ☐ YES   ☐ NO

2. During your *undergraduate training*, did
   you ever have sexual contact with a
   lecturer/tutor? (Tick one box)

   ☐ YES   ☐NO

3. During your *postgraduate clinical training*,
   did you ever have sexual contact with a
   lecturer/tutor/supervisor? (Tick one box)

   ☐ YES   ☐ NO

4. If you have had/are currently having
   personal therapy, have you ever had
   sexual contact with your therapist(s)?
   (Tick one box)

   ☐ YES   ☐ NO
   ☐ NOT APPLICABLE

5. If you are a lecturer/supervisor, have you   ☐ YES ☐ NO
    ever had sexual contact with one of your   ☐ NOT APPLICABLE
    student/trainee psychologists (including
    undergraduates)? (Tick one box)

SECTION FIVE

1. To your knowledge, have you ever treated   ☐ YES ☐ NO
    any patients who have had sexual contact
    with previous therapists? (Tick one box)

If NO, go to *SECTION SIX*

2. What was/were the profession(s) of the   ☐ CLINICAL PSYCHOLOGIST
    previous therapist(s)? (Tick as many   ☐ PSYCHIATRIST
    boxes as apply)   ☐ SOCIAL WORKER
                                                   ☐ NURSE
                                                   ☐ VOLUNTARY AGENCY THERAPIST
                                                   ☐ PRIVATE SECTOR
                                                       PSYCHOTHERAPIST
                                                   ☐ COUNSELLOR
                                                   ☐ OTHER (Please specify)
                                                   ☐ DO NOT KNOW

3. Overall, how would you rate the effects of   ☐ POSITIVE ☐ MIXED
    the sexual contact(s) on the patient(s)?   ☐ NEGATIVE
    (Tick one box)

4. Approximately how many of the therapists   NUMBER REPORTED . . . .
    were reported to their employer,   NUMBER NOT REPORTED . . . . .
    professional body, official agency, etc.?   NUMBER UNCERTAIN . . . .

SECTION SIX

1. Do you know through sources other than   ☐ YES ☐ NO
    your own patients, of clinical psychologists
    who have been sexually involved with their
    patients? (Tick one box)

If NO, go to *SECTION SEVEN*

2. How many such clinical psychologists do   . . . .
    you know of?

3. Was/were the psychologist(s) reported to   NUMBER REPORTED . . . .
    their employer, BPS, official agency, etc.?   NUMBER NOT REPORTED . . . . .
                                                   NUMBER UNCERTAIN . . . .

4. a) To your knowledge, how many   . . . .
    psychologists were sexually involved with
    only one patient?

    b) To your knowledge, how many   . . . .
    psychologists were sexually involved with
    more than one patient?

5. Have you taken any action to prevent the
    continuation of such contacts, for example
    to report a contact or to discuss the
    matter with the psychologist concerned?
    (Tick one box)

    ☐ YES   ☐ NO

    If NO, why not?

    . . . .

    . . . .

SECTION SEVEN

1. Any further comments

    . . . .

    . . . .

    . . . .

    . . . .

Appendix B
Autobiographical account

Fourteen years ago I sought help from a counsellor for relationship problems and depression. I had been living in a long-standing relationship with a man, but the relationship had been unsatisfactory for some time. I felt he no longer loved or respected me, but I still loved him and needed him. At the time, we were living separately because his employment took him to another town. We still came together at weekends and for holidays. I was unable to find a job in the area to which he had moved because I was recovering from surgery. My partner had blamed problems with his employment for our deteriorating relationship and had indicated that a change of job would bring a fresh start for us, but over the months of our partial separation, I became disillusioned and increasingly depressed. I felt unable to make the move, away from friends, family and job without any sense of security that my partner would give me love and support, but neither could I contemplate life without him.

I work in a "helping profession" myself and found it very difficult to admit that I was unable to cope with my own problems and seek help. However, I plucked up courage and saw a counsellor at a local counselling agency. Initially, my counsellor was a social work student on placement; subsequently he obtained employment at the agency and continued as my counsellor. As far as I know at that time his only qualification was a Certificate of Qualification in Social Work, but he is now described as a psychosexual counsellor!

The first few weeks of the counselling were very successful; after only a couple of sessions I started to feel the depression lifting. After a couple of months I started to see myself in a more positive light, my health improved, and I told my partner that I had no immediate plans to move to where he now lived. Meanwhile, I felt so grateful to the counsellor, that when he told me he needed to find alternative accommodation, (his training course and home were in another town), I told him about a vacant flat in the building where I lived.

I had strong transference feelings, which we discussed in a counselling session; he told me that our relationship was a professional one, and that it could not and would not become a sexual relationship. Although I had learned about transference in my professional training, I was quite unprepared for the strength of these feelings.

My sessions were always in the evening because I was working during the day. The building was, I think empty, and certainly no one else was around by the time we left. I expressed to the counsellor my feelings of loneliness without my partner, and my difficulty in meeting new people. After being part of a couple for so long, I found it difficult to operate as a single person socially, especially as I felt I was not "free". I still had a partner even though we didn't live together. My counsellor's response was to invite me to join him in the pub after the session, and this went on for a few weeks.

My partner started to show some interest in me again. My hopes were raised that our relationship could improve. The counsellor offered to see us together, which meant putting himself out as my partner was only in town at weekends. We had one session with the counsellor together. Somewhere around that time, the counsellor told me he'd obtained tenancy of the flat I'd told him about. It had been several weeks, and I'd put it out of my mind, but it dawned on me that it would be difficult living in close proximity to him. At a later session, he informed me he'd had some furniture delivered and asked me for a lift back to the flats. He asked to borrow a screwdriver and for some help putting a bed together. Then he asked if he could come and see my flat. He looked round, had a drink and announced he'd forgotten or lost his keys and wouldn't be able to get into his then current bedsit, which was some distance away. His "new" flat had been unoccupied for some time during the winter and was cold and damp. I offered him a sleeping bag on my living room floor and set out cushions as a makeshift mattress. I had noticed extra interest from some male friends since I'd been living separately from my partner, but if they stayed too late, I asked them to leave, and they did. There was never any hassle. I had even more reason to trust this man, who was my counsellor. He'd told me our relationship was professional, that it would not become a sexual relationship. I believed him. He turned out to be the one man I couldn't trust. He raped me in my own home, in my own bed. It wasn't violent—there was no need. I was in bed, undressed, and I trusted him. I couldn't believe what was happening. I didn't sleep at all that night. I begged him not to leave me alone to cope with what I now realize was a very traumatic experience. I can't find the words to describe it.

He came back to my flat again the next night. I felt so dependent on him, I felt in a state of shock, I was frightened of losing him altogether, but I really didn't know how to cope with the situation—I was having an affair, being unfaithful to my partner, with a counsellor we'd seen together as a couple. It was impossible for me to resolve this situation alone. I fell hopelessly in love with the counsellor—the most intense emotional experience I can remember. It was like being swept out to sea by a tidal wave, losing sight of land and all reference points.

My partner knew something was wrong. I admitted to having an affair, but not with whom. He threatened to kill or injure my lover. I twice tried to break off the relationship with the counsellor, but each time I went back. He was too close by, I couldn't avoid him. And I was so alone, so isolated. I couldn't talk to anyone; I was so afraid he would lose his job, that I would lose him, that I couldn't cope without him. But of course, I had lost the therapeutic relationship I had valued so much. I wanted to see another counsellor but my original counsellor warned me that our relationship would come out and he would lose his job—I couldn't face that responsibility or loss. I also somehow felt guilty because I was a professional myself, I knew our relationship was unethical, and I felt responsible for colluding. For several months, I continued in both relationships, but pretended to my partner that the affair was over. It was all unbelievably stressful. The counsellor was trying to move in with me. I was afraid someone would guess and tell my partner; the consequences were too horrendous to contemplate. I couldn't sort out the relationship one way or another with my partner while this intense affair was going on. I needed to establish my own identity, independence and social life but this was difficult to do while keeping this secret, when he might pop up any time or stay when he wasn't wanted. He was jealous—of my partner, of other male friends. I felt paralysed and unable to resolve the situation.

The "relationship" was not entirely negative. He could be very loving and affectionate. He was a good listener, but there were now "no go" areas. I experienced good sex for the first time and he helped to build up my confidence. But he was also extremely manipulative, using information gained in counselling sessions to criticize and undermine me, especially as I became more independent of him. He told me lies and tried to stop me from seeing people whom I presume he found threatening. I tried hard to make the relationship work, but we shared few interests. We met his supervisor socially; he told me she was aware I had been a client. He wanted to "go public" with the relationship, even asked me to marry him, but for me he was denying the origins and reality of our relationship; his lack of honesty made the relationship unviable for me. I knew it couldn't last; as well as having little in common so much of his behaviour was unacceptable to me.

It was over a year before I broke off the relationship with my partner. There was no way, it seemed, we could have a good relationship now. How could he ever forgive me for doing such a terrible thing? I couldn't possibly keep that secret in a relationship, not the sort of relationship I wanted. It was another nine months before I could break off the relationship with the counsellor. I had other family problems to cope with, including the death of my father. I couldn't cope alone, and I couldn't cope with ending the relationship until other parts of my life had calmed down. Keeping the relationship secret isolated me from support and love from others, making me even more dependent on him.

I lost three important relationships within one year. Soon after breaking up with the counsellor, I became ill. I suffered from viral illnesses and post-viral fatigue syndrome when I'd never previously had so much as 'flu. The last one left me with a chronic illness. I don't know how far the abuse and the illness are connected, but my current therapist and a therapist from the Prevention of Professional Abuse Network (POPAN) think they are.

It wasn't until a year and a half ago that I told anyone about this experience. It was all I could do at the time to get him out of my life, it didn't occur to me to complain. I thought that because I'd colluded and had a relationship with him for two years, I would be blamed and that any complaint wouldn't be taken seriously. I kept it a secret, I didn't want anyone to know, I felt foolish and weak for allowing it to happen. I was afraid of being professionally embarrassed if our relationship became known to my colleagues.

It's only since I shared this with another counsellor/therapist that I've come to see the experience as abuse. I feel less responsible now and less guilty. Having met other women abused by therapists and knowing that this man is working with vulnerable people, I feel I should do something to protect others. When I challenged him after we'd split up, about having a relationship with a client, he said I was "very gullible" and still took no responsibility for his unethical behaviour.

I have telephoned the counselling agency. They have no written complaints procedure. I would have to tell my story to the supervisor, then to the committee chair (who could well be someone I know professionally) and possibly to a tribunal. I'm trying to pluck up courage, but I haven't been able to face it yet. I still fear professional embarrassment and not being believed. It's still difficult to reconcile my feelings of intense love, of being loved, when I so desperately needed love, and of being abused. It's very, very complicated, and excruciatingly painful. When I started telling my current therapist and working on this, I became deeply depressed for a couple of months. When I have therapy sessions or talk to my new partner about it, I have sleepless nights, 14 years on. I don't know if I have the strength to go through with a complaint. I'm afraid of becoming depressed, of being unable to function in my job, of being "found out".

It has been very disturbing to recall these events and feelings, but I hope my account will help to draw attention to the damage and distress caused by abuse by therapists. I hope also that professional organizations such as the British

Association of Counselling and agencies that provide direct counselling services will give greater consideration to the needs of those abused in their complaints procedures.

Appendix C
Autobiographical account

In 1976 I battered my son, then aged three. At the school where I taught it had been a difficult year. My son had had three illnesses: whooping cough, measles and chicken-pox. My pupils, or rather some of them, had jeered at me for being unattractive and divorced. As usual I had been unable to make my son go to bed and in despair had repeatedly kicked the back of his pedal car, bruising his back. I was immediately horrified. In desperation I rang my father, a medical official in London, and he came early the next morning. He took charge of the situation and decided that the first priority was my keeping my job. The episode was kept from my school and my son's nursery. A health visitor was called in to keep an eye on me. My parents had my son for a month to give me a rest. He was not seriously hurt. I insisted on an X-ray to make sure. There was more concern for my state of mind, so a psychiatrist was called in privately. He came to my home instead of making an appointment at his consulting room.

So, Dr A arrived. He was about 50, no gift to look at but slim and with a glib manner. He was in my house for less than half an hour and asked very few questions. He was little interested in the now transmitted parenting difficulties caused by my mother's early insanity, rejection of me and subsequent suicide, or in my immediate overwhelming practical and disciplinary problems, or my wish to get my life on some sort of better basis than it had been in my relationship with my ex-husband, whom I had got rid of when my son was eight months old. Dr A's interest in my marriage was less about our relationship in general, or the fact that my ex-husband had not worked, than in our sexual relationship. He asked how we had got on in bed. Even at such a time the oddness of the question struck me. I replied that our sex life had never been much good. How often had I had an orgasm? "Never", was the answer. Dr A nearly fell out of his chair, "You poor thing". Soon afterwards he concluded the interview with the statement that he did not think that my case was very serious but would recommend the prescribing of three brands of tranquillizers and a course of high oestrogen tablets. He left after arranging a further appointment, this time at his consulting room.

Dutifully I took the prescription to my G.P., Dr B, a gruff elderly man who held little truck with mental illness, let alone nervous disturbance; he had not thought my son's bruises more serious than the shakings inflicted on half the children in the country. He read out Dr A's letter. In this it was claimed that in addition to the tranquillizers, I needed the contraceptive pill for menstrual pains which contributed to my exasperation with my son. I exclaimed, "But I don't get menstrual pains". Dr B asked, "Are you calling Dr A a liar then?" Puzzled, I subsided, took the prescription and in due course swallowed the pills and tablets. I positively rattled with them. The drugs and the absence of my son for a month enabled me to relax, have proper meals and fill out from my stone underweight to my normal few pounds overweight. I kept my appointment with Dr A. He patted me and said he would come round "for a talk". I thought that this was a euphemism for making sure that I was not sticking my head in the gas oven. The health visitor, a very nice and helpful woman, had used the same phrase.

Dr A came round on a Friday night. He brought a bottle of wine and made conversation. After a while he took my hand in his and said what a nice little hand it was. I was full of the cares of the week and my situation. He talked of giving me driving lessons and helping me with babysitting. The thought that he might be on the make crossed my mind, but it seemed incredible. As a doctor, my father had had to discourage women admirers. Subconsciously, I assumed that all doctors were either unmoved or scrupulous where their patients were concerned.

A few weeks later Dr A came again. By this time the new term had started. I was now being plagued by an older girl who continually told me in many ways that I could not get a man to take me out and that it was therefore beneath her dignity to learn history from someone like me, deserted by her husband and having to work to support her son and herself instead of getting another husband. It only occurred to me years later that Dr A probably thought that this girl was a fiction conjured up to convey the message, "If you want to screw me, you'll have to take me out, and properly. I come more expensive than a drink in front of the T.V." So he suggested that we go out. To my enquiry about his marital status, he replied that he was separated and spent most of the week at a flatlet in his elderly mother's house in Bristol. His wife and sons lived in the area but not with him. Thus reassured, I agreed to go out with him—but insisted on first being pronounced cured in order to avoid technical professional impropriety.

My motives for agreeing were mixed. I was lonely and virtually cut off from social contact by my domestic situation. It was possible, though difficult, to obtain babysitters. I had no circle of friends to go out with. In any case, I had for the first three years of my son's life felt exhausted. I certainly needed someone to make me feel attractive. And my attitude to Dr A? His clothes were from Aquascutum and he was socially presentable. The idea of going round in a car was irresistible. I expected a medium-term supportive relationship—in a word, company—and for this I was prepared to have sex. For Dr A as a man I had no real desire. In my heart I knew that the intended liaison was wrong. Otherwise I would have let Dr B and my family know. If the relationship had worked out, then, and only then, would I have told them.

Dr A took me for a drive and then for a meal. It was rather a hurried ritual. There were some surprises. He made it obvious that he had a hearty contempt for many of his patients and little human sympathy for any of them. A simple mechanistic approach to treatment was his favourite one. For many of his patients, he thought, the best place was a mental hospital. Indeed, this simplicity was apparent in more personal judgements. He boasted that he was one of the three best psychiatrists in the city and an expert in dealing with the cases of drunks, shoplifters and prostitutes. Of one of these ladies he spoke admiringly: "Ten children and still slim!" Now I wonder, did she pay in kind for his professional services? Still, he was amusing, entertaining and flattering—and I was out of the house. The evening perked me up no end. When we got back to my house and he became demonstrative, I said truthfully that it was my menstrual period. It was clear that he did not entirely believe me. After a relatively chaste goodnight kiss, he departed.

The next time he had clearly decided to make a big investment; he bought a huge box of chocolates and took me, on already booked tickets, to a film. This was followed by a lot of drinks. I was willing to give him his return on his investment but when I was already half-undressed the mixture of chocolates and sherry overcame me and I had to retire to the bathroom to be sick while Dr A took his leave.

A couple of Fridays later he came again. This time he telephoned first and said he would be round in an hour. He told me not to bother to get a babysitter; we would just stay in. Bottle in hand, he appeared and made conversation. We had sex, in my case for the first time for years. It was not physically exciting. Then we had a cup of tea and he left, saying he had the Saturday morning shift at the mental hospital where he worked part-time.

As soon as Dr A had sex with me the relationship changed. He stopped taking me out. Claiming that he was snowed under with work, he made it clear that weekends were out of the question. This was depressing as a single mother feels her isolation and immobility most at the weekends. But Dr A knew that my particular condition—fear of one-to-one confrontation, which had brought all my domestic and professional problems on me since childhood—would prevent me from putting my views and interests forward. Of course, his attitude made sex at first indifferent, then distasteful. He could not understand why I did not think it worth going to bed to make love, instead of doing so on the sofa. From my point of view, twenty minutes were not worth remaking the bed for. Although he was always somewhat mechanical and rushed, he never realized how unarousing he was. The situation had its built-in compensations; if one isn't aroused, one can't be disappointed or frustrated.

His idea was that he should come round for a couple of hours every other week with drink, have some chat, screw me and then, within half an hour of screwing me, go away—just as he had hoped to do in the first place without the tiresome palaver and expense of actually taking me out and giving me the impression that we were kindred souls who just happened to have met through his job. His visits developed a pattern; he was always dropping in to see me on the way from one appointment or engagement to another, or before going home to his mother's house for an early night. Glancing at his watch, gulping his tea down and telling me how pretty I was constituted his passionate farewell. No doubt he thought that the brilliance of his lovemaking reconciled me to this. To be fair, he sometimes brought a couple of chicken legs or a small box of chocolates.

On one occasion Dr A was even more perfunctory than usual. For me, sex was definitely unpleasant. My suspicions about the reason for the haste of his visits was hardening. I tried to phone him at his alleged home, which I had never done before. The voice of a youngish woman replied. The set-up was obvious. I still feared confrontation. As I debated with myself what to do, or rather how to get rid of him tactfully and discreetly, he rang to say that he would be round on his way back from a social engagement. At ten o'clock he had still not arrived so I locked up and got ready for bed. There was a great banging on the door. I opened it and let him in. He had obviously had a few drinks. At such an hour he could spend little time on the attempted establishment of the appropriate mood. Passively, I let him have me; anything to avoid a scene. I was stiff with revulsion. He felt my nipple. It was hard with my disgust and self-disgust. But he seemed to think it was excitement and continued. After the usual cup of tea he left with the usual speech about having to get up early the next day. He had been in my house for one hour and twenty minutes. It was the most revolting sexual experience I had ever had—and many of them have been gruesome. Despite the lateness of the hour I immediately had a bath and washed my hair. I also washed and disinfected the nightdress and dressing-gown I had been wearing. Neither of us had bothered to take them off. Later they were given to a jumble sale.

Now I was most anxious to get rid of Dr A. Paradoxically, he dimly perceived that he had behaved unacceptably and wrote offering to take me out to the cinema again or to come round on an evening of my choosing. I ignored the letter. Then he appeared unexpectedly in the early evening with a trug of strawberries. However, he found another man at my table, having a cup of tea and a cigarette. So he stammered something about coming again some other time and disappeared. In fact the strange man was only the painter but I did not explain. A few weeks later Dr A rang back to ask if I'd got a new boyfriend. I replied, "Yes", knowing that it was the only reason for dismissal that a man of his kind would respect. He responded as I had hoped: "You don't want me to come round any more?". With a brief, "No", I confirmed this, and that was it—the end of our contact. One could hardly call it a relationship.

To analyse the consequences and implications of the therapy offered by Dr A, one has first to state what his diagnosis, treatment and prognosis of my problem were. His diagnosis was that I was suffering from lack of intercourse and orgasm, his treatment was the provision of this by him and his prognosis was more of the same, from others as well, which would release him from carrying the whole burden while still nobly doing his bit if required. One might describe his approach as priming the pump.

The result of this medical assessment was that I hung on to a job virtually beyond my powers in view of my inability to handle my domestic situation. Jacked up and held together by tranquillizers, I struggled to maintain a pretence of coping. My son was not physically battered again, but he felt my tension and despair so deeply that his behaviour caused him to be sent first to a child guidance clinic and then to a special unit for disturbed children. He had four years of pain until I stopped work. He is still recovering. My relationship with Dr B and his colleagues was affected. I could not tell them what had happened. I feared their comments on my self-deception almost as much as I feared the legal action on which they might conscientiously have insisted. I could not ask for another psychiatrist. The habit of not speaking stuck.

Only when I was about to leave the area did I tell Dr C, one of Dr B's colleagues, who was not surprised, let alone incredulous. He told me that the practice had long stopped referring to Dr A (who had died recently) because patients sent to him had simply been dosed up with drugs then returned to the practice substantially uncured. In other words he had been making a good thing, financially and sexually, out of not doing his job.

Dr A had made a gross misdiagnosis, if one can call it that, of my particular case because he wanted sex. This misjudgement was in its turn based on his ignorance of what women wanted and how to give it to them. He thought of my sexual relationship with my ex-husband as completely separated from our general relationship, if indeed he thought of people having general relationships at all. He did not ask me why my husband had been unable to give me an orgasm or what had been done about it. Nor did he ask what I liked in bed, or rather on the sofa. He just assumed that with his expertise he could give even a comparative stranger a good time: the modern equivalent of the knight on a white horse? He did not consider the improbability of being able to learn enough about someone in two hours every fortnight to give her a thrill. He lied about his marital status—something I would never have expected from an educated man—and misrepresented the amount of time available for us to be together. He did not consider the age gap. He could not even tell whether I'd had or was on the way to having an orgasm. His need for sex and an ego-trip made him misread the situation and deceive himself. Yet on one level he knew he was deceiving himself about my needs. Otherwise he would have stated his assessment of them boldly and without flannel. In short, he behaved exactly like ordinary married men furtively on the make—the sort of men whose distressed wives he treated, or did not treat. In a way he must have known how ridiculous, conceited, inconsistent and unscrupulous he would have sounded in front of a law court or a G.M.C. disciplinary committee. He would have been not so much struck off as laughed off. It is disturbing to think of Dr A's influence on the lives of his other patients.

References

Abramson, L.Y., Seligman, M.P. & Teasdale, J. (1978). Learned helplessness in humans: Critique and reformulations, *Journal of Abnormal Psychology*, **87**, 49–74.

Akamatsu, T.J. (1988). Intimate relationships with former clients: National survey of attitudes and behavior among practitioners, *Professional Psychology: Research and Practice*, **19**, 454–458.

Albach, F. & Everaerd, W. (1992). Posttraumatic stress symptoms in victims of childhood incest, *Psychotherapy and Psychosomatics*, **57**, 143–151.

American Association for Marriage and Family Therapy (1988). *AAMFT code of ethical principles for marriage and family therapists*. AAMFT, Washington, D.C.

American Psychiatric Association (1980). *Diagnostic and Statistical Manual of Mental Disorders* (third edition). AMA, Washington, D.C.

American Psychiatric Association (1987). *Diagnostic and Statistical Manual of Mental Disorders* (third edition, revised). AMA, Washington, D.C.

American Psychiatric Association (1989). *The principles of medical ethics with annotations especially applicable to psychiatry*. AMA, Washington, D.C.

American Psychological Association (1992). Ethical principles of psychologists and code of conduct, *American Psychologist*, **47**, 1597–1611.

American Psychological Association Monitor (1987). Sex with ex-clients judged on intent of termination, June.

Appelbaum, P.S. & Jorgenson, L.M. (1991). Psychotherapist–patient sexual contact after termination of treatment: An analysis and a proposal, *American Journal of Psychiatry*, **148**, 1466–1473.

Armsworth, M.W. (1989). Therapy of incest survivors: Abuse or support? *Child Abuse and Neglect*, **13**, 549–562.

Armsworth, M.W. (1990). A qualitative analysis of adult incest survivors' responses to sexual involvement with therapists, *Child Abuse and Neglect*, **14**, 541–554.

Atkeson, B.M., Calhoun, K.S. & Morris, K.T. (1989). Victim resistance to rape: The relationship of previous victimization, demographics, and situational factors, *Archives of Sexual Behaviour*, **18**, 497–507.

Bancroft, J. (1989). *Human Sexuality and its Problems* (second edition). Churchill Livingstone, Edinburgh.

Bandura, A. (1977). *Social Learning Theory*. Prentice Hall, Englewood Cliffs, N.J.

Bandura, A. (1982). Self-efficacy mechanism in human agency, *American Psychologist*, **37**, 122–147.

Barlow, D.H. (Ed.) (1985). *Clinical Handbook of Psychological Disorders: A Step-by-Step Treatment Manual.* Guilford, New York.

Bartell, P.A. & Rubin, L.J. (1990). Dangerous liaisons: Sexual intimacies in supervision, *Professional Psychology: Research and Practice*, **21**, 442–450.

Bartlett, F.C. (1932). *Remembering.* Cambridge University Press, Cambridge.

Bass, E. & Davis, L. (1988). *The Courage to Heal: A Guide for Women Survivors of Child Sexual Abuse.* Harper & Row, New York.

Bates, C.M. & Brodsky, A.M. (1989). *Sex in the Therapy Hour.* Guilford, New York.

Beauchamp, T.L. & Childress, J.F. (1983). *Principles of Biomedical Ethics* (second edition). Oxford University Press, Oxford.

Beck, A.T. (1976). *Cognitive Therapy and the Emotional Disorders.* International Universities Press, New York.

Beck, A.T. & Emery, G. (1985). *Anxiety Disorders and Phobias: A Cognitive Perspective.* Basic Books, New York.

Beck, A.T. & Freeman, A. (1990). *Cognitive Therapy of Personality Disorders.* Guilford, New York.

Beck, A.T., Rush, A.J., Shaw, B.F. & Emery, G. (1979). *Cognitive Therapy of Depression.* Guilford, New York.

Beck, A.T., Steer, R.A. & Garbin, M.G. (1988). Psychometric properties of the Beck Depression Inventory: Twenty-five years of evaluation, *Clinical Psychology Review*, **8**, 77–100.

Bellack, A.S. & Hersen, M. (Eds). (1990). *Handbook of Comparative Treatments for Adult Disorders.* Wiley, New York.

Bellack, A.S., Hersen, M. & Kazdin, A.E. (Eds). (1992). *International Handbook of Behaviour Modification and Therapy* (second edition). Plenum, New York.

Borenzweig, H. (1983). Touching in clinical social work, *Social Casework*, **64**, 238–242.

Borys, D.S. & Pope, K.S. (1989). Dual relationships between therapist and client: A national study of psychologists, psychiatrists and social workers, *Professional Psychology: Research and Practice*, **20**, 283–293.

Bouhoutsos, J.C. (1985). Sexual intimacy between psychotherapists and clients: Policy implications for the future, in *Woman and Mental Health Policy* (Ed. L. Walker). Sage, Beverly Hills, C.A.

Bouhoutsos, J.C. & Brodsky, A.M. (1985). Mediation in therapist–client sex: A model, *Psychotherapy*, **22**, 189–193.

Bouhoutsos, J.C., Holroyd, J.C., Lerman, H., Forer, B.R. & Greenberg, M. (1983). Sexual intimacy between psychotherapists and patients, *Professional Psychology: Research and Practice*, **14**, 185–196.

Bowlby, J. (1980). *Loss, Sadness and Depression.* Hogarth, London.

Brazier, M. (1992). *Medicine, Patients, and the Law* (second edition). Penguin, Harmondsworth.

Briere, J. (1989). *Therapy with Adults Molested as Children: Beyond Survival.* Springer-Verlag, New York.

Briere, J. (1992). *Child Abuse Trauma: Theory and Treatment of the Lasting Effects.* Sage, Newbury Park.

Briere, J. & Runtz, M. (1987). Post sexual abuse trauma: Data and implications for clinical practice, *Journal of Interpersonal Violence*, **2**, 367–379.

Briere, J. & Runtz, M. (1988). Multivariate correlates of childhood psychological and physical maltreatment among university women, *Child Abuse and Neglect*, **12**, 331–341.

British Association for Counselling. (1992). *Code of ethics and practice for counsellors*. BAC, Rugby.

British Association for Sexual and Marital Therapy. (1991). *Code of practice*. BASMT.

British Association of Social Workers. (1986). *Code of ethics for social work*. BASW, Birmingham.

British Association of Social Workers. (1991). *Determining and regulating standards of conduct: The procedures of the Disciplinary Board*. BASW, Birmingham.

British Psychological Society. (1991). *Code of conduct for psychologists*. BPS, Leicester.

Brodsky, A.M. (1989). Sex between patient and therapist: Psychology's data and response, in *Sexual Exploitation in Professional Relationships* (Ed. G.O. Gabbard), pp. 15–25. American Psychiatric Press, Washington, D.C.

Brown, L.S. (1988). Harmful effects of posttermination sexual and romantic relationships between therapists and their former clients, *Psychotherapy*, **25**, 249–255.

Brownell, K.D., Hayes, S.C. & Barlow, D.H. (1977). Patterns of appropriate and deviant sexual arousal: The behavioral treatment of multiple sexual deviations, *Journal of Consulting and Clinical Psychology*, **45**, 1144–1155.

Burns, D.D. (1980). *Feeling Good: The New Mood Therapy*. Signet, New York.

Bursztain, H.J. & Gutheil, T.G. (1992). Protecting patients from clinician–patient sexual contact, *American Journal of Psychiatry*, **149**, 1276.

Butler, S. & Zelen, S.L. (1977). Sexual intimacies between therapists and patients, *Psychotherapy: Theory, Research and Practice*, **14**, 139–145.

Callanan, K. & O'Connor, T. (1988). *Staff comments and recommendations regarding the report of the Senate Task Force on Psychotherapist and Patient Sexual Relations*. Board of Behavioral Science Examiners and Psychology Examining Committee, Sacramento, C.A.

Cautela, J.R. (1967). Covert sensitization, *Psychological Reports*, **20**, 459–468.

Chemtob, C., Roitblat, H.L., Hamadan, R.S., Carlson, J.G. & Twentyman, C.T. (1988). A cognitive action theory of post-traumatic stress disorder, *Journal of Anxiety Disorders*, **2**, 253–275.

Chu, J.A. & Dill, D.L. (1990). Dissociative symptoms in relation to childhood physical and sexual abuse, *American Journal of Psychiatry*, **147**, 887–892.

College of Physicians and Surgeons of British Columbia (1992). *Crossing the boundaries: The report of the committee on physician sexual misconduct*. College of Physicians and Surgeons of British Columbia, Vancouver.

College of Physicians and Surgeons of Ontario (1991). *Final report of the task force on sexual abuse of patients*. College of Physicians and Surgeons of Ontario, Ontario.

Committee on Professional Practice (1987). *Memorandum on sex with former clients*. Unpublished document.

Committee on Women in Psychology (1989). If sex enters into the psychotherapy relationship, *Professional Psychology: Research and Practice*, **20**, 112–115.

Conte, H., Plutchik, R., Picard, S. & Karasu, T. (1989). Ethics in the practice of psychotherapy: A survey, *American Journal of Psychotherapy*, **43**, 32–42.

Cunningham, J., Pearce, T. & Pearce, P. (1988). Childhood sexual abuse and medical complaints in adult women, *Journal of Interpersonal Violence*, **3**, 131–144.

D'Addario, L. (1977). *Sexual relationships between female clients and male therapists*. Doctoral dissertation, California School of Professional Psychology, San Diego.

Dahlberg, C. (1970). Sexual contact between patient and therapist, *Contemporary Psychoanalysis*, **6**, 107–124.

Davidson, V. (1977). Psychiatry's problem with no name: Therapist–patient sex, *American Journal of Psychoanalysis*, **37**, 43–50.

Derosis, H., Hamilton, J., Morrison, E. & Strauss, M. (1987). More on psychiatrist–patient sexual contact, *American Journal of Psychiatry*, **144**, 688–689.

De Young, M. (1981). Case reports: The sexual exploitation of incest victims by helping professionals, *Victimology: An International Journal*, **6**, 92–101.

Domino, J.V. & Haber, J.D. (1987). Prior physical and sexual abuse in women with chronic headache: Clinical correlates, *Headache*, **27**, 310–314.

Edelwich, J. & Brodsky, A.M. (1991). *Sexual Dilemmas for the Helping Professional* (second edition). Brunner/Mazel, New York.

Edwards, D.J.A. (1981). The role of touch in interpersonal relations: Implications for psychotherapy, *South African Journal of Psychology*, **11**, 29–37.

Edwards, D.J.A. (1989). Cognitive restructuring through guided imagery: Lessons from Gestalt therapy, in *Comprehensive Handbook of Cognitive Therapy* (Eds A. Freeman, K. Simon, H. Arkowitz & L. Beutler), pp. 283–297. Plenum, New York.

Edwards, D.J.A. (1990). Cognitive therapy and the restructuring of early memories through guided imagery, *Journal of Cognitive Psychotherapy*, **4**, 33–50.

Elliot, D.M. & Briere, J. (1992). Sexual abuse trauma among professional women: Validating the Trauma Symptom Checklist-40 (TSC-40). *Child Abuse and Neglect*, **16**, 391–398.

Epstein, R.S. & Simon, R.I. (1990). The exploitation index: An early warning indicator of boundary violations in psychotherapy, *Bulletin of the Menninger Clinic*, **54**, 450–465.

Eyman, J.R. & Gabbard, G.O. (1991). Will therapist–patient sex prevent suicide? *Psychiatric Annals*, **21**, 669–674.

Feldman-Summers, S. & Jones, G. (1984). Psychological impacts of sexual contact between therapists or other health care practitioners and their clients, *Journal of Consulting and Clinical Psychology*, **52**, 1054–1061.

Finkelhor, D. (1984). *Child Sexual Abuse: New Theory and Research*. Free Press, New York.

Foa, E.B. & Kozak, M.J. (1985). Treatment of anxiety disorders: Implications for psychopathology, in *Anxiety and the Anxiety Disorders* (Eds A.H. Tuma & J.D. Maser), pp. 421–452. Erlbaum, Hillsdale, N.J.

Foa, E.B. & Kozak, M.J. (1986). Emotional processing of fear: Exposure to corrective information, *Psychological Bulletin*, **99**, 20–35.

Foa, E.B., Steketee, G. & Olasov-Rothbaum, B. (1989). Behavioral/cognitive conceptualizations of post-traumatic distress disorder, *Behavior Therapy*, **20**, 155–176.

Folman, R.Z. (1991). Therapist–patient sex: Attraction and boundary problems, *Psychotherapy*, **28**, 168–173.

Freeman, A., Simon, K.M., Beutler, L.E. & Arkowitz, H. (Eds). (1989). *Comprehensive Handbook of Cognitive Therapy*. Plenum, New York.

Freeman, L. & Roy, J. (1976). *Betrayal*. Stein and Day, New York.

Fromuth, M.E. (1986). The relationship of childhood sexual abuse with later psychological and sexual adjustment in a sample of college women, *Child Abuse and Neglect*, **10**, 5–15.

Furby, L., Weinrott, M.R. & Blackshaw, L. (1989). Sex offender recidivism: A review, *Psychological Bulletin*, **105**, 3–30.

Gabbard, G.O. (Ed.) (1989). *Sexual Exploitation in Professional Relationships*. American Psychiatric Press, Washington, D.C.

Gabbard, G.O. (1991). Psychodynamics of sexual boundary violations, *Psychiatric Annals*, **21**, 651–655.

Gabbard, G.O. & Pope, K.S. (1989). Sexual intimacies after termination: Clinical, ethical and legal aspects, in *Sexual Exploitation in Professional Relationships* (Ed. G.O. Gabbard), pp. 115–127. American Psychiatric Press, Washington, D.C.

Gartrell, N., Herman, J.L., Olarte, S., Feldstein, M. & Localio, R. (1986). Psychiatrist–patient sexual contact: Results of a national survey, I: Prevalence, *American Journal of Psychiatry*, **143**, 1126–1131.

Gartrell, N., Herman, J.L., Olarte, S., Feldstein, M. & Localio, R. (1987). Reporting practices of psychiatrists who knew of sexual misconduct by colleagues, *American Journal of Orthopsychiatry*, **57**, 287–295.

Gartrell, N., Herman, J.L., Olarte, S., Localio, R. & Feldstein, M. (1988). Psychiatric residents' sexual contact with educators and patients: Results of a national survey, *American Journal of Psychiatry*, **145**, 690–694.

Gechtman, L. (1989). Sexual contact between social workers and their clients, in *Sexual Exploitation in Professional Relationships* (Ed. G.O. Gabbard), pp. 27–28. American Psychiatric Press, Washington, D.C.

Gelinas, D.J. (1983). The persisting negative effects of incest, *Psychiatry*, **46**, 312–332.

Geller, J.D., Cooley, R.S. & Hartley, D. (1981–2). Images of the psychotherapist: A theoretical and methodological perspective, *Imagination, Cognition and Personality*, **1**, 123–146.

General Medical Council (1992). *Professional conduct and discipline: Fitness to practise*. General Medical Council, London.

Glaser, R.D. & Thorpe, J.S. (1986). Unethical intimacy: A survey of sexual contact and advances between psychology educators and female graduate students, *American Psychologist*, **41**, 43–51.

Gonsiorek, J.C. (1989a). Sexual exploitation by psychotherapists: Some observations on male victims and sexual orientation issues, in *Psychotherapists' Sexual Involvement with Clients: Intervention and Prevention* (Eds G.R. Schoener, J.H. Milgrom, J.C. Gonsiorek, E.T. Luepker & R.M. Conroe), pp. 113–119. Walk-In Counseling Center, Minneapolis.

Gonsiorek, J.C. (1989b). Working therapeutically with therapists who have become sexually involved with clients, in *Psychotherapists' Sexual Involvement with Clients: Intervention and Prevention* (Eds G.R. Schoener, J.H. Milgrom, J.C. Gonsiorek, E.T. Luepker & R.M. Conroe), pp. 421–433. Walk-In Counseling Center, Minneapolis.

Gonsiorek, J.C. (1989c). The prevention of sexual exploitation of clients: Hiring practices, in *Psychotherapists' Sexual Involvement with Clients: Intervention and Prevention* (Eds G.R. Schoener, J.H. Milgrom, J.C. Gonsiorek, E.T. Luepker & R.M. Conroe), pp. 469–475. Walk-In Counseling Center, Minneapolis.

Gonsiorek, J.C. & Brown, L.S. (1989). Post therapy sexual relationships with clients, in *Psychotherapists' Sexual Involvement with Clients: Intervention and Prevention* (Eds G.R. Schoener, J.H. Milgrom, J.C. Gonsiorek, E.T. Luepker & R.M. Conroe), pp. 289–301. Walk-In Counseling Center, Minneapolis.

Goodman, M. & Teicher, A. (1988). To touch or not to touch, *Psychotherapy*, **25**, 492–500.

Gottlieb, M.C., Sell, J.M. & Schoenfield, L.S. (1988). Sexual/romantic relationships with present and former clients: State licensing board actions, *Professional Psychology: Research and Practice*, **19**, 459–462.

Greenson, R.R. (1974). Loving, hating and indifference towards the patient, *International Review of Psycho-Analysis*, **1**, 259–265.

Grossman, C.M. (1965). Transference, countertransference and being in love, *Psychoanalytic Quarterly*, **34**, 249–256.

Grunebaum, H., Nadelson, C.C. & Macht, L.B. (1976). *Sexual activity with the psychiatrist: A district branch dilemma*. Unpublished paper presented at the annual convention of the American Psychological Association, Miami, F.L.

Gutheil, T.G. (1989). Borderline personality disorder, boundary violations, and patient–therapist sex: Medicolegal pitfalls, *American Journal of Psychiatry*, **146**, 597–602.

Gutheil, T.G. (1991). Patients involved in sexual misconduct with therapists: Is a victim profile possible? *Psychiatric Annals*, **21**, 661–667.

Gutheil, T.G. & Gabbard, G.O. (1993). The concept of boundaries in clinical practice: Theoretical and risk management dimensions, *American Journal of Psychiatry*, **150**, 188–196.

Hall, J.E. (1986). Issues and procedures in the disciplining of distressed psychologists, in *Professionals in Distress: Issues, Syndromes and Solutions in Psychology* (Eds R.R. Kilburg, P.E. Nathan & R.W. Thoreson), pp. 275–299. American Psychiatric Press, Washington, D.C.

Hall, R.L. (1989). Relapse rehearsal, in *Relapse Prevention with Sex Offenders* (Ed. D.R. Laws), pp. 197–206. Guilford, New York.

Halsbury's Laws of England (1980). (4th edition). Butterworths, London.

Harney, P.A. (1992). The role of incest in developmental theory and treatment of women diagnosed with borderline personality disorder, *Women and Therapy*, **12**, 39–57.

Harrop-Griffiths, J., Katon, W., Walker, E., Holm, L., Russo, J. & Hickok, L. (1988). The association between chronic pelvic pain, psychiatric diagnoses, and childhood sexual abuse, *Obstetrics & Gynaecology*, **71**, 589–594.

Hawton, K. (1985). *Sex Therapy: A Practical Guide*. Oxford University Press, Oxford.

Hawton, K., Salkovskis, P.M., Kirk, J. & Clark, D.M. (Eds.). (1989). *Cognitive Behaviour Therapy for Psychiatric Problems: A Practical Guide*. Oxford University Press, Oxford.

Hayes, S.C., Brownell, K.D. & Barlow, D.H. (1978). The use of self-administered covert sensitization in the treatment of exhibitionism and sadism, *Behavior Therapy*, **9**, 283–289.

Head, H. (1920). *Studies in neurology*. Oxford University Press, Oxford.

Herman, J.L., Gartrell, N., Olarte, S., Feldstein, M. & Localio, R. (1987). Psychiatrist–patient sexual contact: Results of a national survey, II: Psychiatrists' attitudes, *American Journal of Psychiatry*, **144**, 164–169.

Herman, J.L., Perry, J.C. & van der Kolk, B.A. (1989). Childhood trauma in borderline personality disorder, *American Journal of Psychiatry*, **146**, 490–495.

Hildebran, D. & Pithers, W.D. (1989). Enhancing offender empathy for sexual-abuse victims, in *Relapse Prevention with Sex Offenders* (Ed. D.R. Laws), pp. 236–243. Guilford, New York.

Hippocrates (n.d., a). *Oath*. (Translated by W.H.S. Jones). Heinemann, London.

Hippocrates (n.d., b). *Epidemics I*. (Translated by W.H.S. Jones). Heinemann, London.

Hoge, S.K., Jorgenson, L.M., Goldstein, N., Metzner, J., Patterson, R. & Robinson, G. (1993). *Mental health professional–patient sexual misconduct: Legal sanctions. A resource document*. American Psychiatric Association, Washington, D.C.

Holroyd, J.C. & Bouhoutsos, J.C. (1985). Biased reporting of therapist–patient sexual intimacy, *Professional Psychology: Research and Practice*, **16**, 701–709.

Holroyd, J.C. & Brodsky, A.M. (1977). Psychologists' attitudes and practices regarding erotic and nonerotic physical contact with patients, *American Psychologist*, **32**, 843–849.

Holroyd, J.C. & Brodsky, A.M. (1980). Does touching patients lead to sexual intercourse? *Professional Psychology*, **11**, 807–811.

Howard League (1985). *Unlawful Sex*. Waterlow, London.

James, J. & Meyerding, J. (1977). Early sexual experience as a factor in prostitution, *Archives of Sexual Behavior*, **1**, 31–42.

Janoff-Bulman, R. (1989). Assumptive worlds and the stress of traumatic events: Applications of the schema construct, *Social Cognition*, **7**, 113–136.

Janoff-Bulman, R. (1992). *Shattered assumptions: Towards a new psychology of trauma*. The Free Press, New York.

Jehu, D. (1979). *Sexual Dysfunction: A Behavioural Approach to Causation, Assessment, and Treatment*. Wiley, Chichester.

Jehu, D. (1988). *Beyond Sexual Abuse: Therapy with Women who were Childhood Victims*. Wiley, Chichester.

Jehu, D. (1989). Mood disturbances among women clients sexually abused in childhood: Prevalence, etiology, treatment, *Journal of Interpersonal Violence*, **4**, 164–184.

Jehu, D. (1991a). Clinical work with adults who were sexually abused in childhood, in *Clinical Approaches to Sex Offenders and their Victims* (Eds C.R. Hollin & K. Howells), pp. 229–260. Wiley, Chichester.

Jehu, D. (1991b). Post-traumatic stress reactions among adults molested as children, *Sexual and Marital Therapy*, **6**, 227–243.

Jehu, D. (1992). Personality problems among adults molested as children, *Sexual and Marital Therapy*, **7**, 231–249.

Jenkins-Hall, K.D. (1989). The decision matrix, in *Relapse Prevention with Sex Offenders* (Ed. D.R. Laws), pp. 159–166. Guilford, New York.

Jorgenson, L.M. & Appelbaum, P.S. (1991). For whom the statute tolls: Extending the time during which patients can sue, *Hospital and Community Psychiatry*, **42**, 683–684.

Jorgenson, L.M., Bisbing, S.B. & Sutherland, P.K. (1992). Therapist–patient sexual exploitation and insurance liability, *Tort and Insurance Law Journal*, **27**, 595–614.

Jorgenson, L.M. & Randles, R.M. (1991). Time out: The statute of limitations and fiduciary theory in psychotherapist sexual misconduct cases, *Oklahoma Law Review*, **44**, 181–225.

Jorgenson, L.M., Randles, R.M. & Strasburger, L.H. (1991). The furor over psychotherapist–patient sexual contact: New solutions to an old problem, *William and Mary Law Review*, **32**, 645–732.

Jorgenson, L.M. & Sutherland, P.K. (1993). Psychotherapist liability: What's sex got to do with it? *Trial*, May, 22–25.

Kane, A.W. (1992). *The effect of criminalization of sexual misconduct by therapists: Report of a survey in Wisconsin*. Unpublished paper.

Kanfer, F.H. (1980). Self-management methods, in *Helping People Change: A Textbook of Methods* (second edition) (Eds F.H. Kanfer & A.P. Goldstein), pp. 334–389. Pergamon, New York.

Kardener, S.H. (1974). Sex and the physician–patient relationship, *American Journal of Psychiatry*, **131**, 1134–1136.

Kardener, S.H., Fuller, M. & Mensh, I.N. (1973). A survey of physicians' attitudes and practices regarding erotic and nonerotic contact with patients, *American Journal of Psychiatry*, **130**, 1077–1081.

Kardener, S.H., Fuller, M. & Mensh, I.N. (1976). Characteristics of "erotic" practitioners, *American Journal of Psychiatry*, **133**, 1324–1325.

Kaufman, P.A. & Harrison, E. (1986). Open-ended group therapy for victims of therapist sexual misconduct, in *Sexual Exploitation of Patients by Health Professionals* (Eds A.W. Burgess & C.R. Hartman), pp. 172–177. Praeger, New York.

Kelly, G. (1955). *The Psychology of Personal Constructs* (two volumes). Norton, New York.

Kennedy, I. & Grubb, A. (1989). *Medical Law: Text and Materials*. Butterworths, London.

Kitchener, K.S. (1988). Dual role relationships: What makes them so problematic? *Journal of Counseling and Development*, **67**, 217–221.

Klopfer, W.G. (1974). The seductive patient, in *Problems in Psychotherapy* (Eds W.G. Klopfer & M.R. Reed), pp. 35–46. Wiley, New York.

Kluft, R.P. (1989). Treating the patient who has been sexually exploited by a previous therapist, *Psychiatric Clinics of North America*, **12**, 483–500.

Kluft, R.P. (1990). Incest and subsequent revictimization: The case of therapist–patient sexual exploitation, with a description of the sitting duck syndrome, in *Incest-Related Syndromes of Adult Psychopathology* (Ed. R.P. Kluft), pp. 263–287. American Psychiatric Press, Washington, D.C.

Kuchan, A. (1989). Survey of incidence of psychotherapists' sexual contact with clients in Wisconsin, in *Psychotherapists' Sexual Involvement with Clients: Intervention and Prevention* (Eds G.R. Schoener, J.H. Milgrom, J.C. Gonsiorek, E.T. Luepker & R.M. Conroe), pp. 51–64. Walk-In Counseling Center, Minneapolis.

Landecker, H. (1992). The role of childhood sexual trauma in the etiology of borderline personality disorder: Considerations for diagnosis and treatment, *Psychotherapy*, **29**, 234–242.

Lanyon, R.I. (1986). Theory and treatment in child molestation, *Journal of Consulting and Clinical Psychology*, **54**, 176–182.

Laws, D.R. (Ed.). (1989). *Relapse Prevention with Sex Offenders*. Guilford, New York.

Letters to the Editor (1992). *American Journal of Psychiatry*, **149**, 979–989.

Levenson, J.L. (1986). When a colleague practices unethically: Guidelines for intervention, *Journal of Counseling and Development*, **64**, 315–317.

Levitan, A.A. & Johnson, J.M. (1986). The role of touch in healing and hypnotherapy, *American Journal of Clinical Hypnosis*, **28**, 218–223.

Lichstein, K.L. & Hung, J.H.F. (1980). Covert sensitization: An examination of covert and overt parameters, *Behavioral Engineering*, **6**, 1–18.

Lindemann, E. (1944). Symptomatology and management of acute grief, *American Journal of Psychiatry*, **101**, 141–148.

List, A. (1989). A first experience in co-facilitating a group for victims, in *Psychotherapists' Sexual Involvement with Clients: Intervention and Prevention* (Eds G.R. Schoener, J.H. Milgrom, J.C. Gonsiorek, E.T. Luepker & R.M. Conroe), pp. 195–200. Walk-In Counseling Center, Minneapolis.

Litz, B.T. & Keane, T.M. (1989). Information processing in anxiety disorders: Application to the understanding of post-traumatic stress disorder, *Clinical Psychology Review*, **9**, 243–257.

Luepker, E.T. (1989a). Clinical assessment of clients who have been sexually exploited by their therapists and development of differential treatment plans, in *Psychotherapists'*

Sexual Involvement with Clients: Intervention and Prevention (Eds G.R. Schoener, J.H. Milgrom, J.C. Gonsiorek, E.T. Luepker & R.M. Conroe), pp. 159–176. Walk-In Counseling Center, Minneapolis.

Luepker, E.T. (1989b). Time-limited treatment/support groups for clients who have been sexually exploited by therapists: A nine year perspective, in *Psychotherapists' Sexual Involvement with Clients: Intervention and Prevention* (Eds G.R. Schoener, J.H. Milgrom, J.C. Gonsiorek, E.T. Luepker & R.M. Conroe), pp. 181–194. Walk-In Counseling Center, Minneapolis.

Luepker, E.T. & O'Brien, M. (1989). Support groups for spouses, in *Psychotherapists' Sexual Involvement with Clients: Intervention and Prevention* (Eds G.R. Schoener, J.H. Milgrom, J.C. Gonsiorek, E.T. Luepker & R.M. Conroe), pp. 241–244. Walk-In Counseling Center, Minneapolis.

Marks, I. (1981). *Cure and Care of Neuroses: Theory and Practice of Behavioural Psychotherapy*. Wiley, New York.

Marmor, J. (1972). Sexual acting-out in psychotherapy, *American Journal of Psychoanalysis*, **32**, 3–8.

Maroda, K.J. (1991). *The Power of Countertransference: Innovations in Analytic Technique*. Wiley, Chichester.

Marshall, W.L., Jones, R., Ward, T., Johnston, P. & Barbaree, H.E. (1991). Treatment outcome for sex offenders, *Clinical Psychology Review*, **11**, 465–485.

Mason, J.K. & McCall Smith, R.A. (1991). *Law and Medical Ethics* (third edition). Butterworths, London.

McCann, I.L. & Pearlman, L.A. (1990). *Psychological Trauma and the Adult Survivor: Theory, Therapy and Transformation*. Brunner/Mazel, New York.

McCartney, J.L. (1966). Overt transference, *Journal of Sex Research*, **2**, 227–237.

Meichenbaum, D. (1985). *Stress Inoculation Training*. Pergamon, New York.

Meichenbaum, D. & Genest, M. (1980). Cognitive behavior modification: An integration of cognitive and behavioral methods, in *Helping People Change: A Textbook of Methods* (second edition) (Eds F.H. Kanfer & A.P. Goldstein), pp. 390–422. Pergamon, New York.

Milgrom, J.H. (1989a). The first group for clients sexually exploited by their therapists: A twelve-year perspective, in *Psychotherapists' Sexual Involvement with Clients: Intervention and Prevention* (Eds G.R. Schoener, J.H. Milgrom, J.C. Gonsiorek, E.T. Luepker & R.M. Conroe), pp. 177–179. Walk-In Counseling Center, Minneapolis.

Milgrom, J.H. (1989b). Secondary victims of sexual exploitation by counselors and therapists: Some observations, in *Psychotherapists' Sexual Involvement with Clients: Intervention and Prevention* (Eds G.R. Schoener, J.H. Milgrom, J.C. Gonsiorek, E.T. Luepker & R.M. Conroe), pp. 235–240. Walk-In Counseling Center, Minneapolis.

Miller, E. (1992). Statutory registration, *The Psychologist*, **15**, 466–467.

Miller, E. (1993). Non-professional relationships with clients (Letter). *Division of Clinical Psychology Forum*, **54**, 164–169.

MIND (n.d.). *Your right to say no*. MIND, London.

Mogul, K.M. (1982). Overview: The sex of the therapist, *American Journal of Psychiatry*, **139**, 1–11.

Mogul, K.M. (1992). Ethics complaints against female psychiatrists, *American Journal of Psychiatry*, **149**, 651–653.

Morrison, J. (1989). Childhood sexual histories of women with somatization disorder, *American Journal of Psychiatry*, **146**, 239–241.

Murphy, W.D. (1990). Assessment and modification of cognitive distortions in sex offenders, in *Handbook of Sexual Assault: Issues, Theories, and Treatment of the Sexual Offender* (Eds W.L. Marshall, D.R. Laws & H.E. Barbaree), pp. 331–342. Plenum, New York.

Nelson, C. & Jackson, P. (1989). High-risk recognition: The cognitive-behavioral chain, in *Relapse Prevention with Sex Offenders* (Ed. D.R. Laws), pp. 167–177. Guilford, New York.

Noel, M.M. (1988). Reporting colleagues who are sexually intimate with clients: It's time to talk, *Women and Therapy*, **7**, 87–94.

Ogata, S.N., Silk, K.R., Goodrich, S., Lohr, N.E., Westen, D. & Hill, E.M. (1990). Childhood sexual and physical abuse in adult patients with borderline personality disorder, *American Journal of Psychiatry*, **147**, 1008–1013.

Paris, J. & Zweig, F.H. (1992). A critical review of the role of childhood sexual abuse in the etiology of borderline personality disorder, *Canadian Journal of Psychiatry*, **37**, 125–128.

Parkes, C.M. (1972). *Bereavement: Studies of Grief in Adult Life*. International Universities Press, New York.

Pattison, J.E. (1973). Effects of touch on self-exploration and the therapeutic relationship, *Journal of Counseling and Clinical Psychology*, **40**, 170–175.

Pearlman, L.A., McCann, I.L. & Johnson, G.B. (1993). *McPearl belief scale: A new measure of cognitive schemas*. Unpublished manuscript. (Available from L.A. Pearlman, The Traumatic Stress Institute, 22 Morgan Farms Drive, South Windsor, Connecticut 06074, U.S.A.).

Perkins, D. (1991). Clinical work with sex offenders in secure settings, in *Clinical Approaches to Sex Offenders and their Victims* (Eds C.R. Hollin & K. Howells), pp. 151–177. Wiley, Chichester.

Peterson, C. & Seligman, M.E.P. (1983). Learned helplessness and victimization, *Journal of Social Issues*, **39**, 103–116.

Piaget, J. (1926). *The Language and Thought of the Child*. Harcourt Brace, New York.

Piaget, J. (1970). *Structuralism*. Harper & Row, New York.

Piaget, J. (1971). *Psychology and Epistemology: Towards a Theory of Knowledge*. Viking Press, New York.

Pithers, W.D., Kashima, K.M., Cumming G.F. & Beal, L.S. (1988). Relapse prevention: A method of enhancing maintenance of change in sex offenders, in *Treating Child Sex Offenders and Victims: A Practical Guide* (Ed. A.C. Salter), pp. 131–170. Sage, Newbury Park.

Plaisil, E. (1985). *Therapist*. St. Martin's/Marek, New York.

Pope, K.S. (1987a). Preventing therapist–patient sexual intimacy: Therapy for a therapist at risk, *Professional Psychology: Research and Practice*, **18**, 624–628.

Pope, K.S. (1987b). Sex with patients: New data, standards and liabilities, *Independent Practitioner*, May, 15–20.

Pope, K.S. (1989a). Malpractice suits, licensing disciplinary actions, and ethics cases: Frequencies, causes and costs, *Independent Practitioner*, **9**, 22–26.

Pope, K.S. (1989b). Sexual intimacies between psychologists and their students and supervisees: Research, standards and professional liability, *Independent Practitioner*, **9**, 33–41.

Pope, K.S. (1990). Therapist–patient sex as sex abuse: Six scientific, professional, and practical dilemmas in addressing victimization and rehabilitation, *Professional Psychology: Research and Practice*, **21**, 227–239.

Pope, K.S. (1991). Rehabilitation plans and expert testimony for therapists who have been sexually involved with a patient, *Independent Practitioner*, **22**, 31–39.

Pope, K.S. & Bajt, T.R. (1988). When laws and values conflict: A dilemma for psychologists, *American Psychologist*, **43**, 828–829.

Pope, K.S. & Bouhoutsos, J.C. (1986). *Sexual Intimacy between Therapists and Patients.* Praeger, New York.

Pope, K.S., Keith-Spiegel, P. & Tabachnick, B.G. (1986). Sexual attraction to clients: The human therapist and the (sometimes) inhuman training system, *American Psychologist*, **41**, 147–158.

Pope, K.S., Levenson, H. & Schover, L.R. (1979). Sexual intimacy in psychology training: Results and implications of a national survey, *American Psychologist*, **34**, 682–689.

Pope, K.S., Tabachnick, B.G. & Keith-Spiegel, P. (1987). Ethics of practice: The beliefs and behaviors of psychologists as therapists, *American Psychologist*, **42**, 993–1006.

Pope, K.S. & Vetter, V.A. (1991). Prior therapist–patient sexual involvement among patients seen by psychologists, *Psychotherapy*, **28**, 429–438.

Putnam, F.W. (1989). *Diagnosis and Treatment of Multiple Personality Disorder.* Guilford, New York.

Putnam, F.W. (1991). Dissociative phenomena, in *Annual Review of Psychiatry* (Ed. A. Tasman), pp. 159–174. American Psychiatric Press, Washington D.C.

Radloff, I.S. (1977). The CES-D scale: A self-report depression scale for research in the general population, *Applied Psychological Measurement*, **1**, 385–401.

Raphael, B. (1983). *The Anatomy of Bereavement.* Basic Books, New York.

Rappaport, E.A. (1956). The management of the eroticized transference, *Psychoanalytic Quarterly*, **23**, 515–529.

Reiter, R.C. & Gambone, J.C. (1990). Demographic and historic variables in women with idiopathic chronic pelvic pain, *Obstetrics & Gynecology*, **75**, 428–432.

Rieker, P.P. & Carmen, E.H. (1983). Teaching value clarification: The value of gender and psychotherapy, *American Journal of Psychiatry*, **140**, 410–415.

Rook, P.F.G. & Ward, R. (1990). *Sexual Offences.* Waterlow, London.

Ross, C.A. (1989). *Multiple Personality Disorder: Diagnosis, Clinical Features and Treatment.* Wiley, New York.

Roth, S. & Newman, E. (1991). The process of coping with sexual trauma, *Journal of Traumatic Stress*, **4**, 279–297.

Rotter, J.B. (1954). *Social Learning and Clinical Psychology.* Prentice Hall, Englewood Cliffs, N.J.

Runtz, M. & Briere, J. (1988). *Childhood sexual abuse, revictimization as an adult, and current symptomatology.* Paper presented at the National Symposium on Child Victimization, Anaheim, C.A., April.

Russell, D.E.H. (1986). *The Secret Trauma: Incest in the Lives of Girls and Women.* Basic Books, New York.

Rutter, P. (1990). *Sex in the forbidden zone: When men in power—therapists, doctors, clergy, teachers, and others—betray women's trust.* Mandala, London.

Sanders, B. & Giolas, M.H. (1991). Dissociation and childhood trauma in psychologically disturbed adolescents, *American Journal of Psychiatry*, **148**, 50–54.

Saul, L.J. (1962). The erotic transference, *Psychoanalytic Quarterly*, **31**, 54–61.

Schoener, G.R. (1989a). Supervision of therapists who have sexually exploited clients, in *Psychotherapists' Sexual Involvement with Clients: Intervention and Prevention* (Eds

G.R. Schoener, J.H. Milgrom, J.C. Gonsiorek, E.T. Luepker & R.M. Conroe), pp. 435–446. Walk-In Counseling Center, Minneapolis.

Schoener, G.R. (1989b). Problems in the use of direct observation in probation plans for professionals who have sexually exploited clients, in *Psychotherapists' Sexual Involvement with Clients: Intervention and Prevention* (Eds G.R. Schoener, J.H. Milgrom, J.C. Gonsiorek, E.T. Luepker & R.M. Conroe), pp. 447–449. Walk-In Counseling Center, Minneapolis.

Schoener, G.R. (1989c). The role of supervision and case consultation: Some notes on sexual feelings in therapy, in *Psychotherapists' Sexual Involvement with Clients: Intervention and Prevention* (Eds G.R. Schoener, J.H. Milgrom, J.C. Gonsiorek, E.T. Luepker & R.M. Conroe), pp. 495–502. Walk-In Counseling Center, Minneapolis.

Schoener, G.R. (1989d). Self-help and consumer groups, in *Psychotherapists' Sexual Involvement with Clients: Intervention and Prevention* (Eds G.R. Schoener, J.H. Milgrom, J.C. Gonsiorek, E.T. Luepker & R.M. Conroe), pp. 375–389. Walk-In Counseling Center, Minneapolis.

Schoener, G.R. (1989e). The assessment of damages, in *Psychotherapists' Sexual Involvement with Clients: Intervention and Prevention* (Eds G.R. Schoener, J.H. Milgrom, J.C. Gonsiorek, E.T. Luepker & R.M. Conroe), pp. 133–145. Walk-In Counseling Center, Minneapolis.

Schoener, G.R. (1989f). Filing complaints against therapists who sexually exploit clients, in *Psychotherapists' Sexual Involvement with Clients: Intervention and Prevention* (Eds G.R. Schoener, J.H. Milgrom, J.C. Gonsiorek, E.T. Luepker & R.M. Conroe), pp. 313–343. Walk-In Counseling Center, Minneapolis.

Schoener, G.R. (1989g). Administrative safeguards, in *Psychotherapists' Sexual Involvement with Clients: Intervention and Prevention* (Eds G.R. Schoener, J.H. Milgrom, J.C. Gonsiorek, E.T. Luepker & R.M. Conroe), pp. 453–467. Walk-In Counseling Center, Minneapolis.

Schoener, G.R. & Conroe, R.M. (1989). The role of supervision and case consultation in primary prevention, in *Psychotherapists' Sexual Involvement with Clients: Intervention and Prevention* (Eds G.R. Schoener, J.H. Milgrom, J.C. Gonsiorek, E.T. Luepker & R.M. Conroe), pp. 477–493. Walk-In Counseling Center, Minneapolis.

Schoener, G.R. & Gonsiorek, J.C. (1988). Assessment and development of rehabilitation plans for counselors who have sexually exploited their clients, *Journal of Counseling and Development*, **67**, 227–232.

Schoener, G.R. & Gonsiorek, J.C. (1989). Assessment and development of rehabilitation plans for the therapist, in *Psychotherapists' Sexual Involvement with Clients: Intervention and Prevention* (Eds G.R. Schoener, J.H. Milgrom, J.C. Gonsiorek, E.T. Luepker & R.M. Conroe), pp. 401–420. Walk-In Counseling Center, Minneapolis.

Schoener, G.R. & Milgrom, J.H. (1989). False or misleading complaints, in *Psychotherapists' Sexual Involvement with Clients: Intervention and Prevention* (Eds G.R. Schoener, J.H. Milgrom, J.C. Gonsiorek, E.T. Luepker & R.M. Conroe), pp. 147–155. Walk-In Counseling Center, Minneapolis.

Schoener, G.R., Milgrom, J.H. & Gonsiorek, J.C. (1989). Therapeutic responses to clients who have been sexually abused by psychotherapists, in *Psychotherapists' Sexual Involvement with Clients: Intervention and Prevention* (Eds G.R. Schoener, J.H. Milgrom, J.C. Gonsiorek, E.T. Luepker & R.M. Conroe), pp. 95–112. Walk-In Counseling Center, Minneapolis.

Schoener, G.R., Milgrom, J.H., Gonsiorek, J.C., Luepker, E.T. & Conroe, R.M. (Eds) (1989). *Psychotherapists' Sexual Involvement with Clients: Intervention and Prevention.* Walk-In Counseling Center, Minneapolis.

Searles, H.F. (1979). *Countertransference and Related Subjects.* International University Press, New York.

Sedney, M.A. & Brooks, B. (1984). Factors associated with a history of childhood sexual experience in a nonclinical female population, *Journal of the American Academy of Child Psychiatry,* **23**, 215–218.

Seligman, M.E.P. (1975). *Helplessness: On Depression, Development and Death.* W.H. Freeman, San Francisco.

Shepard, M. (1971). *The Love Treatment: Sexual Intimacy between Patients and Psychotherapists.* Wyden, New York.

Silbert, M.H. (1984). Treatment of prostitute victims of sexual assault, in *Victims of Sexual Aggression: Treatment of Children, Women and Men* (Eds I.R. Stuart & J.G. Greer), pp. 251–282. Van Nostrand Reinhold, New York.

Silbert, M.H. & Pines, A.M. (1981). Sexual child abuse as an antecedent to prostitution, *Child Abuse and Neglect,* **5**, 407–411.

Silbert, M.H. & Pines, A.M. (1983). Early sexual exploitation as an influence in prostitution, *Social Work,* **28**, 285–289.

Simon, R.I. (1989). Sexual exploitation of patients: How it begins before it happens, *Psychiatric Annals,* **19**, 104–112.

Simon, R.I. (1991). Psychological injury caused by boundary violation precursors to therapist–patient sex, *Psychiatric Annals,* **21**, 614–619.

Simon, R.I. & Sadoff, R.L. (1993). *Psychiatric Malpractice: Cases and Comments for Clinicians.* American Psychiatric Press, Washington, D.C.

Smith, S. (1984). The sexually abused patient and the abusing therapist: A study in sadomasochistic relationships, *Psychoanalytic Psychology,* **1**, 89–98.

Smith, S. (1989). The seduction of the female patient, in *Sexual Exploitation in Professional Relationships* (Ed. G.O. Gabbard), pp. 57–69. American Psychiatric Press, Washington, D.C.

Sonne, J.L. (1986). An example of group therapy for victims of therapist–client sexual intimacy, in *Sexual Exploitation in Professional Relationships* (Ed. G.O. Gabbard), pp. 101–113. American Psychiatric Press, Washington, D.C.

Sonne, J.L., Meyer, B., Borys, D. & Marshall, V. (1985). Clients' reactions to sexual intimacy in therapy, *American Journal of Orthopsychiatry,* **55**, 183–189.

Sonne, J.L. & Pope, K.S. (1991). Treating victims of therapist–patient sexual involvement, *Psychotherapy,* **28**, 174–187.

Spence, S.H. (1991). *Psychosexual Therapy: A Cognitive-Behavioural Approach.* Chapman & Hall, London.

Stake, J.E. & Oliver, J. (1991). Sexual contact and touching between therapist and client: A survey of psychologists' attitudes and behavior, *Professional Psychology: Research and Practice,* **22**, 297–307.

Stone, A.A. (1983). Sexual misconduct by psychiatrists: The ethical and clinical dilemma of confidentiality, *American Journal of Psychiatry,* **140**, 195–197.

Strasburger, L.H., Jorgenson, L.M. & Randles, R.M. (1990). Mandatory reporting of sexually exploitive psychotherapists, *Bulletin of the American Academy of Psychiatry and Law,* **18**, 379–384.

Strasburger, L.H., Jorgenson, L.M. & Randles, R.M. (1991). Criminalization of psychotherapist–patient sex, *American Journal of Psychiatry,* **148**, 859–863.

Strasburger, L.H., Jorgenson, L.M. & Sutherland, P.K. (1992). The prevention of psychotherapist sexual misconduct: Avoiding the slippery slope, *American Journal of Psychotherapy*, **46**, 544–555.

Strick, F.L. & Wilcoxon, S.A. (1991). A comparison of dissociative experiences in adult female outpatients with and without histories of early incestuous abuse, *Dissociation: Progress in the Dissociative Disorders*, **4**, 193–199.

Taylor, S.E. (1983). Adjustment to threatening events: A theory of cognitive adaptation, *American Psychologist*, **38**, 1161–1173.

Theisen, M. (1993). *Therapist sexual abuse*. Unpublished memorandum, State of Minnesota Attorney General's Office, May.

United Kingdom Central Council for Nursing, Midwifery and Health Visiting (1990). *"... with a view to removal from the register ..."?*. UKCC, London.

United Kingdom Central Council for Nursing, Midwifery and Health Visiting (1992). *Code of Professional Conduct*. UKCC, London.

Valiquette, M. (1989). *Les séquelles psychologiques de l'intimatè sexuelle en psychothèrapie*. Doctoral dissertation, University of Montreal.

Van der Kolk, B.A., Perry, J.C. & Herman, J.L. (1991). Childhood origins of self-destructive behavior, *American Journal of Psychiatry*, **148**, 1665–1671.

Vinson, J.S. (1984). *Sexual contact with psychotherapists: A study of client reactions and complaint procedures*. Doctoral dissertation, California School of Professional Psychology.

Vitaliano, P.P., James, J. & Boyer, D. (1981). Sexuality of deviant females: Adolescent and adult correlates, *Social Work*, **26**, 468–472.

Walker, L.E. (1985). The battered woman syndrome study, in *The Dark Side of Families* (Eds D. Finkelhor, R.J. Gelles, G.T. Hotaling & M.A. Strauss), pp. 31–48. Sage, Beverly Hills, C.A.

Walker, L.E. & Young, T.D. (1986). *A Killing Cure*. Holt, New York.

Walsh, B.W. & Rosen, P. (1988). *Self-Mutilation: Theory, Research and Treatment*. Guilford, New York.

Williams, M.H. (1992). Exploitation and inference: Mapping the damage from therapist–patient sexual involvement, *American Psychologist*, **47**, 412–421.

Wood, B., Klein, S., Cross, H., Lammers, C. & Elliott, J. (1985). Impaired practitioners: Psychologists' opinions about prevalence and proposals for intervention, *Professional Psychology: Research and Practice*, **16**, 843–850.

Wyatt, G.E., Guthrie, D. & Notgrass, C.M. (1992). Differential effects of women's child sexual abuse and subsequent sexual revictimization, *Journal of Consulting and Clinical Psychology*, **60**, 167–173.

Young, J.E. (1990). *Cognitive Therapy for Personality Disorders: A Schema-Focused Approach*. Practitioner Resource Exchange, Sarasota, F.L.

Zanarini, M.C., Gunderson, J.G., Marino, M.F., Schwartz, E.O. & Frankenburg, F.R. (1989). Childhood experiences of borderline patients, *Comprehensive Psychiatry*, **30**, 18–25.

Index

continued from page ii